T0160610

LEXICON DEVIL

THE FAST TIMES AND SHORT LIFE OF DARBY CRASH AND THE GERMS

By Brendan Mullen With Don Bolles and Adam Parfrey

ISBN: 978-0-922915-70-5
ISBN: 0-922915-70-9

FERAL HOUSE
1240 W SIMS WAY #124
PORT TOWNSEND, WA 98368

WWW.FERALHOUSE.COM
INFO@FERALHOUSE.COM

DESIGN BY HEDI EL KHOLTI
COVER PHOTOGRAPH BY RUBY RAY

10 9 8 7 6

"It's not the load that breaks you down, it's the way you carry it."

—Lena Horne

"Only that which can destroy itself is truly alive."

—C. G. Jung, *Psychology and Alchemy*

"Live dangerously..."

—Friedrich Nietzsche

TABLE OF CONTENTS

O

PUBLISHER'S NOTE

To reduce confusion, and to retain a linear time frame to this book, Darby Crash initially speaks as "Paul Beahm," his birth name variant, until he adopts the name "Bobby Pyn," and later, "Darby Crash." Pat Smear's birth name, "Georg Ruthenberg" is used until the punk spasm redefines his image. (Pat insists that Georg is spelled without an "e" at the end.)

The decision was made not to impede the flow of this oral history with authorial interruptions. Whenever possible, the over 100 speakers within introduce other players and contextualize events. Readers interested in knowing more about the quoted witnesses should consult the "Cast of Characters" found on page 269. *Lexicon Devil* is not a comprehensive history of Los Angeles punk rock. For that sort of thing, the reader is referred to Marc Spitz and Brendan Mullen's *We Got the Neutron Bomb*, published by Three Rivers Press. And for further information on the Germs' hardcore aftermath in Los Angeles and elsewhere, there's Steven Blush's *American Hardcore: A Tribal History*, published by Feral House.

ooo

I remember buying the "Lexicon Devil" ep from the Bomp Records store, and listening to it again and again with even more pleasure than Sex Pistols singles. At a Germs show at the Rock Corporation, a Valley biker bar, several short, fat Germettes picked me out of the crowd for the dubious honor of a pounding. As I defended myself, a couple surfer types made sure to join the thrash, screaming in my face, "Don't hit a girl, faggot!"

These were not unknown experiences in punk rock, circa '78-'79, a price I was very willing to pay for feeling connected to a scene in an otherwise culturally barren time and place.

In early 1997 when I handed Don Bolles an advance payment for a Germs book, I did not expect the coming half-decade of dead ends, sorry excuses, as well as a litany of venom from a couple former Germs associates. Brendan Mullen, who had already interviewed a good number of participants, and run across his own portion of trouble, came aboard, and helped us to right a listing ship. But then there were some crucial interviews that Don or Brendan found no way to lasso, so my intervention was required to help complete the book. As it turns out, the additional years needed to finish this project provided enough time to unearth an amazing array of anecdotes and revelations that would never have been discovered if this book was written in a timely manner by just one person.

Lexicon Devil is a natural oral history. When reading a couple interview transcripts, I suddenly became dizzy and broke into a cold sweat, when words, words alone, sunk to the pit of my stomach. What was being said did not affect me as much as *how* it was being said—the 1974 West L.A. juvie style in all its confusion, ignorance and arrogance sucker-punched me in the gut, and brought me back to a time and place I spent so many years trying to forget.

I wish to thank the dozens of participants who agreed to speak—either to me, to Brendan Mullen, or to Don Bolles. Brendan thanks so many in his introduction, but a personal sense of gratitude also goes to: Pat Smear, Kent Beyda, Jenny Lens, Scott Lindgren, Richard Meltzer, Jimmy McDonough, Ruby Ray, Gary Leonard, Michael Yampolski, Jena Cardwell, Will Amato, Allan MacDonell, Pleasant Gehman, Trudie, K.K., David Brown, Robin Boyarsky, Fred Holtby, Caldwell Williams, Bill Bartell, Casey Cola, Amanda Volta, Michael Gira, Kim Fowley, Laura Guerrero, Frank Gargani, and Gerber. The publisher also wishes to thank Faith Baker for being kind enough to lend us family photos and artifacts from the early years of Paul Beahm.

My deep thanks to Brendan Mullen for his ever-surprising resources and (at times) total involvement in the project. I also would like to thank Don Bolles, because his inspired moments overcame much of my frustration. Not only did the designer, Hedi el Kholti, call off a trip to the Philippines to work on this book, but his understanding of the material and remarkably on-target aesthetic made him feel like a co-author. There are others who contributed to this book; may they forgive me for not calling them out by name. R.I.P. to Rik L. Rik, Cliff Hanger, Claude Bessy, Tomata du Plenty, and the rest of us, when our time comes. And for being patient and warm, my love goes to Marti and Alice.

The Germs are more influential today than at any time in their past. Their cultural lifts—let's call 'em homages—were sometimes quite transparent, but their recordings, particularly the *G.I.* album, try so hard and do so much, so well, and so authentically, I can only think of them as being true art brut of psychedelically punctured L.A. of the late '70s.

I wish to dedicate this book to the memory of the original Manimal. As my Portland-based Poison Idea friends said in an early recording of theirs, "Darby Crash Rides Again."

Adam Parfrey
March 2002

DON BOLLES' INTRODUCTORY MUSINGS

O

The Germs were not just about "music." Music was our front, but we were dealing in something a lot more elemental, although it was rarely articulated at the time. There was something in the nexus of that sound, the insanity of the audience, and the Cult of Darby Crash that none of these people, myself included, had ever before experienced; it was like the total amphetamine mania and psychotic mass breakdown of the Third Reich, except a lot more fun and without the blood [well, maybe not as *much* blood—Publisher's note], compressed into one room and 20 minutes, every song a new exhortation for the audience to abandon everything to this blind, idiot messiah, as his need became your need, his sacrifice your freedom, his beer your responsibility.

Between the bad covers of "Sugar, Sugar," the feedback 'n' noise, and the insane antics, and the brilliance of Darby's lyrics, there was something undeniable about this bunch of losers, an almost giddy feeling of danger, like absolutely anything could happen at their shows. Somehow this bunch of ridiculous, bratty no-talents could turn any venue that would have them into a total chaos vortex, and anyone there could feel it. And you didn't have to go through years of hermetic weirdness in some esoteric magickal order to experience it—instant Thelemic ecstasy for under five dollars.

With a little more luck and concentrated effort, Darby could have fulfilled his plan to be the new Jesus/Bowie/Manson/Hitler/L. Ron Hubbard, as he was as a natural Messiah/Leader type whose heroic consumption of LSD helped make him the most psychedelic prankster I've ever known.

Don Bolles
October 2001

INTRODUCTION

You could say I'm just another Germs' fan and Darby Crash was someone I knew best through his work as a lyricist-songwriter and as a stage performer. I also knew him as a fixture on the nightly Bacchanalian party scene we both enjoyed during the mid-to-late '70s. I did enjoy several memorable encounters with him as a club booker-promoter at The Masque, the Whisky, and other venues when the Germs gigged around from 1977 to 1980, and I hung out with him when he played the Mabuhay Gardens in San Francisco—the same weekend the Sex Pistols imploded at Winterland.

One of the few other times I saw Darby without his usual entourage was at a Halloween party in 1980, five weeks before his death, when I intercepted to save him from a beating at the hands of some bodybuilder-type who was foaming on steroids, and shouting back at me, "I don't give a shit who he is! He's fuckin' pissing me right OFF!" This enraged hulk was about to toss Darby off a balcony with a 50-foot drop onto concrete. Darby never even blinked. The strangest thing was that he was quieter than usual that night, and I can't remember what he might have said that got the guy so steamed up—although Darby had certainly been known to revel in winding people up.

When Feral House publisher Adam Parfrey and original author Don Bolles pulled me into this project, I'd already spent a few years interviewing people on and off, some of them in tandem with the late Rik L. Rik, with the idea of eventually creating a serious biography on the Germs. There was no rush, no deadline, not even a publisher. Rik and I bonded over the idea to stay true to one common goal: we wanted to counter a lot of the rubbish that floats around the Internet about Darby's life. And so I'd like to dedicate my end of this book to the memory of Rik (Richard Elerick), who died from brain cancer in July, 2000. I wish you could've lived to see your idea of compiling an oral history of Darby's life come to fruition. A very special thanks is also due to my friend Marc Spitz, co-author with me of *We Got the Neutron Bomb: The Untold Story of L.A. Punk* for his generosity of spirit and endlessly positive attitude.

To some Darby was a quasi-mystical seer, a celestial being, a charismatic poet, a genius; while to others he was an apocalyptic would-be cult leader, a terminally annoying gossip, a psychic bully, a drunken panhandler and a fraudulent boor who plagiarized scraps of musical and philosophical ideas from Bowie, Iggy, Nietzsche, Hitler, Manson, and L. Ron Hubbard. Yet to others he was a son, a brother, an uncle, a fun-loving daredevil kid who got in over his head and deep-sixed on drugs and alcohol. Deep down I sensed he was vulnerable and a movingly committed loyalist to the original Hollywood boho-punk community which gave him and the Germs an audience.

Whatever the Germs did or didn't do—and that, too, varies massively depending on who you're talking to—for me the band and their audience together were one of the greatest rock spectacles ever on a good night. Live they were frequently an instrumental and vocal mess which has only contributed to that you-just-had-to-be-there mystique. Yet once in the studio, the Germs became a caring, dedicated musical entity. They left behind a few classic records, especially the "Lexicon Devil" ep and the essential *G.I.* album, plus a slew of bootlegs from live shows that have become immortalized as the soundtrack to the times Darby lived in and, some will say, for which he died.

I'd like to thank my colleagues Adam Parfrey, a great and extremely patient co-editor, and Don Bolles, a member of the band for two of the Germs' three years of existence for his invaluable input. Special shouts to Kateri Butler, Jim Carberry, and the rest of my extended family.

I am also indebted forever to the following people who contributed directly or indirectly to making this book what it became:

Will Amato, Amber, Trudie Arguelles, Jill Ash, Chris Ashford, Faith Baker, Alice Bag, KK Barrett, Bill Bartell, Nickey Beat, Judith Bell, Michelle Bell (Gerber), Claude Bessy (RIP), Kent Beyda, Bob Biggs, Rodney Bingenheimer, Ella Black (Kari Leuschner), Black Randy (RIP), DJ Bonebrake, Dinky Bonebrake, Robin Boyarksy, David Brown, Lynda Burdick, Dez Cadena, Bruce Kalberg, Jena Cardwell, Belinda Carlisle, Douglas Cavanaugh, Exene Cervenka, Bob Clark, Casey Cola, Kerry Colonna, Edward Colver, Chris D., John Doe, Lorna Doom, Deborah Drooz, Tomata du Plenty (RIP), Maggie Ehrig, Al Flipside, Michael Friend, Kim Fowley, Frank Gargani, Don Garstang, Pleasant Gehman, Terry Graham, Jack Grisham, Cliff Hanger (RIP), Fred Holtby, Gus Hudson, Robert Hill, Joan Jett, David Jones, Michael Jones, Shawn Kerri, Hellin Killer, Tony Kinman, Tito Larriva, Craig Lee (RIP), Jenny Lens, Gary Leonard, Jeff McDonald, Kristine McKenna, Basho Macko (Allan MacDonell), Toby Mamis, Dave Markey, Richard Meltzer, Regi Mentle, Tony Montesion, Thurston Moore, Keith Morris, Mugger, Hal Negro (Marty Goldberg), Mike Ness, Joe Nolte, Margot Olaverra and the Go-Go's, Steve Olson, Genesis P-Orridge, Bruce Osbourne, Nicole Panter, Mike Patton, Jeffrey Lee Pierce (RIP), John Pochna, Kid Congo Powers, The Plungers (Trudie, Hellin, Mary, Trixie), Jack Rabid, Ruby Ray, John Roecker, Paul Roessler, Donnie Rose (RIP), Gorilla Rose (RIP), Penelope Spheeris, Paul Sanoian, Jennifer Schwartz, Andy Seven, Greg Shaw, Pat Smear, James Stark, Rooh Steif, Shawn and Mark Stern, John Sutton-Smith, Rick Van Santen, Tony the Hustler, Amanda Volta, Lori Weiner, Johanna Went, Sandy West, Caldwell Williams, Philomena Winstanley, Geza X, X-8, Michael Yampolsky, Charles M. Young, Billy Zoom ... and to the soul of Darby Crash himself.

Brendan Mullen
Los Angeles, 2002

FAITH BAKER   Paul wasn't a follower. He did pretty much as he wanted to do.

HELLIN KILLER   He took everyone he could at that school and gave them as much acid as possible and tried to convince them of everything he had to say, and he was really good at it, really good at manipulating people.

PAUL ROESSLER   Paul Beahm would take acid, and then take the teachers apart. It wasn't like he could just do it to some bimbo 15-year-old chick, it worked on grown-ups, too.

PENELOPE SPHEERIS   It's really easy to get girls if you don't really want them, and he didn't really want them. So he would get girls trailing after him left and right because he didn't give a shit.

WILL AMATO   He could be incredibly insulting, and attack you, and mind-fuck you, and everything else. In the end he picked a game he couldn't win. There was something kind of sad about the guy...

RIK L. RIK   Darby was the most brilliant person I ever met.

DARBY CRASH   When you have people for friends, and they're not the sort of people you want, what do you do? You make some better ones. So I'm going to take all these idiots and make them into better ones.

PAUL ROESSLER   On one of our excursions, we went down into the reservoir in West L.A. in the middle of the night and went swimming underground. Darby would open up the hatch, and we'd go down into this sewer. He'd close the hatch, and all there was were pillars and water and darkness. No light, nothing. It was just terrifying, but we hung out there anyway.

DARBY CRASH   You know what's fun? You take like ten hits of acid, and drink a six-pack of beer and you go to the Santa Monica Pier; there's a bridge there that goes nowhere, 'cause they're supposed to lower it for boats, and you can go out to the end and jump off, right? And you can swim, and it's so great 'cause it's dark, you know, and you can just swim and it doesn't matter if you live or die or anything, just swim and swim, and you feel the fish nibbling at your feet...

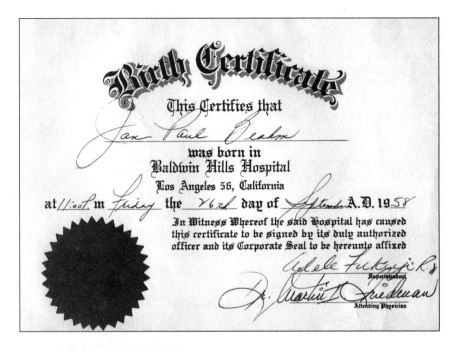

Birth Certificate

This Certifies that

Jan Paul Beahm

was born in
Baldwin Hills Hospital
Los Angeles 56, California

at 11:00 pm Friday the 26th day of September A.D. 1958

In Witness Whereof the said Hospital has caused this certificate to be signed by its duly authorized officer and its Corporate Seal to be hereunto affixed

Adele Fukuji R.N.
Superintendent

Dr. Martin L. Friedman
Attending Physician

Faith Baker with baby Paul.
Family photographs courtesy of Faith Baker.

Faith, Jr. and Christine holding Paul.

THE BOY WITH BLUE HAIR

O

BOBBY   I like the movie, *The Boy With Green Hair* 'cause my father was in it.
X-8   What was he?
BOBBY   The boy with green hair.
(From *Flipside* fanzine, 1977)

CHRIS ASHFORD   Paul Beahm had a photo of Dean Stockwell as a kid in the late '40s … it was a still from the Joseph Losey movie, *The Boy With Green Hair*, that he'd taped up on the wall near his bed. When I asked him about it he said, "That's my dad." The movie is about some war orphan who becomes a social outcast when his hair changes color. That's probably where he got the idea to go to school with blue hair.

PAUL BEAHM   Mainly my reputation started in 10th or 11th grade. I just dyed my hair blue and lost all my friends in one day. I said I wanted to see what it's like being the only black kid in a white school, and my God, nobody would talk to me or anything. But then there's always the few people that see something different after a while, and then after a while it got to be normal because I'd dye it different colors all the time. In the end they all did, too.

PAUL ROESSLER   I was in 10th grade, a recent migrant to L.A., the first time I saw Paul Beahm at Uni High [University High School of West Los Angeles]. It was lunch break … I saw this huge crowd of people coming across the field. There were a couple of people in front and a whole bunch of others following, staring and laughing, getting in fights, and generally acting like a bunch of high school idiots, and right in front was what all these people were flipping out over—Paul Beahm, with bright blue hair. He had hair down a little past his shoulders, like a surfer, but it was bright blue. Everyone was following him. We all reacted in different ways, I said, "What is that?'" Someone else said, "Fucking faggot!" and another person said "That's cool!"

FAITH BAKER   I was born Faith Reynolds. My first husband was Brainard Lucas who was an inventor, he was a manufacturer of picture tubes. We came out West from New Jersey. We had two children, Bobby and Christine, before we split up.

Paul was named after a neighbor's baby that died of a congenital heart defect right before Paul was born, and they asked me to name my baby after him, so he was named Jan Paul; we always liked the name Paul.

When Paul was born, on September 26, 1958, we lived upstairs over a bar in Venice. When he was five weeks old, we moved down to Avenue 33; then over to Pacific Avenue, next to the old Nightingale School. Then we got a big seven-room house right by the beach for $125 a month. We lived there until they tore it down.

Stepdad Bob Baker, Paul, Faith, Faith Jr.

Bobby Lucas, Paul's half brother, a recurrent drug addict, was murdered in 1969.

Then we lived on Grand Canal. Paul had a cat for 13 years until someone stole it. He fed it cantaloupe. My grandaughter named him Tom Kitty, because, if your name is Tom, it had to be Kitty, right?

When we first moved to West L.A., we lived on Brockton, and Paul went to Brockton Avenue School until we moved here. My daughter Faith had a little girlfriend who lived down the street. Once she was mad at Faith, and she hid behind a tree, and she meant to throw a rock at Faith, but when Paul came walking down Brockton, she hit him instead, and chipped his tooth. He was about six years old at the time.

Then he went to Webster Junior High. They had a special class there, and Paul went to that. He went to special classes up at Uni High, too. I used to make food for Uni High, enough for 80 people for when they had their little fairs. Paul and I would take it up there. One year I made stuffed cabbage and the German teacher said it was the best stuffed cabbage he'd ever had in his life. I'm a cooking enthusiast. I always was involved with food. Everybody knows me for my cooking! All my kids like to cook, and all my grandkids like to cook—Paul, too. Georg said that if everybody ever paid me back for what they ate in my house when they were teenagers, I would never have to work again! So I said, "Well, let's start payin' right?" Ha ha ha!

Paul was very into religions; when he was very young, we lived near a church, and he used to walk up the street and go to church by himself. When Paul and Faith Junior were young, there was a woman that used to take care of them if I was working on Sunday. She went to the Salvation Army, and took Paul and Faith with her. I think he got interested in religion there 'cause they went with her for a long time. After he dropped Scientology he was into all religions—he liked to read about them.

Paul was a very vibrant, living human being, and we were very close.

PAUL BEAHM   When I was really small I went to Catholic church, not long, like a year or two. I never got baptized or anything. The only reason I went to church every day was 'cause I'd get See's candy, like a pound or a five-pound bag or something. It was in a rich neighborhood in Venice. Every day See's would throw out fresh candy and they'd donate it all to the church.

BRENDAN MULLEN   Paul thought his father was Hal Beahm, Faith's second husband, who fathered Faith Jr. but vanished without a trace when Paul was a tot. Mr. Beahm was allegedly prone to excessive drinking and violent outbursts which ended in Faith's household after she sent him packing, never to be heard from again. Darby found out when a sibling let it slip during an argument that his father was really a Swedish sailor named William Bjorklund, another man was gone before he could see his then-unborn son. Next up was Bob Baker who Faith married in 1964.

FAITH BAKER   My other boy Bobby was murdered in Venice in 1969 when Paul was 11. They found him dead in his car. He was my first child, and he was 27 years old when he was killed. He was married to the sister of Mike Farrell, the movie star. Mike Farrell and I had a lot of fights—I didn't approve of him, and he didn't approve of me. I remarried when Paul was young—I'm a widow—and we used to go camping, and all that kind of stuff; he liked that. Paul and Faith were teenagers when my husband Bob Baker died—he died in 1972. They became pretty close to him. We used to go on lots of trips—once we went to Oregon. Once I had a broken leg, and when I got the cast off, we all went up to the Kern River for five days to celebrate. We cooked every day in the woods, and my husband and all the kids went fishing—I think we had like six kids—there was Faith and Paul and a bunch of the neighborhood kids.

BRENDAN MULLEN   At age 13, not long after his older brother Bobby (whom he idolized) was found dead in a station wagon in Venice reputedly from a hot-shot heroin O.D. passed to him by a burned dopeman, Paul's stepfather Bob Baker, a kindly man and the only stable male figure in Darby's life, died young from a heart attack. He was 39. Paul loved Bob Baker since the day he'd asked the older man to come home with him and his mother after the two adults had been out on a date. At the age of six Paul asked Baker to marry his mom and to be his new daddy.

FAITH BAKER   Bob Baker was a good solid man. There was never a dull moment when he was around. We were always going somewhere fun.

3

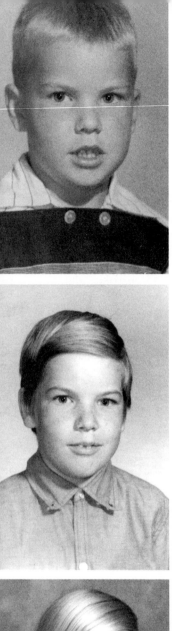

VILE BABIES

O

WILL AMATO I met Georg Ruthenberg in fourth grade. There were only like two, maybe three black kids in the whole school. I was kind of attracted to him for a number of reasons—for one thing being black he was kind of an underdog, and he just lived like two blocks away. He lived right down the street in that house on Bundy and Pico where the Germs used to rehearse. So we got to be friends. I used to go over to his house. He was actually half black—his mom was an opera singer, she had a very beautiful voice; his father was an older German fellow, who didn't say too much. I don't think he was in the greatest health. But Georg was just kind of an odd kid, real imaginative. He *loved* animals—he had this bunch of exotic birds, a collection that grew immensely over time.

FAITH BAKER Georg's father Mr. Ruthenberg was in his 80s. He was one of the inventors of color movies, with Howard Hughes. A brilliant man. He was way older than Georg's mother who is still living. She speaks about five languages, and she lives in a senior citizens' thing now and interprets for the old people.

GEORG RUTHENBERG There was one black kid—Wendel Wainwright III—that used to take my lunch money every day. I hated him, but there were white bullies, too. The black girls were always chasing me and trying to kiss me, which got my ass kicked by the boys, and the white girls were just my friends. Having sisters helped me to be able to be friends with women; a lot of guys don't have any women friends because they're either fucking them or trying to fuck them. Most guys don't know how to be friends with women—they grow up to be guys, with guys, but I was raised more like a girl. My mom had five girls before me, so all she knew how to do was raise girls. Darby was always friends with girls, too, especially girls that were like his mom. The girls that were always around were at least sort of like his mom—big, outspoken girls, like Michelle Baer and Dinky—they went from being Paul groupies, to Bobby Pyn groupies, to Darby Crash groupies.

ROBIN BOYARSKY I met Paul Beahm and Georg Ruthenberg in junior high; eighth or ninth grade. There were all these different groups at school—the surfers, the Chicanos, the blacks, and the stoners. All of them were very regimented, totally unimaginative. I started hanging out with kids who were weirder than everybody else, and Paul was definitely in that group. Paul was beyond weird, he was absolutely a freak, but he was *really* funny. He was always hanging around with Georg, who was also really, really funny.

WILL AMATO Georg and I started hanging out and being "freaks" together in junior high. There were all these various cliques with all their own rituals. The freaks were the ones who either couldn't find anyone to hang with or just had a more eccentric palette of obsessions than simply surfing, or being a jock, or just getting stoned. Around this time Georg met Paul. I didn't know Paul back then—this is seventh grade, early eighth grade.

GEORG RUTHENBERG I was 12 the first time I met Paul Beahm. I had a dollar a day for lunch money, and there was a 300-pound girl who sold whites 10 for a dollar. I remember laughing about how a speed dealer could weigh so much, because speed makes you not eat! She knew us both, and decided that even though we had never met, Paul and I were going to be best friends, and so she *had* to introduce us. We knocked on the door of his house, and Faith came to the door and said, "What?" And we said, "Oh, we're here to see Paul." She said, "He can't come out now. He's hiding in the closet in his underwear!" We said, "Oh, okay..." He didn't want visitors when he hid—"Raaar—keep 'em away!"

ROBIN BOYARSKY So there were Zabra and me, this girl Debbie, and Paul and Georg. We mostly just got stoned a lot on weed, though I know Paul and Georg also took reds. They were more good friends with each other than with anyone else. People used to say "intense" all the time, and if you didn't call pot "weed," you were either a dork or an old hippie. Zabra's dad was a pornographer, and there was porno all over their house. Zabra got arrested because she brought a little kid home to, like, get a Band-Aid or something, and there was this S&M mural with a demon on it in the bedroom. The kid told his mom about it, and she had Zabra arrested. I asked Zabra if she and her father had ever had sex ... it was, after all, the '70s ... and she said that they had talked about it but decided it would be "too weird."

PAUL ROESSLER Georg always had a very intense personality, even back then. He'd wear glitter shirts and carry his books like a girl across his chest, and he'd go mincing up to these hardcore cholo homeboys—he'd do this swishy flaming flounce act and say, (affects extremely girlish voice) "Beat me up," and these Mexican gangbangers would be just like... "Whoa, *putos*!"

WILL AMATO Georg and I started dressing strange. We'd wear formal tails to school, sometimes we'd wear T-shirts with some rock band logo on it, and "I Hate..." scrawled on it with Marks-a-lot, sort of like Johnny Rotten did later on. We started wearing nail polish which freaked many people out. We were listening to Alice Cooper, the Stooges, Bowie ... *School's Out* had just come out.

GEORG RUTHENBERG It was the '70s—I was into rock and roll, New York Dolls, the Stooges, Bowie's *Ziggy Stardust* album, and Alice Cooper's *School's Out*. We tried to dress like Bowie and Alice Cooper.

WILL AMATO I went to my first rock concert with Georg. We saw Alice Cooper at the Hollywood Bowl in '72 with Captain Beyond opening. We were doing our best to be... well, freaks. Glam started coming out in the air, around the Alice Cooper thing. We didn't have the hippie culture anymore, the Beatles had broken up; there was this nascent thing beginning, this vibe in the air, and we just knew it wasn't about jocks or "goody-goods"; it was about something subversive. And it was very young.

CHRIS ASHFORD Nobody ever called it glam rock in L.A. It was called glitter rock. The term "glam rock" became popular in the '80s.

TOBY MAMIS Behind nearly every punk was a record collection of Alice, Iggy, early Bowie, T. Rex, Roxy, the Dolls, all the usual suspects…

RODNEY BINGENHEIMER Punk is just dirty glitter.

KIM FOWLEY The California version was seen by the British rock press as the playpen of overeducated suburban white boy schmucks with nothing to do in this life but rebel against being rich and privileged and not having to shovel snow every winter. If you weren't British you were dog shit.

TOBY MAMIS The original Alice Cooper Band was probably the first rock act who took a stab at commercial success with their hybrid of the '60s punk/garage aesthetic and right-in-your-face "glam rock" … blatant androgyny served up with a big dollop of teen angst. This package also came with a surly lack of respect for musical or cultural norms. And when they had actual commercial success, it was like giving the inmates the key to the asylum.

KIM FOWLEY If you put '60s garage rock and '70s glam rock together, you get, duh—punk rock.

TOBY MAMIS The Alice Cooper Band inspired many other performers in so many ways, and crossed many boundaries. The New York Dolls were on the same track, but without the commercial success. Did they have the same talent? I don't know, but Alice Cooper made it cool for a band to be not technically good musicians, just good enough to rock out. Alice made it possible for bands to perform more than just standing around playing their songs live. These things inspired so many kids to form bands, and some of them ended up spearheading the punk scene.

KIM FOWLEY Punk was kids watching kids, it always works.

WILL AMATO Something as mundane as wearing nail polish was a way to piss off the mainstream. You didn't fit in so you really wanted to stick their nose in it. Then Bowie came out. Bowie provided a blueprint, a vibe that had a huge impact on the other teens I knew. When the *Ziggy Stardust* album came out. I was like "Oh fuck—do I really want to buy this?" When I opened up that gatefold I thought, "It's like homosexual pornography or something—and I've just bought it!" But then the texture of Ronson's guitars came out of the speakers, a very manly guitar sound—it really was like a weird drug, you know?

7

Paul and Faith.

Paul with sister Faith Jr., Mar Vista Bowl parking lot, 12/72.

GEORG RUTHENBERG   I hated anything to do with '50s-based rock, I just didn't wanna do any of those kind of chord changes. I liked bands like Yes that had nothing to do with what the '50s rock bands were about, or even the '60s pop thing. I just hated all that stuff so bad. You know those compilation albums that have a picture of a big gold record, and they say "Oldies But Goodies" on the cover? That's what Paul Beahm was listening to. Doo-wop sort of stuff.

PAUL BEAHM   I used to hate Bowie and rock music, I used to call them all queers and stuff. And I wouldn't listen to it.

GEORG RUTHENBERG   He hated what I listened to—Yes, Bowie, Queen, Alice. He thought it was all crap, just too fucking weird. When the first Queen record came out I was all psyched up to buy it, but somebody, probably Paul, talked me out of it, because it was a "fag record." Nobody at school wanted that, "Oh, you like *fag* music" rep. He just liked lowrider music—that's what he grew up on, that's what his sister liked, that's what his friends liked, that's what his crowd—the cholo crowd—listened to.

BRENDAN MULLEN   The following "non-faggot" 45's—each with the signature Paul Beahm in regular ballpoint ink on the labels—were retrieved and donated to me by sister Faith Jr. whose crew used to party down to "Angel Baby" by Rosie and the Originals and "Viva Tirado Parts 1 & 2" by El Chicano.

> "Everybody is a Star"/"Thank You (Falettin Me Be Mice Elf Again)" by Sly
>   & the Family Stone
> "Color Him Father" by the Winstons
> "A Little Bit of Soap" by Paul Davis

WILL AMATO   Alice Cooper had a song on the *Killer* album called "Halo of Flies" and Georg strung together an actual "Halo of Flies." It was a necklace made of flies, some alive, some dead … you could always find 'em on the windowsills, some he'd concussion bomb 'em with a cupped palm—POOM! Stun 'em and string 'em. The flies would remain alive for like three or four days. It was a really disturbing little relic, like a shrunken head or something. I hated the cruelty, but had to admire the ingeniousness of it. Georg and I went on a lot of shoplifting sprees at the May Co. on Pico. We'd steal all kinds of crap; stuff we didn't even want.

PAUL ROESSLER   One time, though, Georg's luck ran out—he and Paul went a bit too far, and they were caught red-handed…

GEORG RUTHENBERG   We ripped off some pot plants from a Mexican gangbanger, and he found out we did it, but Paul's sister was going out with this huge cholo guy, so he didn't mess with him, but I'd get beaten up every day, and they chased me with knives trying to kill me, so I ran away to this Jesus freak commune. Originally it was in Mendocino, but later they got an apartment building in

Eureka, and I lived in both places for a year. My sister Greta went there, I have no idea why, and when I was 13, we went up to visit her, and I somehow ended up staying. When I was 14, I went home. Then I went back when I was 15, and stayed until I turned 16.

It was originally a regular hippie colony out in the middle of a redwood forest, all log cabins, outhouses, no running water, then suddenly one day the same people turned it into a Jesus Loves You commune. I must have liked it, 'cause I lived there. It was really confusing.

Everyone was like a 21- or 22-year-old ex-hippie with a two-year-old baby, and I was like 13. They didn't know what to do with me. For a while I lived with one of the women because I was just a little kid, and then somebody said, "He's not a kid, we've got to move him to the men's dorm." But I couldn't go out and work with the men, because I wasn't a man; so for a while I was the babysitter.

I was 13, suddenly being dropped off at this far-out commune of weirdos, and so I sorta became a full-on Jesus freak. The only contact I had with anyone was a few letters that I wrote to Darby and a couple of other friends. I'd write, "Jesus loves you... don't fucking ruin your life, dumb shit!" That sort of thing. Now I'm a hardcore atheist. I don't even believe in the concept of the soul. I don't believe in anything! Later, when we wrote "No God," I was confused. It was only a couple of years after the commune thing, recent enough that I still had the "what if?" fear. I had been brainwashed by these Christian nuts for so long.

I really wanted to believe in it but always thought, "What's *wrong* with *me*?" All these people really knew; they actually had talked to Jesus or God direct. They always had a thing that had happened to them! Why didn't I have a "thing" that happened to me? Why does *she* speak in tongues and I don't? At first I couldn't *not* believe it, because these people were all good Christians and all good Christian soldiers wouldn't lie! I thought, "Why do these people have so much proof, and I don't have *any*?"

The first time I came back from the commune, when I was 13, I met up with Paul Beahm, and I was just back to normal. But the second time I came back, when I was 15, I tried to stay like that for a little while longer. I was a Christian who wasn't allowed to like any rock music—it was "of the world." I was taught to think of it as the Devil's music. And then Paul was suddenly into it. I was like, "What the fuck!" So I didn't really hang with him when I came back—but it seemed like he had kind of co-opted my old life. Now he was into all the bands I was into and he was hanging out with Julia my best neighbor-friend; I just felt really weird and left out. I don't know how he got into it; it all happened while I was gone. I didn't want to know. I wasn't interested, it was like, "I don't do this anymore." Darby thought I was an idiot for being so into Christianity and we argued about it.

BOBBY PYN   After I was a lowrider I got into acid.
FLIPSIDE   What did you use to trip out on acid?
BOBBY PYN   Acid.
   (From *Flipside*, circa '77.)

GEORG RUTHENBERG   It was acid, acid, acid, acid, acid! Darby had some free acid connection, so we'd take it every day—acid, acid, more acid, and even more acid and we'd talk for 12 hours at a time. We started thinking stuff like, "I wonder what happens if you take 10 hits? Wonder what happens if you take 20?" It was nuts! I don't know where all the acid came from; it was one of those secret things he liked to have. Paul said some guy gave it to him. Maybe he stole it, maybe he bought it, maybe someone did give it to him—I don't know. I'm sure he probably didn't buy it. He was very coy about it. He'd just say, "I got it from a friend." What friend? "Oh, you know—a friend."

PAUL ROESSLER   The math teacher thought Paul was the greatest, and they'd take acid and do math over at this teacher's apartment, and this dude had supposedly taken over 2000 hits of acid. He wasn't like a regular high school teacher; he would just sort of come in and do special stuff. He was always expressing love and awe that Paul could be as bright as he was.

GEORG RUTHENBERG   Darby liked to hang out with this particular teacher from IPS who lived in an apartment across the street from Uni. I went there a couple of times, and I'd drink with him, or get high, or whatever. He was like 30 years old and he was a raging alcoholic and there were rumors about him and boys and these camping trips. We'd either walk from [Paul's] house to my house, or from my house to his house, and spend the night together on acid. Then we'd walk back to my house to get a blanket and walk to the school with no shoes on, frying on acid. We were rarely separated—and if we were, we were on the phone. He always made things sound so mysterious. When I have a "mysterious secret" that I don't want anyone to know, I don't make sure everybody's wondering about my "mysterious secret!"

PAUL BEAHM   Acid took two years off of my life. I don't remember anything.

Paul Beahm's acid-drenched, homoerotic, high school period drawings.

est, Scientology and IPS

O

KIM FOWLEY Uni High was all rich kids, movie star kids, and TV actor kids during the '50s when I went there. The children of all those people. It was James Dean repressed high school, just like *Rebel Without A Cause*. It was: Thou shalt not fuck, thou shalt not come, thou shalt not get drunk, or get high or have any fun. Thou shalt go to college. Thou shalt be a credit to your parents. You better make 'em proud. You'll all be doctors, you'll all be lawyers, you'll all be castrated, Episcopalian puppets, and you'll all be like Ozzie and Harriet's children because that's what everybody wanted their kids to be like.

PAUL BEAHM I learned it all from Uni High. People thought it was a really weird school. Like one of the teachers was a convicted child molester. Carole King's daughter went there with us, too. And Jeff Bridges used to visit all the time.

KIM FOWLEY By the time Darby Crash and Pat Smear went there in the '70s it was like: You better not smoke dope, you better not go to Hollywood on weekends. You better not suck cock, you better not eat pussy. You better not have a black girlfriend. Ooh, you better not start a band. Ooh, you better not shoot up. You won't be a credit to your family, but, of course, nearly all familes by the '70s, were like single parent, dysfunctional trainwrecks with the Vietnam guilt and the John F. Kennedy mourning and the Beatles suppression of everything.

GEZA X I predated IPS at Uni High during the '60s. Some of my social group were the campus radicals … we were staging demonstrations, putting out underground newspapers, and fucking a lot. A lot of the teachers saw that this was a group of pretty smart kids looking for some direction. I'm sure that's why they allowed something like IPS to come in there later on.

CALDWELL WILLIAMS Whoever [University High School] didn't want... I was directed to take! Paul was a disturbed kid!

PAT SMEAR IPS was the ultimate rebellion. We decided to get into it so we could rebel against it.

CALDWELL WILLIAMS After [California senator] Alan Cranston turned down my plan for a school in South Central, I found myself in a meeting with a group of parents from the Westside that wanted to do something different, so I quickly modified my plan from a full school to a "sub-school"—a "school within a school." I only knew Fred Holtby by reputation until that meeting when he called time out and said, "Caldwell, can I talk to you for a minute?" We went into the kitchen and he said, "When Maynard Hutchens started his think-tank in Santa

Barbara he pulled together all these august minds, but it didn't work because, essentially, all these august minds couldn't get along; so he closed it down and started over again. On his second try, Hutchens picked one guy that he knew he could get along with; and then the two of them had to agree on the third guy that they'd both get along with; that's how they built the second team at his think tank—and it worked! So Fred said, "I propose we use that model; let's see if you and I can get along, and then we'll pick the third, and so on; and I said, "Great!" So he just included himself, brilliantly. So we go back into the meeting, and Fred announced "We have the nucleus of a team," and the group was enthralled that someone was taking the ball.

FRED HOLTBY   To my knowledge we were the first public school, maybe the first school, period, to have a little school-within-a-school like that. It all started with one parent especially who had a daughter who was unhappy with school and wanted to do something else…

CALDWELL WILLIAMS   I was on the front end of the human potential movement, with Esalen and the rest. I checked it all out. I took the est training. Werner Erhardt put together a process that delivered a program to 250 people in 60 hours that produced the impact and insight that six months of group therapy, or *three years* of one-on-one therapy could have produced. After I had done it, some of my students wanted to do it, too, and I said, "Check with your parents." Some of my students did the est training and then my colleagues did it.

FAITH BAKER   I went to a few est meetings at Uni High with Georg's father. We used to take Paul and Georg to these meetings, too, until we got disenchanted. They had … funny beliefs. You know what "Rolfing" is? It was sort of physical— it got kinda rough, heh heh heh!

PAUL BEAHM   The IPS school within a school was based on est and Scientology stuff. It was like the first alternative public school special education program in California, but all they did was screw with people's heads. Every morning you could go to a class like self-hypnosis or something where we'd all do these exercises. If you lost your name tag you weren't allowed in.

GEORG RUTHENBERG   Paul and I went to IPS together. We thought it was *really* weird, but mostly we just wanted it to end so we could get on to the part where we would take acid with the teachers, make our own classes, and grade ourselves.

ROBIN BOYARSKY   IPS stood for "Innovative Program School." Scientology heavily influenced our learning program. Our study setup was designed by a Scientologist, and it was trademarked. The teacher's aide had just been "est-ed," and of course there were the two Scientologists—Fred Holtby, the rhetoric teacher, and G——, the math teacher. One of the other teachers followed Transactional Analysis, and the art teacher was coming out as a lesbian. She played "women's music" in art class.

PAUL ROESSLER   Everyone at IPS would look up any word we weren't absolutely sure about in the dictionary; that was a big Scientology thing, too. I think that was the origin of Darby's "lexicon" obsession … the Scientology dictionary thing was very probably a major influence in developing his fascination with wordsmithing, word sculpting…

PAUL BEAHM   There are 26 meanings for the word "the," and I like to know exactly what they mean. I learned this from Scientology.

CALDWELL WILLIAMS   Fred was one of the most popular teachers on campus, but I think he was more appreciated as a brilliant English teacher than as a human being. Fred was a mind fucker. If you were intelligent, you got off on the gyrations that he put you through. You had to think. You had to figure out. You had to justify. He was an extraordinary rhetorician and a fan of Alan Watts.

GEORG RUTHENBERG   We'd heard stories like, "The IPS teachers take acid with the students!" We thought, "Cool! We've gotta get into this school!" That was really our motivation; and it turned out to be true, at least about the math teacher. We just wanted to try it because it was some weird, new thing.

PAUL ROESSLER   IPS convened in a row of run-down bungalows on campus. They had their own philosophy that would change and evolve, and the students were involved in setting the direction. If you were intellectual with an open mind, IPS was really enlightening. It was incredible to be exposed to all those different contexts, and some of them were actually educational. I learned about Tai Chi and rhetoric because of IPS.

GEORG RUTHENBERG   You had to bring at least one of your parents to "orientation." They just yelled at you and called you "cocks" and "cunts" and wouldn't let you go to the bathroom. If you made it through however many days of *that* without freaking out, or killing yourself, or whatever was supposed to happen to you— *then* you got to go to "Basic Training," which was all these weird yoga exercises called "Body-Mind." It was a bunch of hippie mumbo-jumbo thrown into the Scientology/est bullshit.

PAUL ROESSLER   We had our own language in IPS. Fred Holtby made up a lot of the words. He would also teach us rhetoric. We'd study the Bible, J. D. Salinger, and Kurt Vonnegut. One day Fred had a stack of Bibles, and he was throwing them to each person sitting in a circle on the floor. When he'd throw one to a guy he'd say, "Here, Cock!" When he'd throw one to a girl, he'd say, "Here, Cunt!" Here was this freaky old guy with gold hair throwing a Bible at us going "Here Cock, here Cunt!" I just thought, "Cool!" He'd say "Look what the first line in the Bible says—In the beginning was the word—What does that mean?" It meant that rhetoric was number one, above all.

GEORG RUTHENBERG   The teachers were attempting to brainwash us, while teaching us brainwashing techniques. Meanwhile, we were taking *tons* of acid and acting out as wannabe-rock stars. It was the est/Scientology thing—it's so creepily mind-controlling! We were rebelling against *that*—on top of all the acid. Yeah, I'd say that IPS definitely affected me, sometimes to the present day.

WILL AMATO   Fred was a hard nut for Paul to crack, a challenge, so of course Paul had to fuck with him. Fred was a very bright guy, and he'd fuck with you mostly by being really deadpan. He could look at you, go to level zero, blank out and give you this kind of idiotic grin, but you could see the gears turning behind those eyes; and those eyes never turned dead. He'd look at you and just say "Flunk" and wouldn't elaborate. He'd just say "Flunk."

PAUL ROESSLER   IPS "Basic Training" was one of those "California awareness" things, but it was also like Korean prisoner-of-war brainwashing. It was a two-week thing, in a huge auditorium at UCLA. First thing every morning, in this room with 300 students, you had to just sit and look at the person next to you, stare straight into their eyes and just "be" with them for the first ten or fifteen minutes. You weren't supposed to laugh, joke, or talk; you weren't supposed to think, you weren't supposed to do *anything* but just *be there*, looking straight into this person's eyes. They'd say, "Notice what your brain is doing right now."

ROBIN BOYARSKY   They'd say, "Anything you have to tell us, tell us!" So this one girl confessed that she was drinking codeine cough syrup, and so they toted her off to Narconon, the Scientology drug rehab. We were told by IPS teachers, "Don't tell 'Real Uni' or we'll get closed down." But "Real Uni" quickly found out they were shipping out people to this outrageously expensive Scientology rehab and they had to stop.

GEORG RUTHENBERG   Basic Training was where they yelled at you and said you were assholes for eight hours, and you had to bring a parent with you. If you survived you got to go to this special school.

PAUL ROESSLER   You'd have to get down in front of the class and every boy would have to act like a girl and every girl would have to act like a boy. When you're 16 years old, and doing something really, really embarrassing like that in front of 300 people … it's intense. If someone had a headache they'd make the person describe what color it was and how much water it could hold until the pain was gone. They'd say "Do you remember a time previous to this when you felt that way? And previous to that?" And so on, until you're like two days old, or going back into a previous life, all very silly stuff—yet very cool stuff at the same time.

ROBIN BOYARSKY   K—— S—— was really ugly, because she had this swollen, jowly face with eczema all over it, and she was always rubbing it with her fingertips because it itched. Her mom was the teacher of this sex education class. She was a

IPS Body/Mind ritual. Kira Roessler, bottom, second from left.

IPS faculty as drawn by Will Amato for the yearbook. Fred Holtby, third from left. Caldwell Williams, fourth from left.

big '70s-style Jewish mother—lots of jewelry, big nails, the whole bit. One time we were supposed to go around the room and tell our sex fantasy, and she went first. She and her husband were in bed making love and their son and daughter K—— were each in their rooms masturbating. And poor K—— was right there in the class! Can you imagine if your mom said that? In front of the whole class? It was just appalling!

PAUL ROESSLER   It was all part of a breaking down intimidation process. The military does that, right? Like those psycho drill sergeants in the movies screaming and spitting the fear of god into a bunch of dumb new jarheads. They were saying, "Look, if you want to be in this school; you have to start by admitting you're fucked up and you want to change. To get what we have, you have to say, 'I want more; I want to achieve more.' If you're fine the way you are, then go to regular school."

ROBIN BOYARSKY   Probably the biggest thing that I took away from IPS was the ability to maintain eye contact, staring people down; they taught you how to do that.

GEORG RUTHENBERG   The big thing in IPS was that the teachers were always right, you were never supposed to question anything that they said or told you to do, which, of course, is exactly what we did. Our thing was, "You're not God, not everything you say is right—fuck you!"

PAUL BEAHM   Teachers got mad. You were allowed to say anything to a teacher you wanted and so we'd tell 'em to go to hell, kill yourself, we don't care. And the parents got upset because we went to this other school and caused trouble. And one of the teacher's sons was hanging around with us and we were taking acid, so he was pretty upset.

WILL AMATO   IPS allowed you to form your own classes. As long as you could get one other person to join your class it was legit, and Georg and Paul announced that they had formed a class. Fred [Holtby] said, "Oh, really? What's your class?" They said, "It's a sewing class." Which got a lot of laughs. So Fred said, "Okay, well, you can do whatever you want—so I guess you're going to form a sewing class. When are you going to start sewing?" And Paul said "Right now." "Well," said Fred, "How are you going to do that?" Paul looked at him and said "So?" Fred said "What do you mean? I don't understand you." And Paul said "So?" Fred looking real puzzled said, "You do know you have to fill out this form and keep track of the work you do?" and Paul replied "So?" No matter what Fred or anyone said to them they'd say "So?" And that was their big "so-ing" class!

GEORG RUTHENBERG   Then we had the Fruit Eating class. It was an hour a day, where we'd walk up to the market, eat fruit from the produce department, and hang out in front for a while, and then walk back to school. We, of course, gave ourselves A's.

PAUL BEAHM   Nobody really took what the [IPS teachers] said seriously. You'd go to lunch and still get loaded and stuff. Like you had to make an agreement that you wouldn't take drugs, that you wouldn't be late, that you wouldn't be sick, and so on. And then we started saying, "Okay, we caused it, we're responsible … there's no right and there's no wrong, so now what?"

GEORG RUTHENBERG   Some people saw it as a sort of cushy continuation school. If you screwed up at regular Uni you could almost certainly graduate if you went to IPS, where you could pick your own grades. The IPS kids were misfits, but they weren't stupid misfits, like the people in continuation school. Everyone was really smart and savvy, they were usually in IPS for disciplinary reasons, or that they were too bright for the regular classes. A school like that would never be allowed to exist now.

FRED HOLTBY   Those '70s were something else! I think we really did some good things. We were trying real hard to do well. The one thing that we faculty all agreed on is that we didn't want a completely free-form school, although we certainly wanted a lot of input from the students. We'd start and end the day with a general meeting.

PAUL ROESSLER   The teachers either thought Paul was the coolest, some were even in awe of him … or else they hated him, were scared of him, didn't want anything to do with him. Fred called him a "rhetorician," which meant he controlled reality with his words. Fred was a very good rhetorician himself; never in awe of anybody, so this was a major compliment. He said, "Paul can control reality like us." Rhetoric is the study of argument—if you win your argument you're a good rhetorician; it's got nothing to do with truth. And a really avant-garde rhetorician believes that by winning your argument, you actually affect reality. That makes what truth is. "In the beginning was the word."

WILL AMATO   Rhetoric was a very important class for Paul Beahm. He was trying to crack language into different pieces to discover the secrets of rhetoric. He'd wonder, "Why the fuck does that Bowie album affect us like this?" He'd say, "It's buried in those lyrics, it's somewhere in there; I know it's in the texture of his voice, I know it's in those clever pop tunes, I know it's in that weird look of his, but he's doing *something* in those words. What is it? Why are all the kids in England going nuts over this guy?" He was using rhetoric. That was the key.

GEORG RUTHENBERG   Paul somehow changed the script for the morning announcements to include an item about members of Led Zeppelin being killed in a horrible plane crash; a good percentage of the class burst into tears.

WILL AMATO   A story went around that Paul took this girl who was supposedly having an affair with Fred, and gave her acid, then brainwashed her into hating Fred. Is any of that true? I don't know. Roessler thinks it's true. Robin Boyarsky thinks it's true.

ROBIN BOYARSKY   They made us hug, and there was a rule against giving "A-frame" hugs, which is where you hug someone but you only lean your upper body towards them, as opposed to pressing your entire body against them. They'd say, "No A-frames!" My girlfriends and I would always go in the corner and hug each other, 'cause we didn't want to give non-A-frame hugs to these ugly teenage boys with boners! We made a promise to "play IPS." That was the terminology. We were gonna play, or we were not gonna play, and we had to sign something to say that we were going to play. Fred and G—— were very sadistic with these creepy robotic smiles, always talking in Scientology lingo, like if you didn't understand something you wouldn't say that, you'd say, "I have a misunderstood." Instead of "Homeroom," we did "Frame," which was supposed to be the framework of our day. In Frame we did exercises from Scientology and est. Whoever your Frame teacher was would have their own thing. We did exercises in Frame every morning, and we'd start by doing "TR's" which is from Scientology. TR stands for "training routine" where you'd sit cross-legged across from a partner doing various exercises. Not that many people can sit cross-legged, touching another person they don't know that well, or staring into their eyes for five minutes, and be comfortable.

WILL AMATO   TR-0 was training yourself to maintain a Zen-like indifference to an object. They were big into "You're either Cause or Effect."

ROBIN BOYARSKY   You can see why so many actors are into it. First you'd sit with your eyes closed for a few minutes, until you were comfortable—that's TR-1. TR-2 would be the same, but with your eyes open, without fidgeting or talking. TR-3, I think, was to make someone laugh.

WILL AMATO   Up around TR-9 you're saying, "Please touch that wall," and you are grabbing their hand and yanking them to a wall, and pushing their hand up to the wall, and then you look at them and say, "Thank you." These were communication skills, so that you could be in "cause" rather than in "effect."

ROBIN BOYARSKY   They made you write down all your drug experiences—using real names, dates and places—and turn them in to your Frame teacher, or else you "weren't playing IPS," which meant you got sent back to "real Uni." They were having drug problems, because everyone was taking acid and the parents were complaining. If they caught you with drugs you had to name two other drug users in IPS, or else they sent you back to regular Uni. One person was sent back, which meant that other people were "narcs," and we knew it, so there was this horrible atmosphere of paranoia. The guy who got sent back refused to snitch his friends off. It meant that he was not going to graduate high school.

I didn't really hang around with the people from the school—it was too culty; they were a little too into it. I was just too busy getting stoned. I had to pretend that I was into it, too, of course, or I wasn't "playing IPS." I would never have graduated from high school otherwise, and a lot of people were there for just that reason.

Doug Holtby, Fred Holtby's son and Paul Beahm's friend, IPS yearbook.

Will Amato, IPS yearbook.

GERBER When we met I was still in junior high, I was in Emerson. It was my last year, and I was supposed to transfer to Uni, but I got suspended for fighting and then expelled, so when I transferred to Uni I was ineligible to go to IPS based on my academic probation and my history of violence. I was sent to the remedial school which was still on the campus—but I was always ditching to hang out with Paul and Georg and Paul Roessler … we became very close.

PLEASANT GEHMAN (Diary entry, November 18, 1975)   I went to IPS today. Mixed emotions. Very mixed. I got feelings like, "Hell, I should be going here, why am I submitting myself to Beverly Hills [High School]?" And then, "God, this place is pretty fucked." It was pretty neat, mostly fruits and earthers, which, when hostility ain't included, mix perfectly, because they both aren't "normal." But the one thing that bothered me was the self-righteousness and the self-conscious-ness. Very self-conscious of being unselfconscious, uninhibited, and "free." People always spoke in IPS lingo which goes something like, "I get that you acknowledge me an asshole, but that doesn't mean you don't have the space to play with me. I want you to get that. By the way, it's OK to be fucked to me." They seemed uncom-fortable.

HALLOWEEN DA

RICHIE DAGGER'S CRIME

O

PAUL ROESSLER   Paul had this natural power; it was hard to figure out what it actually was; it was either that he was so much smarter than anybody else so he could do these things, or he had techniques that he learned from the books he read or from IPS. Or he just had magic.

PAUL BEAHM   They finally threw me out of the school and told me if I never came back I could have my diploma equivalency. They got upset because the rest of the school was getting real scared and the teachers wanted to have us committed.

GEORG RUTHENBERG   We had our little group of LSD friends, and Paul and I started convincing them that the teachers weren't right, and we got all these followers that rebelled.

CHRIS ASHFORD   Darby left high school in '76. Pat was a year younger, but I don't think Pat went his last year at all.

GEORG RUTHENBERG   One of our followers was Doug Holtby the head of the school's son, which didn't help our case. The student council kicked us out of the program. Paul's deal was that he'd get his diploma if he never set foot on school grounds again; mine was to go to continuation school off campus provided I saw the school psychologist.

PAUL ROESSLER   [IPS] gave him straight A's and all his credits as long as he would not speak to anyone from the school ever again.

PAUL BEAHM   I said, "Well, does it matter if I hang around here, you know, because I'm not going out of town." And they said sure. And then in a year they wouldn't give me my diploma. Like they did that to Pat, too. They said to us, "They're lost. We threw them away." Finally, we went to the school board and I just told them these IPS teachers were nuts and I explained to the board what they were doing. They said those are pretty serious charges and you may have to go to court about this. Finally they got scared and gave them to me. But they gave me D's in classes like Remedial Reading. At the end of the year they had a list of people who contributed to the school and I was number one or two on it.

GEORG RUTHENBERG   We were accused of "brainwashing" people like Doug Holtby, Fred's son. We were making the other kids part of our "Let's take acid and mock everything they do" group.

PAUL ROESSLER Paul could be really cruel and horrible to his friends. On the way home from dropping people off, he'd have whoever was driving pull up in front of some girl's house that had really conservative parents, and he'd yell "Tracy's on acid! Tracy's on acid!" really loud, and they'd like freak out, ground her forever and send her to boarding school, basically ruin her life, and he would just laugh about it.

PAUL BEAHM They threw us out of IPS for having our own religion... we renamed it Inter-Planetary School ... everyone wore "Certified Space Case" silver stickers. We convinced about half the other kids that I was God and Pat was Jesus, this one girl almost had a nervous breakdown ... 'cause I sat there for like half an hour telling her I was God, and she started screaming and there was all these Bibles in the class and she started throwing them at us. She didn't come back to school for a week.

PAUL ROESSLER When they threw him out I think there was a triumph there, too. They would call it defeat because they got rid of him, but I don't think of it like that at all. I have this picture of the final confrontation—I think he probably looked at them and said, "You guys are hypocrites." I heard there was an IPS staff meeting where they voted to boot him. Lucky Lehrer [the same person who later played drums in the Circle Jerks and even the Darby Crash Band] was part of that meeting. Lucky was the only student who was allowed to participate in staff meetings.

GEORG RUTHENBERG Sometimes we just liked to hang out at school. I don't know why. We'd break in at night, take acid and just... hang out. We'd spend the night there. We loved it! In fact, just after Darby got kicked out—he was already going to SMC [Santa Monica City College]. I got suspended from school, but we used to come back to hang out until cops came and actually arrested us. It was the middle of the day, and we were just going to hang out at our old school ... then out of nowhere there's all these cops and handcuffs; we were all punked out—by now we had our Germs T-shirts on.

LEXICON DEVIL

FAITH BAKER   Paul was always good with words; he talked very young, and he read everything he could get his hands on—we read a lot of the same books; we used to swap. I think it runs in the family, because my father was like that—he was a great reader, and he loved poetry.

PAUL ROESSLER   For a few months I was over at his house all the time, and I would just observe ... he would never sleep. We'd watch *Johnny Carson*, then read 'til four or five, whenever, I'd fall asleep and wake up and he was still sitting there reading.

PAUL BEAHM   Practically all I do is read and write.

PAUL ROESSLER   He was always taking us on field trips. He'd take a bunch of his friends down to the Krishna Temple. They'd feed us, and we'd dance and sing with them. Another day he took us all down to the Scientology place on Holly-wood Boulevard. Pat scored zero on the personality test, and they told him that he was an utterly horrible person; I scored like a regular person, and they said, "Yeah, we can help you for a $500.00 deposit." Of course, Darby scored perfectly on everything, and they asked him to come teach.

CLAUDE BESSY   They said [Darby] was well-read, but I haven't got a fucking clue what he'd read or what he was supposedly reading.

CHRIS D.   Everybody always talks about him reading Nietzsche ... but he told us about this book *Twins* which was a bestseller at the time ... about twin gynecolo-gists who go off their rocker and end up killing each other. [The novel by Bari Wood and Jack Geasland later became the David Cronenberg movie, *Dead Ringers*.]

PAUL ROESSLER   He was way into Nietzsche and Oswald Spengler.

FAITH BAKER   I bought the *Star* and the *Enquirer*, because Paul wanted them—even when he was into the punk scene, he read them every week.

PAUL ROESSLER   He also immersed himself in Bertrand Russell's *Encyclopædia of Philosophy*.

CHRIS D.   He was familiar with both the stuff you'd read in American literature class in high school, back through 19th Century European stuff, but he also loved trash, pulp, bestseller type stuff. Darby didn't discriminate between low-brow or highbrow.

PAUL BEAHM My favorite book, probably, is *Brave New World* by Aldous Huxley. There's a really neat sequel called *Brave New World Revisited* that tells how it's all coming true.

WILL AMATO Paul was reading *Mein Kampf* around '75. And he was reading *The Family* by Ed Sanders, and *Helter Skelter*, too. He was also going to the Scientology Center, and reading L. Ron Hubbard.

PAUL BEAHM'S READING LIST

Dianetics: L. Ron Hubbard
Mein Kampf: Adolf Hitler
The Family: Ed Sanders
Helter Skelter: Vincent Bugliosi
Knots: R.D. Laing
The Politics of Experience: R.D. Laing
The Decline Of the West: Oswald Spengler
Also Sprach Zarathustra: Nietzsche
Twins: Bari Wood and Jack Geasland
I, Judas: Tara Caldwell
The Glass Bead Game: Herman Hesse
Brave New World: Aldous Huxley
Brave New World Revisited: Aldous Huxley
The Prince: Machiavelli
The works of Roald Dahl
Crash: J.G. Ballard
The National Enquirer
Magicians of the Golden Dawn: Ellic Howe
The short stories of Charles Beaumont and Richard Matheson, the two main
    writers for Rod Serling's *Twilight Zone*

PAUL BEAHM When I was in school I kept notebooks and stuff. Not any more. I work on some philosophy stuff. Just Scientology and Nietzsche like *Thus Spake Zarathustra* and *The Prince* by Machiavelli. Manson got thrown out of Scientology the first day, they said he was psychotic.

NICOLE PANTER I suggested he read Machiavelli's *The Prince*. I thought there had to be a more subtle way for him to manipulate people if that's what he really wanted to do. He asked if that would get people to do what he wanted them to and I said yeah, and they won't even know they're doing it. I think he tried to read the book but just didn't see the connection.

PAUL BEAHM

'Tell Me Why' Query Brings Yearbook Award

A West Los Angeles youth has won a new Book of Knowledge Yearbook for his entry in the "Tell Me Why" contest published on the Evening Outlook's comics page.

Paul Beahm, 15, won the award for his question, "What Is A Platypus?"

He is a 10th grade student at University High School.

The son of Faith Baker of 1567 Barrington Ave., he has a brother, Bobby, and two sisters, Christine and Faith.

He lists his hobbies as jewelry and crafts.

Darby at mom's West L.A. house, circa 1979.

FIVE YEARS

O

WILL AMATO   Bowie was to Paul what the Beatles were to Manson.

PAUL BEAHM   My favorite is Bowie. Just because he's done everything.

WILL AMATO   Paul Beahm was a fanatically dedicated student of Bowie. He looked at *Ziggy Stardust* as the *Mein Kampf* of pop. And I think Bowie intended it as such. Just like *Mein Kampf* laid out the ground-plan for what Hitler was going to do, so *Ziggy Stardust* laid it out for what Bowie was gonna do.

PAUL ROESSLER   Paul Beahm turned me on to David Bowie. I said, "I haven't really heard much Bowie stuff; I'm really into the Rolling Stones," and he said something sarcastic like, "Oh yeah, Mick Jagger's really cool," you know; and he'd make me feel like an idiot, like there was something important that I didn't know. He also talked about Iggy, and I said, "Who's that?" "A faded pop star," he said.

WILL AMATO   Paul felt that Bowie was on to something that wasn't explicit. Bowie could give you surface suggestion, but what he *wasn't* saying was what got to him. One time Paul excitedly announced that he had cracked the coded meaning of the *Diamond Dogs* album title. I'd already given it my best shot. I said, "Well, the diamonds are the rarified jewels, the rich people in their towers, and the dogs are the curs, the underclass below?" And Paul said "No, no, no—what's a girl's best friend?" And I said, "Uh, diamonds." Then he said, "What's a man's best friend?" I smacked my forehead. What did it mean that he would take that much time to figure something like that out?

HELLIN KILLER   He had a Bowie shrine in his room … he'd sign himself Astrid and he'd written these letters and put them up at school … he'd say he was a child from the stars.

ASTRID

Astrid was from a planet blue
He spoke of love for me and you
He could set your mind ablaze
With sparkling eyes and visionary gaze
He stood like a remnant from an outbreak past
Wore a ring in his ear and boy was he fast
Had hair like a rocket's nest but
When he cheered he gave his best
He made a noise that stirred our souls

Got us moving out of control
When Astrid moved we changed our tunes

They filled his arms with needles bare
Shot him up and cut his hair
Tied him to an evil plot
Told the kids that he was not...
Their man

He gave us life and dealt us love
Sold us out for the great above—he was

On a starry night in mid-December
Astrid cried—you might remember

(Live it to the end, share it with a friend
Deny me not, 'cause now you're caught)

I'll be with you in the thought—beyond
                —Jan Paul Beahm, 1975 (age 17)

WILL AMATO Paul wanted that magic, he wanted that mojo. He said Bowie was using language to physically affect people, and they didn't even know it. Language was a cause, and all these Bowie kids were the effect. If he could learn to use language like that, if he could harness the power of language to that degree, then he, too, could be cause. Language had the power to sway and persuade and bamboozle and hypnotize, you could even get a bunch of crazed, drug-addled teenagers to form a little killing cult for you if you wanted ... it could have that much power just for the taking.

CLAUDE BESSY Darby thought only of Iggy Pop and David Bowie.

PLEASANT GEHMAN And Joan Jett.

WILL AMATO The fact that Bowie looked the way he did, could sing the way that he did, could crank out lots of super-catchy pop songs, and had one of the most brilliant management teams in pop history behind him may have had something to do with his success. Sadly, Paul had none of this. What it was that he hoped to achieve with the Bowie fixation could not be done. He was never gonna *be* Dave Bowie.

CHRIS ASHFORD Paul Beahm was already starting to erect a myth about himself. We went to a Yes concert with Peter Frampton opening, right after *Frampton Comes Alive.* It was me, Georg, Pleasant, Paul Roessler, and Paul Beahm. We all went together, but Paul disappeared. We couldn't find him, and we left. He was home before we got back, and he said that he had climbed the fence, gotten by the security guards, and had watched the entire concert backstage. We asked him how he got back home, and he remained mysterious about it. Did he really go backstage? I can't say he didn't, but he sure wanted us to think he had; and that he had some mysterious way to get back home before the rest of us. Without a car. He said that he didn't want to spend the whole concert sitting around with a bunch of dumbasses smoking pot, or whatever we were doing. He had other agendas. Somehow he got backstage. Somehow he got home before the rest of us without a car. It gave him an aura.

GEORG RUTHENBERG I met Pleasant Gehman when I was like 15 at a Tubes show. We found out where they were rehearsing and went over there and said we wanted to be in their show. They said, "Okay—we need some plants!" They wanted us to run when Fee Waybill came down the aisle with the chainsaw. I remember that we really didn't want to do it, we just wanted to get in free.

PLEASANT GEHMAN I didn't move to Los Angeles until I turned 16 in '75, but within the first two weeks, I went to see the Tubes at Santa Monica Civic, and I was sitting, like, right behind Tony Curtis! The Civic was a sea of denim. There were a few fun, glittery people, but not that many. It was the *White Punks on Dope* tour. I was wearing lots of rhinestones and a '40s evening gown. I saw Georg and Paul coming down the aisle. Paul was wearing all white—a white denim jacket and white bellbottoms, total hustler white. He had a perfect bright carrot-red Bowie cut, and he had drawn an Aladdin Sane lightning bolt down his face.

Georg was way taller than Paul; he looked really tall because he was wearing a floor-length black cape and his hair was all crazy and he had kind of Alice Cooper make-up on. Everyone was wearing either French jeans or California surfer wear. Any kind of glitter fashion statement like that stuck out. I was looking at them thinking, "Kindred souls, oh my God! They're both so cute!" Georg was wearing black satin pants and no shirt under the cape. I always liked really tall and skinny guys, plus I loved Bowie and Alice—any guy wearing make-up was a huge turn-on.

GEORG RUTHENBERG Pleasant threw us her number on a matchbook, and then we went out for a year. She went to Bev High. She was a year older than me; she was in Darby's grade. Some days we'd cut and go to her school, some days she'd cut and go to ours. I was thrown out of Beverly Hills High by some teacher who dragged me downstairs by my ear! Pleasant lived in Beverly Hills, which was closer to Hollywood. We would take the bus out there just to hang out in the Rainbow parking lot, to see who went in and out—all the adult "rock people" that were all dressed up ready to rock out; we were like 14, 15 years old and we were like, "Wow!"

PLEASANT GEHMAN They were three or four rows down. I got a matchbook and drew stars and Saturn and moons and stuff all over it, and I wrote, "Aladdin Sane, you cosmic orgasm, call me." I put my name and number on it, threw it at them— and they got it! The next day Paul called me and we were talking about Bowie,

Squeaky Fromme and Sandra Good of the Manson Family, an early Circle One influence.
Photo: Kerry Colonna

of course, but we talked about a lot of other shit, too. He called again the next day, and then Georg called, so then I was talking to both of them; we had this phone relationship for like two weeks where I would call right after I got home from school, or one of them would call me. The calls started getting longer and longer, and nobody had call waiting then. I learned about emergency break-throughs from them. The operator would say, "I have an emergency breakthrough from Mick Ronson," or some name of a character in a Bowie song. We'd be on the phone for like four, five, six hours at a time. Typical high school teenage stuff. I'd be talking to Georg and there'd be an emergency breakthrough to him from Paul, or they'd be talking and I'd make an emergency breakthrough to Paul, or whatever—it was crazy. We were probably the reason emergency breakthroughs started costing a dollar.

We found out what books we liked and where we went to school. Since Georg and Paul lived in West L.A. and I lived on borderline Beverly Hills and none of us had a car, we decided on a common meeting ground in Westwood. Chris Ash-ford drove them there in this beaten-up old mid-'60s giant blue car; he was the only person they knew who had a car, so we did a lot of stuff with him. We wound up going out and hanging out with each other, getting really stoned and vandalizing things and knocking over sand ashtrays in bank buildings...

We also used to go to the *Rocky Horror Picture Show* in Westwood all the time, but we were never like the people that would throw toast at the screen. Of course we knew all the words, who wouldn't, when you'd seen it so many times?

GEORG RUTHENBERG   We'd go to midnight showings of *Yessongs*!

WHAT WE DO IS SECRET

O

PLEASANT GEHMAN   We saw this Manson documentary that was playing at a theater in Westwood, like five times. We'd go there for the midnight show and get ridiculously stoned.

GEORG RUTHENBERG   We liked the Manson thing in high school. It freaked people out! We would carry around copies of *Helter Skelter* and say it was our Bible; we'd put X's on our foreheads with Magic Markers.

RIK L. RIK   Darby's group, the whole Germs Circle One clique, were accused of being like a Manson Family type situation by some people.

PLEASANT GEHMAN   We used to do "creepy crawls" in neighbors' houses, like the Manson Family—we'd get in their houses and rearrange furniture and stuff.

HELLIN KILLER   It was a small group of teenagers, some of them were still into the glitter rock scene. Darby and Pat were the aftermath of the whole Bowie-Alice Cooper-Tubes-*Rocky Horror* culture and the effect it had on young kids our age who were running around cross-dressed in make-up … we were basically free-wheelin' teenagers emulating the '70s clown rock thing … we just didn't have anywhere else to go. Pleasant and [Georg] and [Paul]. They were weird oddballs who just hung around and somehow merged together.

PLEASANT GEHMAN   We were taking anything we could get, a lot of Quaaludes, a lot of acid. We hardly ever went to Georg's house. We'd hang out at my house because my mom was working during the daytime, but somehow we wound up mainly hanging out at Paul's house. His room was really cool. It was covered with pictures of Bowie and he had a stack of great bootlegs, and it was like really dark. Paul's house became the central focus where we could hang out and talk about everything … we'd do dream interpretation, listen to records, and generally get fucked up.

[Paul] used to jump off the roof of the church that was right next to his mom's place. We used to do crazy shit in his mom's place! One time Paul and Georg made me walk through all this mud on the side of the house, where the hose was; then they would both hold me upside down and I would make muddy footprints all over the ceiling! When his mom would wake up or come in from whatever it was she was doing she would inevitably look up and say, "Paul, what did you do? How are those footprints on the ceiling?" And he'd say "Oh, we were just walking on the ceiling, mom!" She'd just shake her head and go into her room.

GEORG RUTHENBERG   Darby and I were like total best friends, from 12 to 22. It seemed like every couple of years there would be some new boy—like a Doug

Pleasant Gehman, Pat Smear, circa 1975. From a 50-cent photo booth.

Raw Power back cover.

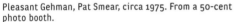

Holtby or a Paul Roessler or a Donnie Rose, or somebody else—who'd be best buds with him for a while, and I'd be on the outs. Not like we'd ever fall out or anything but just, like, it was not us 24-7 anymore.

WILL AMATO Roessler was a lot tighter with Paul Beahm than I was. I remember talking to him about Paul. I said, "Man, you fell for that shit?" but really, I was jealous—he was stealing all my friends! And I said, "He's just using these transparent fucking gimmicks, can't you see that? Don't fall for it!" His gimmicks were really entertaining, but at the time I resented it.

PLEASANT GEHMAN Paul was doing crazy experiments like seeing how long he could go without sleeping. He claimed that once he went for 14 days without sleeping.

WILL AMATO He'd researched that humans could only stay up so many nights before either mental collapse or a lapse into waking hallucinations. He announced that he was going to stay up two days longer than that—a week straight with no sleep. He had his circle setting their alarms for three and four in the morning to call him to make sure he was awake. They'd call him at two AM, they'd call again at four in the morning. Was he really awake? In my opinion, no, he was actually asleep, but was primed so he could seem awake when the phone rang. But I know people who called him at four AM, and he had music on, was watching TV and could talk about what he was watching, so who knows?

CHRIS ASHFORD He used to qualify that and say that he was "meditating"; the staying up involved "meditating," not actually laying down and going to sleep.

RAW POWER

O

CHRIS ASHFORD I was working at a record store on Wilshire called Music Odyssey around late '74-early '75 and Paul Beahm used to come around and we started talking ... and then he brought Georg [Ruthenberg] along and we all talked. Paul was a little surfer kid with really long, straight blonde hair, down past his shoulders.

GEORG RUTHENBERG The [Music Odyssey] record store by Uni High was really high school kid friendly, it had a couch. The store clerk was Chris Ashford who was into Iggy, too, so now that we had that in common, we took him more seriously. Chris knew all the cool stuff, but he was into all that boring East Coast "rock critic" rock—Jonathan Richman, the Velvet Underground, Patti, Television—and we didn't think most of it was all that good. Some of it was okay, very clever and all, but like, none of it ever actually seemed to rock. We wanted things less cerebral, less intellectual ... we wanted a fun spectacle to stomp around to ... like the Runaways or the Stooges, or something...

CHRIS ASHFORD Somehow we started talking about Iggy Pop and *Raw Power*. I told them I knew where Iggy lived so we decided to go over to visit. I drove since neither of them had a car. Iggy and James Williamson were living in an abandoned apartment building next to the Riot Hyatt on Sunset. To us going to see Iggy was what it would be like for someone from the previous generation going to see Elvis. We drove over there and banged on the door, but nobody answered, so we left. Paul and Georg went back later, though, and went inside. They'd go hang out over there occasionally. If Iggy was there, he'd let 'em in; but if Williamson was there and Iggy wasn't, he wouldn't. He'd just tell Iggy, "Your little hippie hoodlum friends came by."

GEORG RUTHENBERG We found Iggy Pop on our own in the cut-out bins and used sections. That's how we discovered the *Raw Power* album. We saw the cover, and went, "Oh, SHIT!" The *cover* totally made it! It wouldn't have made any difference what the record sounded like—you could just tell what it was like from the cover! We'd just go for the records with weird covers—we found some cool records that way—the *Witchcraft Coven Destroys Minds and Reaps Souls* album—that totally Satanic album with a nude girl being sacrificed in the gatefold, and a black mass on side two. There's no way that record could come out today! We were little kids, listening to the black mass in the dark.

> PAT Iggy's a fucking bastard; he's a fart. He used to be a friend of ours, but he's an asshole now.
> BOBBY PYN Last time we saw him he acted like he didn't know us; "I don't know yooouu!"

PAT   He used to be a friend of ours; we used to give him our money. Now he…
BOBBY PYN   … lives in Topanga with three faggots!
(From Germs interview, *Flipside*, 1977)

CHRIS ASHFORD   We were in Westwood one night and we had a little bit of money, so we went to McDonalds, bought 13 hamburgers, and threw them all over the place. We walked around with some Hawaiian Punch and called it "Iggy Pop," and told people there was acid in it and tried to sell it to them.

GEORG RUTHENBERG   We'd read the stories about Iggy—the peanut butter, cutting himself up, and putting cigarettes out on himself. Paul said, "I'm gonna take that to the extreme." You know; there's the real version of what Iggy may have been doing, and there's the teenage exaggeration version, and Darby was going for that one.

Hellin Killer, Trudie, Pleasant, Darby, Nicky Beat, Alice Bag, Delfina, Lorna, Pat, Jena. Photo: Jenny Lens.

SOPHISTIFUCK & THE REVLON SPAM QUEENS
AT THE DAWN OF PUNK

O

CHUCK E. STARR The Odyssey opened in 1976 in the heat of the disco era. Everything went all disco after Rodney's glam mecca closed in late '75. The Odyssey had a huge mirror ball, but they replaced it with this huge spaceship that hung from the ceiling. Oh, God, if it ever fell down it would have killed somebody. And we had neon. And neon was really new then. And there were these huge towers like Studio 54 had with these huge rotating lights that would just cut through the audience like knives. The DJs were gods, even back then. The DJs had their names up in lights.

PLEASANT GEHMAN There was a big mix between the rock 'n' roll people, the hardcore music freaks, and also like gay disco club people that went to places like Gino's and the Odyssey.

TRUDIE It was the end of the glitter era, and we'd *just* found out about it. We'd gone to Rodney's all dressed up in glitter and this guy goes, (high pitched voice) "I thought glitter was dead!" We were so disappointed.

HELLIN KILLER After Rodney's closed all us too-late-for-glam kids hung out at the Sugar Shack in the Valley. We used to take tons of Quaaludes and go there 'cause they played lots of Bowie. Kim Fowley and Rodney were like the only people over 21 who were allowed in—you had to have an ID to prove you were under 21! So Gino's, the Sugar Shack and the Odyssey were where everybody went.

RODNEY BINGENHEIMER The L.A. punks took more from the English scene. During glam everybody had names like Chuckie Starr or Sable Starr, Lori Lightning, so these new glitter kids all changed their names, too. Belinda Carlisle was there. She called herself Dottie Danger. Jane Wiedlin was there. She was Jane Drano.

GERBER I had just moved to West L.A. from Manhattan Beach, which is white upper class, with my mom. We moved right by this Mormon Temple on Manning, which is no longer there. I started looking around for places to hang out. I didn't know what anybody did here, because I had grown up on the beach, where all the loadies hung out under the pier—we would smoke pot, drink, and sometimes do hard narcotics, but I didn't know anybody in West L.A.

JEFF MCDONALD Gerber was one of the very first "scene" type persons that I met; she was after my brother 'cause he was like 10. She told us a story about how she was best friends with Donny Osmond when she was a kid, because she lived behind the Mormon Temple in Westwood, and she like hung out with him there.

GERBER   The Taco Bell in Westwood somehow became a favorite hang for local teens and that was where I first met Darby Crash when he was still Paul Beahm. He had a red Bowie haircut, a Bowie belt buckle, a Bowie T-shirt, and some kind of emblem painted on his forehead, the thing off the *Pin-ups* cover. I considered myself totally Bowie freakazoid, but this guy looked like he thought he was Bowie! I walked over and asked, "Can I sit here?" and he's all, "Yeah," or whatever. I sat. "So," I said, "I take it you're into Bowie?" And he flipped fuckin' out! He stood up, with all this garb on, screaming at me, "Who the fuck are you? You don't know anything about Bowie! Get the fuck away from me!" and made this big scene in a busy restaurant. I said, "I will fucking not! You're the one with the stupid big belt buckle! You're the one making an ass out of yourself. Just siddown!"

Then we ate our tacos and started talking about drugs. Once we had Bowie and the drugs in common we just clicked. He invited me over for purple microdot, and soon we were taking LSD in his bedroom regularly. It was real speedy shit. During these "micro-dot sessions" he'd get into this psychological game-thing, his big philosophy trips, the Scientology, all this fuckin' weird shit. I'd just get irritated because the acid was too speedy and we'd fight all the time.

He had one of those dress mirrors in his room, and on the bottom he had cut out the letters from some Bowie song, I can't remember which one, but the line was, "And I would take a foxy kind of stand." They were just hand cut and taped at the bottom of the mirror. I was like, "Dude, you are a fucking *geek!*" He wasn't one of the most physically attractive boys and I had like the perfect little 14-year-old surfer babe bod; tiny, tight, but curvy, who could get, like, anybody at the pier I wanted. Physically he was kind of a dog, but personality-wise, he was *gold*. Darby and I tried to have sex on one of those micro-dot trips. Instead we both figured out that we must be gay. I was certain that I was, and he was pretty certain he was; but you know, when you're peaking with someone to the point where you don't even need to say it, it's understood—and, yeah, we just *knew*. He still always liked me to be naked. I guess that was visually appealing to him when we were on acid.

CHRIS ASHFORD   When they first started Paul and Georg had a great sense of humor to it. They were huge Bowie and Iggy fans, basically, and when they first started with the name Sophistifuck and the Revlon Spam Queens, you couldn't get much more vulgar glam than that. They were the Revlon Spam Queens for at least four or five months during late '76, early '77. Originally they didn't play at all, they just had shirts. It was a while before they got around to picking up any actual musical instruments and really doing it.

This fantasy group never even made it past the rehearsal stage, which may have been a lucky thing for all concerned! "The Spam Queens" first of all recruited schoolmates Michelle Baer and Dinky [who later became Germs inner circle stalwarts]. Their job was to help the group move beyond imaginary duo status, but then Paul Beahm's gang went right ahead and did what all great fantasy bands do anyway—not practice, not play, and not, under any circumstances, write or record any actual music. Mostly we used to sit and play records since I worked at the record stores and always got the new records right away. They used to call me at the store whenever they wanted to hear something they didn't have. We used to change our names; even before "Sophistifuck" I remember Georg re-spelling his name "Ge5orque." The 5 was silent, of course, and the "que" was for "Queen." I was "Chris 2-4." I was "KRIS Radio."

NICKY BEAT Venus and the Razorblades wasn't punk. Kim Fowley tried to pass that off as punk. I mean we thought it was punk, right, but we thought the Tubes were punk. And if the Tubes were punk, then so was Alice Cooper, and, no, Alice Cooper was whatever Marilyn Manson is—and that's not punk, that's rock.

Kim told me, "Look, I am the weirdest motherfucker you are ever going to come across—I'll fuck a donkey if I think I can get a headline out of it ... don't even think that you can ever be weirder than me!" I guess I seemed weird enough during this phone interview to be asked to come for a drum audition. I think they had already auditioned 35 drummers so they were getting desperate.

I was only in Venus and the Razorblades for like two weeks. I told Kim, "I want to dye my hair black and I want to have 13 blood-red streaks in it, I think that would look really cool." Nobody had that back then, and I wanted black and red ermine hair. I had this long, "beach hair," wavyish but not curly. He looked at me and said, "You're not touching your hair, your hair looks like Peter Frampton and we need to cash in on that." Kim was so antiquated in his thinking, he thought that I should keep my hair as it was, because Frampton was still huge, and we needed it for our "image." He still needed to have elements that you could sell to the masses; you've gotta be able to give the people something they can relate to—they can relate to Peter Frampton hair. We were "punk rock" because we'd got this punk rock name, Venus and the Razorblades, but Kim didn't put this group together as an art project—he put it together to fucking cash in! He didn't have the look or the youth to be able to sell himself, but he figured he could be the puppeteer behind the new punk thing and cash in on it.

PAUL ROESSLER [Paul] thought, "Now that I'm out of high school—now that I'm an adult, how can I take this thing I do and make it huge?" [Georg] had this amazing love for [Paul], and he thought that being a rock musician was the ultimate vehicle for [Paul's] special talents. When they eventually figured out that they could sort of pull off a punk band, that was it!

PAUL BEAHM Punk has an image of mainly being really dumb and stuff, not being able to write. So lots of people think, "Well, they can write, so they must not mean it. They're just doing this for the hell of it. Just taking a year off from college or something."

GEORG RUTHERNBERG Chris Ashford would play us all the new singles from England while we sat on the couch reading British rock mags like *NME* and *Melody Maker*. We fell in love with the Sex Pistols just by reading about them— that's how we learned about punk rock. You couldn't find it on TV or in most record stores. It didn't even have a name yet. There were just some singles and Rodney On the ROQ. And that was it. We'd listen to Rodney religiously.

CHRIS ASHFORD The Ramones or the CBGB scene in New York weren't factors in the formation of the Germs. It was all about the Stooges, Bowie, and Joan Jett … and then it was all about the Sex Pistols and the Damned.

GEORG RUTHENBERG When the Ramones album came out, we thought, "Fuckin' hippies!" It was like, "What? Oh no! Are we going back to that? Fucking long hair, ripped jeans and T-shirts?" We were really disappointed. Then we heard it and we were totally blown away!

HELLIN KILLER Faith thought I was Paul's girlfriend. I was to a certain extent but Paul didn't have sex, which was another one of his big issues. I was naïve at first, just assumed he was a shy, virginal straight teenage guy, but looking back I think he knew he was gay but was in denial. There was stuff that went on, all hearsay, about him having a Christian big brother who molested him as a little kid, or a teacher at Uni High who'd had sex with him and that was one of his big issues … he didn't want anything to do with sex 'til the very end … maybe that's what broke him, who knows?

GERBER If it's true he was molested in childhood he might have thought he was in the loop for continuing the classic cycle where the victim passes the abuse along to somebody else by becoming the abuser, something which would eventually turn him into one helluva sick fuck, too, just like the perv who had originally messed him up … it was like he just couldn't find a place where he was okay with suckin' and fuckin' a buncha darlin' young boys…

AMBER He had had man-on-man experiences since he was very young, and he told me that all the men he had relationships with were men who had also been misused. Donnie Rose, Robbie and Tony—I don't know if Donnie was sexually misused, but he was definitely abused and hit by his father—I saw the bruises and I saw the tears.

RIK L. RIK Occasionally I'd glimpse Darby's mom through the slightly open door of her bedroom, and she just looked like this big snoring monster lady. She was like 300 pounds, with this flaming red hair. She looked like something out of a John Waters movie. He never talked about his father.

REGI MENTLE One time Darby's mom came pounding at the door. Darby screamed, "Get the fuck outta here!" She yelled, "Now Paul—open this door!" Darby yelled back, "Go away, you stupid bitch!"

HELLIN KILLER Darby's mother was intense, she was a scary lady. She was the screaming voice from the other room, the disembodied voice of Faith Baker … she worked nights and was usually asleep all day and if you made noise she'd scream from the other room, "Shut the fuck up!"

NICOLE PANTER I thought Faith Baker was mentally ill, schizophrenic. When I was in that house there was shit piled everywhere … weird, scary stuff … years worth of magazines you had to walk through. She was always in another room and she'd scream, "What, are you drunk, again, you little bastard?!" She was either intoxicated or having some kind of psychotic schizophrenic episode. I never saw the woman drink. It was the middle of the day and we were going into his room to look at the snake. That's pretty embarrassing—you come into your house with three friends in tow and your mother is shrieking at the top of her lungs. It was like something out of *Mommie Dearest*.

GERBER I've heard a lot of people say this, but I don't recall him being intimidated by Faith, or her busting his chops over things. And I spent a lot of time over there, I slept there a lot. She just wasn't around a lot, but when she was she barked and screamed a lot. She was a very bizarre woman, Avon collections that should be in the *Guinness Book of World Records*, weird shit—she's fuckin' weird, man. His sister Faith did not like me at all—I think she wanted him to have a girlfriend, even though it was never spoken about, but these chicks would come around.

LORNA DOOM I remember Faith yelling at Paul a lot when he would leave his room and him coming back in as if nothing happened.

TONY THE HUSTLER Darby kept his door locked because his mom was this hideous monster, and a lot of his friends were just like totally scared of her. This woman was strange. There was no regular furniture in her house. She used to have plastic lawn furniture in the living room with inflated air pillows and water toys hanging from the ceilings … with rafts hanging on the walls. She'd come home from work and would pace the halls back and forth screaming, "Paul, you dirty, rotten, son of a bitch! It's all your fuckin' fault!" When this happened, Darby would totally freak out and would start crying and shit. This would go on for hours and hours. I didn't know what to do for him. I felt really bad.

GERBER I was traumatized deeply by conversations with Faith while I was ripped out of my skull on LSD in his room. I was like blazing, flying out of my body, naked; we were playing that chicken game, where you throw the knife between your fingers, but we were on acid so there were all the trails and stuff. He was always trying to get me naked and playing this chicken game on acid. And then every so often his mom would barge in. She was kind of Divine-like when you're on acid. His mother would barge in and growl, "Do you want some potato chips?" while I'm like blazing on acid. No, I don't think so. She was trying to be friendly, but like while on acid, naked with her son, with the two of us just figuring out that we're faggots, you know, it was all too weird, she looked like this horrible …like this really scary creature from the lagoon with a big rubbery liquid face and this rumbling underwater voice. We'd be terrified until the monster beast would finally give up and go away and leave us alone. His room was creepy, always in blacklight, with posters and lots of Frampton junk and a lotta Bowie shit, too. The Frampton stuff disappeared shortly after the perm did, sometime before the Orpheum [show].

FORMING—THE GERMS BEGIN

O

SLASH   How did the Germs start?

PAT SMEAR   Four months ago, we went into a record store, and some lady said she wanted to be a manager, so we said we'd start a group. We walked down to Uni High School and picked up three girls and we called it Sophistifuck and the Revlon Spam Queens, and then all three girls quit, but we found Lorna and Donna.

SLASH   Why the new name The Germs?

PAT SMEAR   Because we make people sick; isn't that obvious?

BOBBY PYN   Because we wanted to have T-shirts printed, and we didn't have enough money for that long of a name. That's the truth.

(First Germs interview—*SLASH* magazine, 1977)

BELINDA CARLISLE   Terri Ryan [Lorna Doom] and I met in art class at Newbury Park High School in Thousand Oaks. She introduced me to a lot of music like Iggy and the Stooges, New York Dolls, and Roxy Music. We were into the same things—England, for one, and we started going to clubs around 16 or 17. I'd pick her up and we'd go to the Rainbow. We were, like, the local freaks in school. I went from being a cheerleader, fitting in, to being a total freak. We'd smoke colored Shermans and make up really wild stories about partying with Ted Nugent, really gross, unbelievable things! We'd go into Hollywood and hang out at the Rainbow; that's where we got most of our "education."

PAT SMEAR   Queen was staying at the Beverly Hilton, and we had met them in the lobby. The next day we went back and we were hanging around the pool, watching Freddie Mercury on his balcony. We met these two girls from the Valley, total twins with matching poodle haircuts. We snuck into the room below Freddie's and Darby tried to climb the balcony to get into his room, but he couldn't. We hung out with them, and they gave us a ride home; we didn't exchange numbers or anything, and we thought we'd never see them again.

BELINDA CARLISLE   I was totally in love with Freddie Mercury, and Terri was in love with Brian May; we'd find out what flights they were coming in on, and be there at the airport with gifts, flowers, the whole groupie bit. A guy from a record store introduced us to punk. He'd just come back from England and brought the English papers, and we read about the Sex Pistols, and got really excited and curious. But at the same time, we still *loved* Queen.

PLEASANT GEHMAN   Georg and Paul and I loitered for hours on end in the lobby at the Beverly Hilton, I mean just fucking loitering there. We met Belinda Carlisle and Terri Ryan—Lorna Doom. They were really cute, really fun, and they were totally into Queen, so of course we liked them. But they were also way more like girls that would hang out at the Rainbow—they were really quite disco-y looking chicks.

BELINDA CARLISLE We met Bobby and Pat in the lobby at the Beverly Hilton. They were like the weirdest guys we'd ever met—they were great! Bobby had figured out what room Freddie was in, so he went up to his room and knocked on his door; we were pretty annoying. We were all trying to get Freddie Mercury's autograph. We actually knocked on his door, which was really obnoxious. A no-no. It's the most annoying thing when a fan knocks on his door, and there were four of us knocking on Freddie Mercury's door. He never came out. Bobby and Pat thought we were bizarre. These two girls with little hairdos from Thousand Oaks.

CHRIS ASHFORD Pat and Darby began posting flyers around town, looking to form a band with "two untalented girls."

PAT SMEAR We put one up at Licorice Pizza; some time later—it was a while—they called us up and said, "Are you those Queen guys?" And that's when we started hanging out and we formed the band.

BELINDA CARLISLE That's when they put together the Germs—I think my name was Dottie Danger. I was the drummer although I never actually played. Then I got really sick with mononucleosis, and had to go home and live with my parents, which is basically why I didn't do it.

LORNA DOOM She never told me why she decided not to play drums. It seemed like she always had something else to do when we had to meet. I read somewhere that she was ill—who knows? But I have my suspicions that Paul and Georg were just too much for her.

PAT SMEAR We made T-shirts with iron-on letters, that said "The Germs," and our "band" name in the front, and "After You" on the back. We were a band long before Lorna ever had a bass. We'd make posters and put them around town, not for gigs, just to advertise the band. Belinda wanted to be responsible when she quit, she didn't want to fuck us over; so when we said we wanted to buy our instruments, she brought in her friend Becky to replace her.

BELINDA CARLISLE Becky Barton was also a student at Newbury High. She knew all about Aleister Crowley and Jimmy Page. When I got sick, she took over on the drums, which was fine by me, since I wasn't sure I really wanted to try and be a drummer anyway.

GUS HUDSON Bobby and Pat were totally using Becky to get access to things 'cause she had a credit card. She would rent all the equipment they needed …

L to R: Terry "Dad" Bag, Lorna, Belinda Carlisle, Unknown, Hellin Killer, Cliff Hanger, Pleasant Gehman, circa early '77. Photo: Jenny Lens.

we'd drive out to Pasadena and rent everything and we'd crate it into Hollywood. She was willing 'cause she so badly wanted to be part of it. Becky could barely keep a beat … they knew she was terrible but I think they sort of liked that. They'd practice maybe once or twice a week in Pat's parents' house … in the garage. They would just go through the songs. It didn't seem like they cared. They had an idea of what songs they wanted to play and they'd just run through them.

PAT SMEAR Lorna eventually bought a vintage Gibson SG bass for $100. The salesperson misread the tag, because the prices were all in code. A few days later, the store noticed the mistake and called us up, saying that the bass was stolen property, and to bring it back and they'd give us the $100. Darby's mom called them and said, "If you sold these kids stolen property, I'm reporting you to the police!" They let us keep the bass.

> **BOBBY** Tell them how Becky got it.
> **LORNA** She told her grandmother she was dying of leukemia, and she needed to pay the medical expenses.
> **PAT** You gotta call her Donna, even though…
> **LORNA** You know, that fat girl.   (*Flipside* interview, 1977)

FAITH BAKER I think I bought them their first microphone. At that time, nobody was into punk music, you know—and everybody said, "Weren't you mad when they got into it? Didn't you fight with them?" I said no, because I figured that if that interested them then they must have had some talent, you know? Of course, they say that in the beginning they didn't know they had it.

PAT SMEAR   Paul's mom bought him a little Rickenbacker, and we would sit in his backyard and he'd laugh at me, and make fun of my words, and tell me they were shit. And the opposite happened; I could play guitar, he couldn't, so we decided he'd write lyrics and I'd write the music. He could sort of play—like two-chord ideas, and tell me, "Play like this," and I'd make up progressions around them, or sometimes I'd write a whole song, tape it, and give it to him for the lyrics.

JENA CARDWELL   Pat and Darby were sort of in unison; obviously, with Darby's personality, he was in charge; but with Pat, it was more of a partnership. I never got the feeling that Darby was ordering Pat around or telling him what to do, but Pat had a respect for him. I never remember them disagreeing or quarreling.

PAUL ROESSLER   Pat Smear was [Bobby's] "enabler." They became the Glimmer Twins of the L.A. punk scene.

BOBBY PYN   I usually just think of the name for the song and we just go from there.

PAT SMEAR   With the Germs we went out of our way to say and do things that most people would never say or do—it was a reaction to our disappointment in other rock stars—specifically finding out that Alice Cooper played *golf!* That really upset us—really freaked us out—"Alice Cooper does *what?*" It was like, "We're gonna fucking start a band, and we're gonna change our names, and we're gonna fucking be this thing—we're gonna really be like that, 24-7, we're not going to fake it! And we're gonna be the most this, or that, or whatever; and we're never gonna puss out! Whatever it is we're gonna be, we're gonna be the most—if we're gonna be punk, then we're gonna out-punk the Sex Pistols! If we're gonna be the worst band ever, then we're gonna be the fucking *worst* band ever!"

BOBBY PYN   The name Bobby Pyn was more of a joke. I just changed it because you know, that was the easiest way to make people aware that we'd changed. That we were doing something different.

PAT SMEAR   Guitar playing just came to me very easily. I'm probably no better today than I was when I first started! I never practiced. It got to the point where I said, "This is really easy, and I can do what I want to do—I don't need to go [makes noise like fast guitar noodling]—as long as I can play Alice Cooper songs, Yes songs, the Germs songs, and Queen songs, then I'm okay."

BOBBY PYN   You've got to have people around you that can understand what you're trying to do, and if there aren't people like that around you already, what you do is you make them. Except we don't want it on a level like groupies, but there aren't enough people that can understand that so you have to sit down and explain it to them. Maybe it's not like that with the other bands that aren't trying to say anything.

PAT SMEAR   We always tried to play just above our abilities, so it came off badly sometime, but when you are self-taught it always comes out fucked up anyway. My guitar style came more from that than Brian May or Steve Howe. I could listen to a Yes or Queen song and pick it out, but at first I couldn't write a two-chord song without it coming out weird.

TOMATA DU PLENTY   When I first knew Darby, he was a teenager who barely talked. I first saw him hanging out in the donut shop across from the Starwood. He would come in there usually with three or four young women. I don't remember him ever saying one word, but they waited on his every need. The girls talked loud and laughed, and then he would give the signal and they would silently parade out. And this was in 1976, before the Germs had ever played.

GERBER   Paul and Georg, or Bobby and (laughs) I love to say this—*Je'tah*, which was the first name he picked, before Pat Smear—Je'tah!—made those original Germs shirts before they ever even rehearsed! They were yellow, and on the front said, "The Germs" and on the back, "After You … Bobby Pyn; After You … Je'tah; After You … Lorna Doom; After You … Donna Rhia."

TRUDIE   Hellin and I met the Germs at the Capitol Records swap meet…

TOMATA DU PLENTY   Darby was fascinating in a parking lot. I think that's where he was really a star. Watching his behavior in a parking lot, that's what made Darby Crash, that's what made him a legend, certainly not his onstage performances! Oh, they were so boring! I couldn't sit through a Germs' set, please. Torture! But I could certainly sit on the curb with a 40-ounce and listen to him for hours. He was an interesting, interesting person. Lorna Doom was beautiful.[1]

TRUDIE'S DIARY   (4/3/77) At dawn we went to the record swap meet at the Capitol Records parking lot on Vine Street. Two geeky guys, ugly redhead with zits and messed up teeth is named Bobby Pyn. Jeans completely covered in little safety pins. He gave me xeroxed sheets of their lyrics and info. The other one was a tall brown guy with a funny Egyptian pyramid shaped hairdo and snaky grin who is named Pat Smear. They are such a funny looking couple.

PLEASANT GEHMAN   Everybody that was into music went to the Capitol Records swap meet in the parking lot. We'd go there like two or three in the morning after a party or something. Paul would always look for Bowie bootlegs while I'd be looking for retarded, crazy records, any weird stuff. It was like 10 cents, 30 cents, maybe a dollar. You could get cool English imports and bootlegs and also punk rock which was barely starting. Everybody that hung out at the Rainbow, the Roxy, the Starwood, or the Whisky, or at after-hours parties would end up there. Phast Phreddie, Don Waller, Danny Shades, the Screamers would go there. Punk rock was just beginning to take hold, so it was mostly people looking like '50s beatniks or James Brown-ish white collar minister-thugs, and the girls' looks ran the gamut from S&M and, like, vintage '40s fashions to that Cycle Sluts from Hell meets *Rocky Horror* camp rock look of the time…

HANGING OUT WITH THE RUNAWAYS

O

There's nothing hard to understand (or believe) about five young girls trying to work out their fantasies of being rock stars on stage. Rather than try to break commercial patterns in the stark manner of the Ramones, the brighter Runaways have latched onto every riff, hook, or technique that has seemed appealing on teen-oriented, punk-rock efforts by such outfits as Suzi Quatro and the Sweet. The group's themes rely heavily on proven teenage rock concerns: sex, alienation, a craving for excitement and independence.
(Robert Hilburn, *Los Angeles Times*, August 1, 1976)

CHRIS ASHFORD   Pat was a big Runaways fan and he'd go to all their shows.

PAT SMEAR   Our real inspiration was the Runaways, because we thought, "If they can do it, anyone can!"

CHRIS ASHFORD   Joan [Jett] saw them all the time. She lived on San Vicente, off Sunset, and they'd go hang out in her apartment, or at the Whisky, or the Licorice Pizza parking lot.

JENA CARDWELL   When Joan was living on San Vicente just below the Whisky, Darby, Pat and Lorna started hanging out with her. That was a common ground for all of us—we were obsessed with the Runaways.

RODNEY BINGENHEIMER   People would meet Joan at clubs and start talking her up. She took the Germs under her wing.

KIM FOWLEY   Joan became fond of the Germs and she sort of took on the mommy/older sister role.

JOAN JETT   [My apartment] was on San Vicente and Sunset—it's still there, actually; the ugly green building right behind the gas station. That became like the party place for young punks, because nobody was old enough to drink or really party anywhere else. It was a nice, safe place to go before going out until cops started hiding out across the street in the Licorice Pizza parking lot, and sometimes they'd harass people coming out of my apartment. They would shine spotlights on me, and tell me they were going to get my friends for jaywalking, that they were going to get me for something *big*. And I'd say, "What? What are you talking about? I'm just in a *band*, man; leave me alone!"

GERBER   I remember hanging out in the Licorice Pizza parking lot, in the car, getting loaded, going across the street to Joan Jett's house getting loaded, and then just going in for the show and sitting on the side of the stage, handing Darby his drinks.

Bobby wrestles Pat, Joan, Lita Ford, Rodney Bingenheimer. Photo: Jenny Lens.

JENA CARDWELL   I had heard a rumor or two regarding Ms. Jett. One of these involved "Pissicles," which were Popsicles that you could get the kit for and make your own, only these were made from urine. Joan was sick of guys coming over to her house and disrespecting her by brazenly hitting on her girlfriends. She had used them to hilarious effect on at least one occasion. One recipient of these evil confections burst into some very unmanly tears when told of the ingredients …

JOAN JETT   Oh God, the Pissicles! That was a thing that me and my friends did as a defense against assholes; I don't know if we ever even actually utilized them, but we always had them at the ready.

JOAN JETT   We were working on our second album when Darby and Pat showed up at the studio one day to say they were gonna start a band. They'd seen us play gigs in Hollywood and they got inspired. Darby liked the tough girl thing. The rebel aspect. He got a real kick out of that. We were really flattered.

SANDY WEST   The Germs were really sweet people who told everybody that we influenced them. That's cool. I liked them. They were fun to be around.

TRUDIE'S DIARIES   (4/15/77) Bobby Pyn had written a letter to Bowie and he was so excited about giving it to him when Bowie pulled up in his limo. After Pat Smear saw Bowie in person in the parking lot, he was so excited that he ran straight into a pole while hurrying over to tell us about it.

TONY KINMAN   We did one show in L.A. at the "Punk Palace," with the Nerves and the Weirdos, who played without a drummer 'cause they didn't have one yet, and this awful band of, like, rockers who were trying to be punk. They called themselves the Dirty Diapers, and they were like all these long-haired rock-dudes, playing what they thought was some kind of punk rock, and they thought the Weirdos and us were like total shit—"Man, you guys are too young; ya haven't paid your dues," and all this crap! We were like, "What are you guys doin' here?!"

JOHN DENNEY   We thought The Dils were playing old-fashioned rock like Led Zeppelin, with a slight Ramones touch to it to make it seem contemporary.

BOBBY PYN   The Dils are fakes ... they are not Communists. Malcolm McLaren tried to do the same things with the Dolls a long time ago. He didn't do anything, why try to do it again? Their manager Peter Urban is the one who's doing that from what I've heard. Unless you're willing to give it all up and do that I don't think you can be serious about it. One time the Dils auditioned a drummer where we used to practice and they said to him, "Well, you know, there's three things. Number One: you gotta cut your hair. Two: you gotta wear straight-leg jeans, and three: don't act like a college kid."

PLEASANT GEHMAN   When the Damned came to town [April, 1977] they were like the first English punk band, and they were playing at the Starwood. The girl I went with was going home after the first show because she had a curfew. So did I, but I was like "forget it, I am NOT going home." I had this home-made Damned T-shirt on ... the street buzz on punk rock had been growing and growing, and when I went to see that show I thought it was the best thing I had ever seen in my entire life. When my friend left she asked me, "How are you getting home?" and I said, "I don't care!" Rodney ended up dropping me off at school the next morning, and I was totally hungover, a complete mess.

NICKY BEAT   There were all these unruly little punky kids at the Damned in-store. It was Darby, who was still Bobby Pyn, and Pat Smear and Lorna Doom and Donna Rhia.

PLEASANT GEHMAN   I convinced The Germs that they should be ready to play when we were at Bomp Records for The Damned, which is also the first time I saw Angelyne. She was in a baby blue corset with blue maribou trim.

CHRIS ASHFORD   At the Damned in-store, they started throwing food around and they were trying to steal the records, and so Greg and Suzy [Shaw] kicked them out. We used to go to late-night diners and coffee shops and have food fights all the time, throw food all over the table, get people upset, then they'd throw us out.

PAT SMEAR   We went to Bomp Records where the Damned were doing an in-store. We were drunk out of our minds causing trouble. We kept bragging about how we were a band, and someone said if we were a band, why didn't we play at the Weirdos' show tonight? We had no songs or anything. It was a dare.

The original gutter punk, '77. Photo: Jenny Lens.

GERMS' WORLD DEBUT

JOHN DENNEY We crashed the [Damned] in-store at Bomp to try and call some attention to ourselves and this gig the Weirdos were promoting at the Orpheum Theater on Sunset. Darby and Pat were there. He was calling himself Bobby Pyn at that time. Darby came up to me and said in quite a timid small boy's voice: "We have a band ... can we play?" I called over to Cliff Roman, "Hey, Cliff, these guys wanna play the show ... what do you think?" It was the perfect set-up for us. A band of young kids who could barely play at all wouldn't threaten us because we were a fairly shaky new band with no live stage experience and we were playing out with no drummer.

RODNEY BINGENHEIMER The Orpheum was this tiny little theater across from Tower Records where Jim Morrison once read poetry.

FAITH BAKER Paul used to buy old clothes at Aardvarks and at thrift shops, and I would remake them for his stage costumes when the Germs first started playing out.

PLEASANT GEHMAN The Orpheum was pretty crowded. I remember Tomata and K.K. [Barrett] sitting on the tops of the chairs during the Germs set. We all thought it was really cool 'cause the Screamers were there. Then the Damned came in and I remember consciously thinking "Okay, now this is valid."

I saw Belinda wearing this baby blue Qiana jumpsuit with a total cowl-neck halter, draped with these sort of like harem pants coming down really tight around the ankles, stiletto heels and a huge fake flower in her hair. She looked like a cross between a '30s glamour queen and a really sick housewife—but it was, like, total disco clothing! And Lorna I could remember wearing stuff like straight jeans, with high heels and striped shirts with a beret; and they both had really permed hair.

ROBERT LOPEZ There were a lot of people with longish hair, jeans, and T-shirts. Nobody was as fashionable as you might think. Except The Weirdos. They were from art school so they all had spray-painted pans, and plastic wrappers wrapped around their legs. Shirts made of trashbags. The Germs were wearing tight jeans and homemade white T-shirts that were stenciled with the Germs in front and stuff like "Comin' At You!" on the back. It was their first show and they were horrible. Really bad. That's why when their first 45 came out and then "No God," it was such an amazing thing. It didn't resemble them at all. Darby was calling himself Bobby Pyn then. He didn't have his stage thing down yet.

HAL NEGRO I was one of two roadies for the Weirdos, we were just friends of Dix and John and Cliff helping them out, we'd schlep their gear around and help them to set up. The Germs showed up at the Orpheum all fucked up on Quaaludes.

Bobby, Pat, Lorna Doom and Donna Rhia. They had cute names but to us they were just drags who seemed stuck in glam rock. They were Bowie freaks. Quaaludes were a glam rock drug. That was the snobbery that I had. I thought The Germs weren't on the same page. Here we were in this new world of punk rock and now here comes these glam rock geeks ... these leftovers trying to drag their glam rock asses into our world. There was this feeling of us and them. The Weirdos and Zeros jumped right out of the box, but the Germs were just this mess. There was nothing there. They didn't have any songs and they played very slow compared to the speed and the energy of the other bands.

NICKY BEAT The Germs came on, the least professional kind of band you could ever imagine ... tuning up for ten minutes on stage, and then starting a song and then stopping and starting it over again, total amateur bullshit. It was really painful and hard to watch; and not really all that entertaining—

JOHN DENNEY When the time came for the Germs to go on, it was obvious very fast they had no music. They were just snickering, massively intoxicated kids who were literally just playing random feedback and banging around and smearing mayonnaise and peanut butter over themselves and the P.A. It was very amusing, but the gag wore out ... it became tedious and unfunny after about ten minutes. I hate to bust a few myths, but what really happened was that Dave Trout, Cliff and I looked at each other and we all agreed it was time to move on with the next band. They'd made their statement and we thought it very cool and gutsy. We escorted them offstage, it was a lot more low-key than the folkloric version of them being pelted and forcefully dragged off.

NICKY BEAT Bobby Pyn had a big can of peanut butter ... he was stumbling around the stage and knocking into stuff doing "Forming" but really slow with this bad girl drummer.

HAL NEGRO Bobby smeared all this peanut butter on the Zeros' bass amp. There was this outrage ... these precious, homemade amplifiers. Anything else goes, but you don't fuck with another musician's gear, that was the only taboo ... even in punk rock. We were like, "You can't do that. You have to go now, you glam rock posers." Me and Kelly Quinn, the other roadie, grabbed them and threw them off the stage and out into the parking lot where they sat around smashing beer bottles 'til the sheriffs came. I think Darby hated me for that 'til the end of his life.

PAT SMEAR Lorna wore her pants inside out; Darby covered himself in red licorice whips that melted into a sticky goo, and stuck the mic in a jar of peanut butter. We made noise for five minutes, until they threw us off.

BELINDA CARLISLE I remember people being absolutely appalled—it was the greatest thing!

The Germs came on first and were the biggest joke of the year. None of the Germs could play their instruments whatsoever. They took an hour to get set up and then played for two minutes. The lead singer smeared peanut butter all over his face and everybody's in the group, and they all were spitting on each other until they were kicked off. You can bet they won't be back either.

(*Raw Power* magazine, May 1977)

GREGG TURNER   The Germs: self-explanatory. Stay away from these virulent strains at all costs.[2]

D.D. FAYE   With three-quarters of Hollywood now donning their one-week-old leather jackets, learning a couple of chords, and standing around posing tough, it's very easy to see that not much is required to call yourself and your friends a band.

GUS HUDSON   After the Orpheum, all you heard about was "peanut butter" this and "Iggy Pop" that … he only messed with the peanut butter that one time, it was more like a joke at Iggy's expense, it was never intended to be some grand scheme to rip off Iggy's stage act … it was satirical, it was goofy, it was spontaneous, it was just Darby's humor, but it seemed to go over a lot of people's heads … he only did the peanut butter thing one time, yet people talked about it for years, they still do!

PAT SMEAR   After the Orpheum show, Jack Lee from the Nerves called me and said he loved us and wanted to do a single, and asked for a tape, so we got my mom's little cassette, and a bottle of booze, and did an awful version of "Forming" … just me and Darby out of our minds. We mailed a tape to those guys. We never heard from them again.

NICKY BEAT   After the Orpheum show they quickly got rid of Donna Rhia who had no clue how to play drums. Then they got Cliff Hanger. With Cliff on drums, they were a completely different band … everyone knows a decent drummer can often carry a shaky band.

CHRIS ASHFORD   Donna was a complete beginner as a drummer who could kind of hold it together well enough for them at that point, but she was not with the band long enough to develop or grow into it. All the stuff was kind of slow on the Live at the Whisky recording. As soon as they got Cliff Hanger then everything changed. Pat would teach Lorna her bass lines—they'd work on it together—then they'd go to practice at Pat's mom's house. They became serious, and would try to practice as much as they could.

MATT GROENING   I was working at Licorice Pizza, this record store which was kitty-corner from the Whisky. There were lots of British imports and there was a punk corner where various punk 45s and 'zines were sold. That's where I sold my little self-made xeroxed comic "Life In Hell." I liked X, the Weirdos, and the Germs. I loved Geza X and the Deadbeats … and for comedy reasons, I liked The Mentors and Black Randy, and the Dickies and the Go-Go's. I was a huge fan of the local punk scene. The punks that came into Licorice Pizza were a combination of idealistic kids who were totally into the scene, and then there were these kids who would create a ruckus in order to distract us so they could shoplift. Most of the latter category were associated with the Germs. Every catastrophe, every outrageous misdeed or act of vandalism was always blamed on the Germs and their entourage. I remember one time some punk came in and lit Rodney Bingenheimer's hair on fire. Then there was the time punks took the dumpster at the back of the store and rolled it out onto San Vicente and all the way down the street where it smashed into cars. I told that story years later and this quite respectable woman in her '30s said, "That was me!"

○○○

TONY KINMAN   We were in Carlsbad when our manager Peter Urban called about the *Up in Smoke* shoot. We drove up to the Roxy and there was literally a line of bands waiting to go in. To the production people it was, "We got a whole bunch of punk rock bands today, so whatever!" The Dils set up and played, and our drummer couldn't hear himself or something and so it ended in like a jumble, and that was it, then we signed this thing and left. Later on, I heard we were in the movie. We were thinking less about playing for a scene in a movie, it was more like "Hey, we're going to play a real nightclub!" No punk rock band in L.A. had ever been allowed to play in one of these rock places like the Whisky or the Roxy. All we'd done up 'til then was playing like pizza joints or some German restaurant.

ANDY SEVEN   I threw a chair at Darby. Hell yeah, 'cause he was throwing stuff at everybody. He thought it was funny … and it sure was fun to watch 'cause it was so boring, just sitting and waiting around. Darby started throwing stuff, screaming and tearing shit up. The Dils did "I Hate the Rich" and the Berlin Brats did "So Psycho."

BOBBY PYN   The Germs played in the Cheech and Chong movie *Up in Smoke* … just like the one shot of us in the parking lot. They cut it out because they got pissed 'cause of what we did. We were under the impression that it was a punk movie or something, you know, and when we got there they were telling everybody to act bored when the Brats and the Dils came on and stuff. And we said we don't like this, this really sucks. So we went out there and like we just knocked over the tables and broke the glasses and things and ruined the place and the guy's yelling "set set" and he pulled us off the stage. The Dils and the Brats, the bands that did what they wanted, ended up in the film.

ANDY SEVEN   The kids were just happy to be there at the Roxy seeing these bands for free … maybe Darby knew that the joke was on them but that was the way the Germs played it anyway … they always trashed stuff. As soon as he started singing he started kicking stuff over … the stage hands were freaking out 'cause they realized it wasn't a joke … this 'punk band' was the real thing! Before they'd even finished the song the soundman turned off the P.A. and bouncers threw

Hellin Killer, Pleasant Gehman and Bobby Pyn at the Devo concert at the Starwood, circa October, '77. Photo: Jenny Lens.

them out ... the audience was booing these obese long-haired gorilla-like stage hands in Hawaiian shirts.

EXENE CERVENKA Bobby Pyn and I were both extras on the Cheech and Chong movie ... that's where I met him. They were filming at the Roxy ... it was boring as hell and they didn't even feed us. It was 50 dollars, an open cattle call. 50 bucks for a couple of hours was a big score for me.

JENA CARDWELL I saw the Germs perform for the first time at the Roxy during the Cheech and Chong shoot. I was more attracted to Bobby/Darby at first—I thought he was really cute. Everybody was screaming at him—you can hear it at the end of "Sex Boy"—because he'd literally run across our table, kicking and smashing the glasses ... the ice and drinks went all over us. Darby was standing around with this little group of people and I said something really stupid to him, and he just looked at me with those intense blue eyes, and said "Fuck you." I was mesmerized from that moment, and just wanted to be around these people, because I'm a glutton for punishment. Darby was so intense and rude and hardass, and I'd never met anybody like that. He was wearing Levis covered with safety pins and had dyed blonde hair. It was during this weird transitional period when nobody really quite knew what punk was exactly. When he looked at you, you were frozen; he had that kind of intensity. And the whole scene on stage—pissing everybody off, causing trouble—that was fascinating to me. I was still just a little surfer girl, and I loved the blonde hair, the blue eyes, the bad boy thing.

SEX BOY

BOBBY PYN People should understand there must be something if everybody's doing our songs, practically every L.A. punk band has done "Forming," a few have done some of the other ones. The Screamers do "Sex Boy," so there must be something about them, but people still turn around and try to get us kicked off gigs.

TOMATA DU PLENTY The Screamers did a Germs song. K.K. found Bobby Pyn's lyrics to "Sex Boy" and both Tommy Gear and I thought they were brilliant. Gear and I sang it as a duet with some kind of *Solid Gold* dance steps he'd thought up. I remember Darby standing dead center in front of the stage at the Whisky. I was very intimidated by the lack of expression on his face, but told me later he dug it. Was he being kind? I thought we sucked at it. It's interesting now to me that two older queers would pay such homage to a young gay like Darby at the time.

K.K. BARRETT We did "Sex Boy," which was sorta the equivalent of the Stones doing "I Wanna Be Your Man" written by the Beatles.

TOMMY GEAR When we heard "Sex Boy," we were so amazed 'cause it portrayed Gear and Tomata so well. He really is a prophet, Bobby Pyn.[3]

SEX BOY

I like it anywhere, any time that I can
I'm the fucking son of Superman
I got a weapon that's as deadly as life
It's the well-trained tool of a master guy

Every day it's the same flirting
A dozen girls are on my scene
They sent four million into my hands
They're all on the floor, I better do what I can
Take a number, it's supply and demand

Any time that I can
I'm the fucking son of Superman
I got a weapon that's as deadly as life
It's the well-trained tool of a master guy

I put my knife into your arms
You gotta be above when you wanna make love
Say it exactly, such a sex boy, such a doctor

After such a sweet, sweet slut
Any time that I can
I'm the fucking son of Superman
I know what it takes
What in the time I can and can't do
I know what it takes to satisfy you
I know what it takes
That's why your time is due in the house of fortune
I take it out, and you know it's gonna come from behind
Just like you, and you, and you, and you and you

("Sex Boy" lyrics by Bobby Pyn, circa '77) Publishing: Peer/Fowley Music.

K.K. BARRETT   They had a coming-out party for *Slash*, and the Screamers were invited to play at this storefront loft space on Pico. We'd been rehearsing pretty solidly for a few months, and so we were pretty tight. The place was packed. Everybody was drunk. That's when I met Trudie again. She'd been to New York where she'd been called "L.A.'s Favorite Punk Rocker" in a photo caption.

PLEASANT GEHMAN   I remember being horrified that Steve Samiof [*Slash* magazine publisher] had a beard. I kept trying to get him to shave. Claude and Philly and Steve and Melanie were really nice but they all seemed really old!

JENA CARDWELL   The first time I saw the Germs was at a *Slash* party where the Screamers were playing. I saw Pat, Darby, and Lorna winding their way through the crowd, wearing these handmade Germs T-shirts, yelling "The Germs!" I was 16, and lived in Highland Park on Avenue 53. My friend Christie's older sister was involved in the glitter scene, we'd gone into Hollywood to try and find some glitter club action, but accidentally ran into punk instead.

TRUDIE   I had a big black eye from crashing Hellin Killer's mom's Nova on my 18th birthday.

HELLIN KILLER   I was there on crutches.

ANDY SEVEN   The Screamers came on and it was like nothing I'd ever seen or heard before. In 1977, outside of Kraftwerk and maybe Suicide, you never saw a band with no guitars and this one had just two small keyboards and a drummer backing up a lead singer. This was radical, it was completely new to everybody.

K.K. BARRETT   That night the Screamers were kind of baptized, legitimized by the growing new punk scene makers of Bowie club kids barely out of high school and the older mid-to-late-20s art swingers from Venice.

GARY PANTER   When Tommy and Tomata entered a room it was really electrifying. They just came in like exploding heads! Ha ha.

kim
fowley
presents
at the whisky

NEW WAVE MUSIC

3 DAYS--FIRST WEEK OF SUMMER

GUEST HOST RODNEY BINGENHEIMER---- AND OTHER SPECIAL GUESTS

MON JUNE 20
JUICE ZEROS LA RUE WEIRDOS

TUES JUNE 21
GERMS ZIPPERS SCREAMERS

WED JUNE 22
BACKSTAGEPASS WILDCATS DILS

2 shows nitely 9 & 11:30
all ages welcome!

THE WHISKY
8901 SUNSET BLV
652-4202

KIM FOWLEY PRESENTS

O

KIM FOWLEY Californian punk rock has roots in two things: '60s garage rock, like the Count Five, the Music Machine, the Syndicate of Sound, and The Standells ... mixed up with Rodney's version of glam rock ... the Alvin Stardust records, the T. Rex records.

BOBBY PYN The '60s was the last time this country had any major changes. Bands aren't new if they're just playing what everybody else was doing about 30 years ago or something. Most of the people that do those old songs do them as more of a putdown. They do them sarcastically ... like when we played the Whisky and we did "Sugar, Sugar," you know, with a smirk.

KIM FOWLEY One day in the summer of '77 Elmer Valentine, owner of the Whisky, said, "We need a gimmick to get tickets sold. What do you have?" And I said, "Well, punk rock." And he said, "What's that?" "English stuff," I said. He said, "Oh yeah, well get punk rock in here—whatever it is." I said, "Okay." So I called up Rodney and said, "Rodney, you gotta put me on the air, so we can invite all the garage bands in L.A. to show up at the Whisky. We'll call it punk rock no matter what it is, okay?" So I went on Rodney's show and said: "Attention, unsigned new bands in garages! Guys and girls who are playing the weird underground music. Whoever shows up at the Whisky on Friday will be guaranteed a spot. In other words, if you show up, you get to go onstage, even if you're horrible. I don't care. English punk is horrible and they get to go onstage—so if you're horrible, you get to go onstage, too. English punk and American punk can't be that much different."

GUS HUDSON When we were driving to the show, Bobby was sticking his head out the window screaming and yelling at any of the guys who would drive by us ... "You fucking fag! You fucking fag!" He wanted to make a scene. They were all wearing World War II bomber jackets ... old Army surplus leather jackets and they had Germs spelled out with bandages on the back.

KIM FOWLEY The scene was like Kosovo meets Auschwitz. It was displaced persons, refugees from the suburbs ... it was urine-stained, safety-pin-wearing, shit-ass motherfucker out-of-control fuckboys, fuckgirls, puking, shitting, farting, anger angst madness indifference—white dopes on punk.

GUS HUDSON Kim Fowley was real intense that night.

KIM FOWLEY I had seen Pat Smear and Darby Crash before. They were male groupies lurking for The Runaways. More like baby brothers, but there was some male groupie veneer within their shtick.

Kim makes the wave. From ad in *Slash*, June '77.

RODNEY BINGENHEIMER   I went onstage with the Germs when Kim Fowley was presenting his punk shows at the Whisky. Belinda was there. She used to be in the Germs. She was fat and ugly with really short hair.

GUS HUDSON   Rodney introduced The Germs and was mercilessly heckled by the crowd of kids from Uni High, Newbury High and from God knows where else. They weren't diggin' on the "New Wave" hype, or the fact that many of the bands were these funny beaten-up old bar bands that had about as much to do with punk as Donny Osmond ... or Led Zeppelin.

BOBBY PYN   Rodney has the highest ratings on KROQ but he's very scared. I think he uses it for his own good. "Well if I play this single, they're gonna like me." He's really scared that people won't like him. And he gets upset over the littlest things. You say a wrong word, and he'll say, "I'm never playing you again, you're never going to get booked anymore." And for such a little person, he can do it, too.

GUS HUDSON   I helped them load the equipment in to the Whisky. One of the songs they were gonna do was "Sugar, Sugar" and it was my job to hand Bobby the bag of sugar on cue so he could dump it all over the place. During the rest of their set, we were opening up all these condiment packs and throwing them at the audience. Rodney was backstage and he came up to them and said, "If I get any peanut butter on me, you guys are banned from the club scene in L.A."

PLEASANT GEHMAN   The Germs told everyone they knew to bring some kind of food, and the results resembled a hurricane in a Safeway produce department. Sickening concoctions of salad dressings, beans, sour milk, and Campbell's soup flew from the balconies onto the stage below, as the Germs rammed through their killer version of "Sugar Sugar" and Pat and Bobby emptied two-pound bags of sugar over the stage and the crowd.

JENA CARDWELL   Darby was covered with some kind of powder, and Pat was squirting whipped cream around—they were covered with food, and the whole audience was trying to get as far away from the stage as possible.

BELINDA CARLISLE   I helped make flyers and I was the prop person on the side of the stage, handing over salad dressing and whipped cream.

BOBBY PYN   I smelled like a restaurant after. This guy mixed up rotten beans, mayonnaise, salad dressing and bread, and threw buckets of it on us. It was horrible!

PLEASANT GEHMAN   When the set ended, the Germs were banned from the Whisky for the first of many times. The club manager charged like a loon through the dressing rooms, asking people if they'd come to see the Germs. If the answer was affirmative, the patron would be told "Get the fuck down on that stage and clean it up, or you're out!"

The first Whisky performance, June '77. Bobby Pyn with Donna Rhia on drums, her final performance with the Germs. Photo: Diane Grove.

X-8 and Craig Lee. Photo: Al Flipside.

Kira Roessler, tomboy siren of the Masque.
Photo: Michael Yampolsky.

KIM FOWLEY We had a truck outside the Whisky. A live sound truck parked in the alley. A porta-studio. We recorded what eventually came out as *The Germs Live at The Whisky*, produced by me and Ralph. I remember running back and forth, getting the sound right.

GREG SHAW Kim Fowley made a deal with Peer Music [song publishers] to pay to record the whole Fowley-promoted Whisky show on remote 8-track, with the idea that if anything historic happened, it would be documented, and Fowley/Peer would own the publishing. I was to cover the record-releasing side of the deal, and all the bands signed recording/publishing contracts. There are still unreleased tapes by a lot of good bands, including The Weirdos; somehow it was only the Germs session that got released.

HAL NEGRO The Germs sort of crept up on us. The next time I saw them, they were part of the new punk scene.

X-8 In the first issue of *Flipside* we interviewed the Germs in Pat's parents' garage. Darby was talking about taking acid on Santa Monica Pier. I zeroed in on the Germs 'cause they were so non-traditional. The Germs captured that expressionistic trash aesthetic well onstage. Musically it was just, "What the fuck?" The majority of the early *Flipsides* were us getting drunk in somebody's living room and just putting the tape recorder on and saying what was crap and what we didn't like and what we did like and it ended up sounding like a bunch of real adolescent brats.

PAT SMEAR   The week we recorded "Forming," we recorded a lot of songs; probably the same set that's on the live at the Whisky album, *Germicide*. But we did "Forming" specifically for a single. We did it with my parents' reel-to-reel, one mic for the instruments, and Darby sang into the other one. He couldn't hear what he was singing, and didn't know enough to put his finger in his ear! We started each take with a different instrument—one with guitar, one with bass, and one with drums, and kept the one Becky played best on—the one with the bass.

CHRIS ASHFORD   We set up a two-track reel-to-reel in Pat's garage, ran off a whole bunch of takes of stuff while I was at work and then we just picked the best one and put it out. The B-side was recorded on cassette at the taping of the Cheech and Chong movie. On the first pressing, the pressing plant goofed up and flipped the labels, and they threw like 800 of them over a hill at some houses.

PAT SMEAR   The whole neighborhood was there crammed inside my garage. There were surfers sitting on the roof, lowriders on the fence, and my family was throwing things at us. The echo on the vocals was by accident; somebody just bumped into this knob. The black square on the back cover was supposed to be a picture of a friend with Band-Aids on her nipples, but somehow it never got used. I'm sure she's glad—she became a famous model later.

BOBBY PYN   [The B-side of "Forming"] was done at the Roxy during the Cheech and Chong movie … you can hear the breaking glass and stuff. Somebody snuck a tape recorder in. It's supposed to be "Sex Boy," but you can't tell.

PAT SMEAR   The only reason there weren't many indie records then was because it was down to how were we gonna sell them. Out of our homes? But Chris Ashford worked at a record store and made a deal with Peaches. They said, "Yeah, we'll let you sell the single here if this is the only store in the world you'll sell them at." When our single came out we called Rodney up and asked him to play it. We were like brats. We called him all night, every night, and he finally just got mad and said, "Look, I'll play your record if you'll just stop calling me." So we made this deal and stuck to it, and he played our single, and it started selling. At the time Billboard had this New Wave chart, and it made it onto the New Wave Top Ten. Which was hilarious, of course, since there were only 1,000 pressed, it's the only song out of one store in the world. This chart must be pretty fuckin' weak if we're charting on it, you know it had the top five—Blondie, the Ramones, whatever—and it had this bottom five which was these dumb little nobody bands like us … but we got shows from it.[4]

CHRIS ASHFORD   *Back Door Man* hated the single. *Slash* loved it.

CLAUDE BESSY   (writing in *Slash*): Beyond music … mind-boggling … inexplicably brilliant in bringing monotony to new heights…

THE MASQUE—OUT OF THE WOODWORK
AND INTO THE BASEMENT

O

DARBY CRASH   The Masque was just a party. People weren't paying to see it. The people who play there don't have any money.

SEAN CARRILLO   It was like there was this military general who said "Okay, we have a really dangerous mission and it's possible that nine out of ten of you aren't gonna make it, most of you are gonna die. Any volunteers?" The volunteers were at the Masque.

NICOLE PANTER   We were all there because we grew up in really fucked-up environments in one way or another—whether it was suburban Covina or me in Palm Springs with my gangster father. I think all of us came to punk generally unhappy and needing to act out a lot of things. I'd tried to off myself twice. Punk rock to me was not light and funny, it was an extremely dark environment.

KIM FOWLEY   It went down to Hollywood Boulevard. Brendan Mullen and the Masque. That was the next step. He took over the punk rock impresario thing and it proceeded in whatever direction it went.

BLACK RANDY   So this excitement started and all these people came out of the woodwork and identified with this new subculture, and everybody had missionary zeal. All of us really wanted something to happen. We also wanted it to happen differently than things always had with these other art movements and subcultures. There was a definite anti-commercial feeling—new forms had to be taken rather than just new costumes. There was a lot of argument in the early days about who was a poseur and who wasn't, but everybody was a poseur; it was a very abused term.

BRENDAN MULLEN   I was bored with the UK; it was dead, there was nothing happening. By late 1974, just in time for the end of glitter, I moved to Hollywood. I was living with these two guys in a house, and we would jam in the basement. It wasn't anything serious—just a sort of masturbatory fantasy band; get drunk and have these self-indulgent jams. We never had any delusions of being some underground band or anything. Cops kept shutting shut us down all the time—one time we finished up in jail—so I went out to try to find a place to set up. I wasn't looking to start a club or anything—the inspiration was Cornelius Cardew, who said that musicians of all levels of playing from beginners up should intermingle.
   I started calling around rehearsal studios, and they all said "eight to ten dollars an hour," and I thought, "That's crazy!" I wasn't going to spend eight to ten dollars an hour to basically jerk off—we weren't that good as musicians. Why not look for a storefront or something that we could rent by the month—we'll go in, fix it up, and be able to jerk off anytime night or day with no cops. And that's when I stumbled on the basement on Hollywood and Cherokee. It was all beaten to shit—it was like

going down into a labyrinth; there was no power, it hadn't been used in 15 years, so, like Theseus with his string, I dragged this decomposing garden hose in with me so I could find my way back out! I was literally sparking matches to see where I was going. There was trash all over the place—but it was only $850 a month, for 10,000 square feet. I just wanted one room where we could be left alone, but this real estate agent—the true creator of the Masque—said, "Listen, I'll make you a good deal; for a couple hundred bucks extra, why don't you take a 60-day first option on it, and lease the whole goddamned basement! I mean, why one room?" And so The Big Bulb flashed over my head! I had 60 days to come up with first and last? I could rent out some rooms, and subsidize the big room that I really wanted!

BLACK RANDY Everybody would go there on weekends and all these people were getting drunk and getting high and fucking in the bathrooms and they were pogo-ing and it was just insane in this basement. The cops didn't know about it for a long time, it was so underground. And Brendan did keep it pretty quiet, but pretty soon there was spray paint all over the neighborhood, and weird looking kids ... then the first heat started to come.

EXENE CERVENKA The Masque was kinda a speakeasy and a clubhouse for misfits. It was amazing that people could find it, like a 45-year-old graphic designer from San Francisco could wander in and find a place next to a 16-year-old runaway from Fullerton. How did that person find it? I didn't have people's phone numbers ... I didn't know where people lived. You got a sense of something really big going on and you'd go, "How come I'm one of these people?" It was an overwhelming sense of awe that it was even happening ... mingling with people from different social backgrounds was great ... Claude Bessy was completely different from Belinda Carlisle and there they were. Even though a lot of us didn't have much in common, we were together because there was nowhere else for us to go.

HELLIN KILLER The Masque was like heaven and hell rolled into one ... it was the greatest thing since sliced bread. You could always go there ... it was like the clubhouse ... it was just the coolest. It was like a bomb shelter, a basement ... all these weird rooms, stairways going up to a cement ceiling ... it was so amazing, such a dive ... but it was our dive and you could just scrawl all over the walls. The bands were great when they were just starting, all the best bands played their best shows at the Masque.

DON BOLLES A lot of weird stuff happened in that basement. One day Joan Jett and her girlfriend Lisa were chasing each other around the big room, wasted on 'ludes, pulling each other around by the hair and generally beating the crap out of each other. They were just going nuts, yelling, screaming, and cussing like sailors, and when they hit each other, it sounded like a Kung Fu movie. Another time, as everyone was making their way toward the stairs at the end of one of the Masque's legendary "private parties," there was this big, bearded, flannel-wearing lumberjack guy walking backwards with his wenus out, peeing on the concrete floor, and there was Geza X, following the stream on all fours, happily lapping it up as it splashed on

Tops off! The Germs' first Masque gig, Labor Day weekend, '77. Gerber, center; others unknown. Photo: X-8.

the ground! Out of about 150 people, I think I was the only one that seemed to find this the least bit noteworthy.

KIRA ROESSLER   I broke up with Geza on the spot!

EXENE CERVENKA   It didn't even have anything to do with bands, it was about people being bohemian, even though they didn't know what bohemian meant. It was pure, as opposed to Ginsberg wearing khakis in a Gap ad and everyone going out and buying a certain brand of pants 'cause they think it's bohemian.[5]

BRENDAN MULLEN   While I was cleaning up the trash, I took out an ad in the *Recycler*, advertising the new rehearsal space.
  Coincidentally, there were all these bands—they used to call them "street bands"— rehearsing at the old Columbia lot on Gower—that's where Backstage Pass came from. I was aware of these bands, but I didn't know they rehearsed at the Columbia Lot. The space was abandoned, and this guy that was managing it let bands rehearse there for $100 a month, each one had a huge soundstage.

EXENE CERVENKA   It was better to pick someone up at the Masque to get laid than to pick somebody up at the mall. It was unbelievable how we all found each other and knew we were supposed to be together outside society, like in *Close Encounters of The Third Kind*: everybody thought they were crazy, and then they get there and there is a spaceship, and there's people throwing bottles and yelling "Devo" at us the whole way.[6]

BRENDAN MULLEN   I met the Controllers and the Skulls about the same time, and they started rehearsing there. They were so passionate about rocking they were doing all this rehearsing. I remember asking the Controllers one night, "Where do you guys play?" and they said, "Nowhere!" "Nowhere?" I said; "You mean you're rehearsing with no gigs? Very odd..." "Well," they said, "We're hoping to get a gig at a place called the Orpheum, where this band the Germs just played." I think it was their first bass player Field Marshall DOA Dan whatever-he-was-called who said, "Yeah, but the Germs suck—they can't fucking play—it's not a real band; it's a joke. Instead of playing music, they just throw food around—they're for shit, a joke. Just a bunch of fucking kids." That was the first I heard about the Germs, and that kind of stuck. I just thought, "Oh, okay..." and didn't really think about it any more.

CLAUDE BESSY   We went from gig to gig, from parking lot to parking lot with a bottle of ... usually it was tequila because it's cheaper, or vodka.

KIM FOWLEY   Misfits need misfits to worship. It was white kids trying to avoid being white adults; all of them going through the detour of punk culture to expend and waste their youth, because they all knew they were gonna die some-day, bald, fat and stupid.

EXENE CERVENKA   Even though punk was nihilistic and railed against everything that had come before—like "kill the hippies"—it was actually a continuation of the freedom of expression of the hippie and beat movements, a rejection of the middle-class values, the hypocrisy, and the commercialism.[7]

PHILOMENA WINSTANLEY   The people who had no money to buy drinks at the Whisky would drink anything in paper bags outside in the parking lot. We'd just lie on top of cars and whoever got drunk would slide down the roof of the car and lie under the car. Everybody was always dead drunk. That's how I remember the beginning of the punk scene ... drinking outside the Whisky and stumbling around the Masque.

GEZA X   I lived in the Masque when it first opened up. It was so cheap a bunch of unsigned local bands moved in. It was like a bomb shelter. There was a giant storage room filled with food rations from World War II. They were stored in these tins. We were all starving so we started opening them up and they were full of crackers and dried food. We'd go back there, drunk out of our minds and eat these food rations.

LEONARD PHILLIPS   The Spastics went on right before us when [The Dickies] played our first gig at the Masque, and then Darby or one of his little buddies from Uni High turned a fire extinguisher on them. I was scared to death from that. I didn't know if we'd even get to play. We knew our music was tailor-made to what the Masque crowd should have liked ... but you never fucking know. Thank God they loved us, we were an instant hit.

TERRY GRAHAM   The Spastics got booed off stage at the Masque, so Darby got the fire extinguishers out and the Dickies thought they'd get the same treatment.

DON BOLLES   The Masque had the best graffiti I've ever seen, hands down. Not very artistic, but scathing and absurd...

MASQUE GRAFFITI
KILL GOD!
The Doomed
The Metro Squad Stole From Arthur J.
Fuck a Dog—Statutory Rape
The Dils—think
Eraserhead—ALRIGHT!
I love bondage by Marcy
I don't care if C. loves Bruce—if you're happy, do it
White Dopes On Punk
Masque Confussion!
Punish or be Damned
Monitor—art rock
"The only way to escape horror is to bury yourself in it." Jean Genet
The Fucked
Rock Bottom's a faggot
Geza is gay!

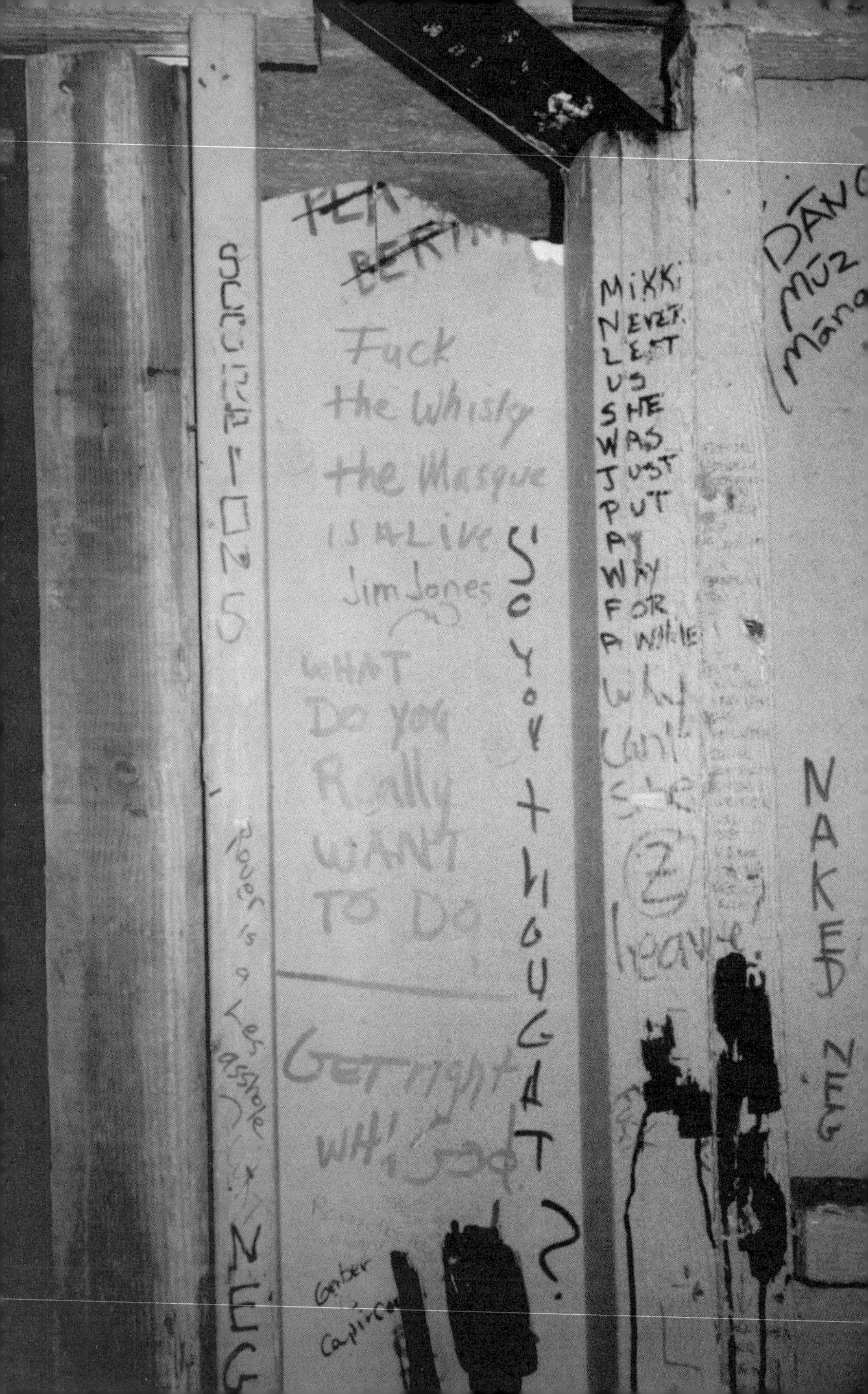

Fuck
the Whisky
the Masque
IS ALIVE
Jim Jones

WHAT
DO YOU
REALLY
WANT
TO DO

GET right
WHORE

So you thought?

SCORPIO 1025

Rover is a Les
asshole

NEG

Gober
CapirCor

MIKKI
NEVER
LEFT
US
SHE
WAS
JUST
PUT
A
WAY
FOR
A WHILE!

Why
Can't
She
(2)
leave

DANG
MU2
Mang

NAKED
GENZ

Jerrys suck
Not all fags are wimps
DIE, NAZIS! Nope; not so simple.
Remember the Plungers
Crickets make tasty snacks for reptiles
The Germs are microscopics
Darby is microscopic
SHOCK
The Germs steal stuff
I Knew This Would Happen
Anarchy = Peace
Freedom is Loss
Let All the Poison that Lurks in the Mud pass out
Brainless Sten Guns in Bel Air
Blow God
Kill a Cop
Suicide Pole—Hit Head Here 50 MPH
Fear has only one homosexual—me, Derf Scratch
Punks Rule—fuck disco
Kay Oss
Kill the 70s
Go-Go's, Plugz, Germs, Elvis Costello
Sell out now!
Everything is wrong
Fuck punks!
Kill yourself
Long Live Bormann
Kill a pig
the Fartz
Kill Hippies!
Yvonnes
Long hair forever!
Bong Ludes!
Peace, Pot and Microdots
No No No!
No Drugs No Pussy No Future No Bags
Quadraplegics Can't Masturbate
Who Cares About Cows
Barry Manilow was here
You are ugly
Quoth the Raven; "Nevermore!"
Mercy is 30 years old—ha ha!
Cal Worthington Was Here—He's a Commie!
Stamp Out Inferiors!
Pussy Power
I'm MAD! So What—I'm Mau Mau!

Masque graffiti. Photo: Michael Jones.

The original lobby of the Masque. Photo: Michael Yampolsky.

"HOW TRENDY" LIST (on Masque office door, circa Aug. '77)
be a punk—how trendy
wear buttons—how trendy
wear pointy boots—how trendy
wear safety pins—how trendy
spike your hair—how trendy
dye your hair—how trendy
have a fanzine—how trendy
only go to major punk shows—how trendy
be in a band—how trendy
hate newcomers—how trendy
try not to be trendy—trendy
trendy trendy trendy trendy trendy

Gerber at the Masque. Photo: Al Flipside.

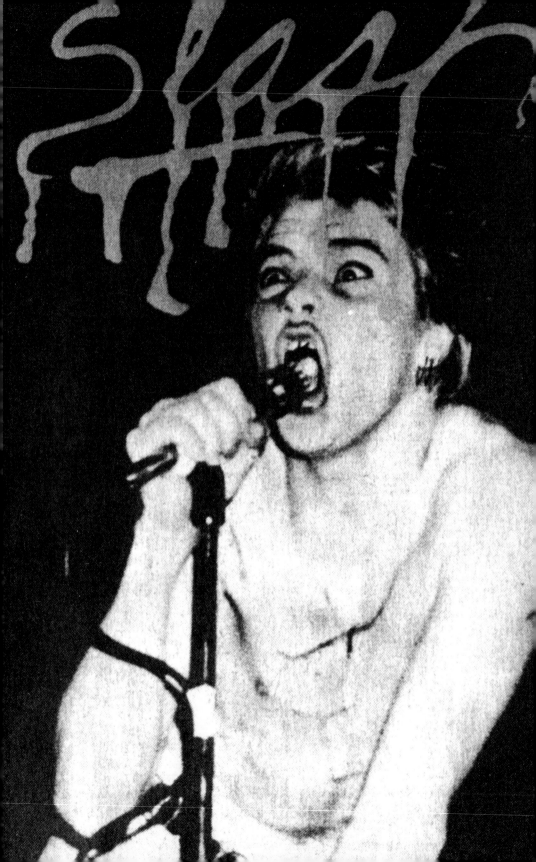

STREET DREAMS

O

JENA CARDWELL I met Pat when they were loading out their equipment. He let me carry his leather jacket and I think I gave him a ride home. That was one of my big "ins"—I had a car! Pat's room was covered with photographs of Pleasant! It was like a shrine to Pleasant. He was really drunk so I just tucked him in and left. Our first date was going to see Kiss and Cheap Trick at the Forum. By this point, his walls were covered with pictures of Farrah Fawcett-Majors—he had thankfully finally moved on. Pat loves to talk on the phone! He's legendary! We would just talk for hours, to the point where my mother came to me with a phone bill: "Do you know that the phone bill is $100?!" That was a huge phone bill back then—and it was only from Highland Park to West L.A.! We would literally spend all night talking on the phone. Most of our relationship was built on that at first, because I was still living at home, until I finally jumped ship, and ran off to live with his family.

When I first started going out with Pat he just listened to Yes and Queen—then later, we got into Shaun Cassidy! We got Yes' *Going For the One album*—the not-so-cool post-Rick Wakeman Yes—and we listened to that obsessively for a while … it was so completely unlike punk rock—it had absolutely nothing to do with it. And of course there was the Bowie fixation … they shared that, too, but Darby had a much deeper obsession with Bowie than Pat did.

HELLIN KILLER Everyone was new and pretty accepting. We cut people's hair off sometimes as a joke. We took in this blind guy that came there, who had really long hair … he was really into the music and we were like "this is great." We'd take him to parties at our house. It was just a really great time and everyone was really close and everyone knew everyone, it was almost family … even if you really hated someone, it was like hating some kind of distant relative or something.

JUDITH BELL I didn't realize at first that many of these younger punk kids came from really fucked-up families for real … broken homes … and that what they were creating was a surrogate family. I never realized how desperate a lot of those people were for real.

THE FIRST *SLASH* INTERVIEW
(by "new contributor," Pleasant)

SLASH What do you think of New Wave?
PAT I think it sucks!
BOBBY I got one yesterday.
PAT I think the Pistols suck.
SLASH The Damned?
BOBBY I think they're good for 13-year-olds.

SLASH   How did you get your hair so blue?

BOBBY   I had polio when I was a baby.

SLASH   Give us some titles of songs you do.

BOBBY   We don't have any … Umm, "Sex Boy," "Death of an Immortal," "Jet Scream," which is about a guy who steals an airplane and it crashes in Lithuania. Umm … "Teenage Clone," and our single, which is "Forming," about breaking down the government and forming our own.

SLASH   Who writes the songs?

BOBBY   Me; well, I write most of them.

SLASH   Where do you get your ideas?

BOBBY   From other peoples' songs!

PAT   Where else?

SLASH   What does your stage act involve?

BOBBY   It ain't an act. It involves about three bottles of champagne and some Quaaludes … I used to sniff spot remover, the 29-cent kind—it tastes like candy, and you put it on a sock and … (gasps) and you walk down the street and you get this thing called the flingin' zingers, where it looks like little meteors are coming at you.

SLASH   Tell us about your fans.

PAT   We don't have any. Well, there are these surfers, Lorna's groupies, that follow us around going, "Wow, man, Bobby Pyn really gets down! He kicks ass!"

SLASH   What was your first sexual experience?

BOBBY   When I stuck my arm down a garbage disposal.

PAT   That wasn't a garbage disposal.

BOBBY   Who was it?

SLASH   What do you think of your music?

BOBBY   We try to ignore it … it's repulsive.

SLASH   Talk about some of the concerts you've played.

PAT   They loved us [at the Whisky] … they were screaming for more, and everyone ran away.

LORNA   And whipped cream.

PAT   And milk of magnesia.

SLASH   What do you think of the Runaways?

BOBBY   Cute. Very cute. I think they're a bad joke, but I like Joan.

PAT   I think they're a good joke. I think Kim Fowley is very witty (giggles). Wait a minute! FUCK!—there, that's better, didn't want this to be too clean.

SLASH   What do you think of the L.A. punk bands?

BOBBY   There are only three real ones. The Screamers, the Weirdos, and us.

PAT   The Screamers are terriff!

SLASH   What do your parents think of the Germs?

PAT   My mom wants to do opera back-up vocals. I'm serious. I swear.

DONNA   They envy us.

SLASH   Do you have any plans for more singles or an album?

BOBBY   Yeah, but nobody else does! (laughter)

SLASH   Are you real punks?

PAT   Yeah, I guess—you shoulda seen what happened at the Orpheum. After we played they closed it down. We trashed the place, they called the police and no punk bands can play there now … we're really sorry, guys.

SLASH   Is your music political?

BOBBY   Kind of; we talk about overthrowing everything. We've been ruined by society. I like to refer to us as social heaps.

SLASH   Did you have a bad childhood?

BOBBY   Yeah—ooh, once I had a day off from school and a bicycle fell on my head and cracked my skull.

LORNA   That's how you got this way, right?

BOBBY   She lived in suburbia. She played on swings and ate peanut butter and jelly, she made mud pies…

BOBBY   Bad childhoods is what causes punks. I bet Johnny Rotten was a battered baby. Pat is such a punk that a dog came up to him on the street and peed on his leg!

SLASH   What's the most disgusting thing that's ever happened to you?

BOBBY   The most disgusting thing that ever happened to me was the Germs! (laughter)

KIM FOWLEY   I like bands that have dirty women like with The Germs, pudgy white girls from the Valley, from the suburbs, from the beaches, from the South Bay, from Orange County, affluent porker chicks who didn't want to marry the doctors and the lawyers—the future farmers of America, or the future schoolteachers. They wanted to go get pissed on and shit on and beat up and shot up and desecrated in Hollywood. And there were The Germs to do it for them. That was their appeal. Some people designed the rock and roll legacy, and the other half just stumbled in. Darby Crash was one of the stumblers. I'd see him on the street and we'd wave. It was like "Hey dude, what's up, motherfucker? Hey man, any pussy at your gigs?" But Darby was very likeable, and from somewhere within his stupor he wrote some nonsense songs that if you were on heroin in the Midwest, you might enjoy. If you were in the ninth grade it probably changed your life. If you were like me, a man in his late 30s, it was just another teenage trend.

PLEASANT GEHMAN   My mom named Cliff Hanger … and she named Hellin Killer.

JENA CARDWELL   The Germs first "real" drummer, Cliff Hanger, is usually described as a "drug dealer in the Rainbow parking lot." He dealt mostly Quaaludes, a little cocaine—whatever was around. He got his punk name from Darby's mom. Now that they had a drummer that could actually play to some degree, the Germs started to rehearse more often. The songs slowly began to sound like songs, and the tempos got a bit faster.

DON BOLLES   The one time I actually hung out with Cliff Hanger was after running into him in the Rainbow parking lot. He invited me up to his conveniently located apartment—a little messy, but not like gross or anything. I had a joint of angel dust with me. We had heard that when you smoked dust, you were supposed to go berserk—you know, bite your best friend's nose off, kill your mom, suddenly acquire the strength of ten men and bench-press a car, that sort of thing—so we decided to try a little experiment. Cliff had a .45 automatic, no doubt for work-related reasons, and we loaded it with a full clip of ammo. Then we sat in these chairs, facing each other across a little round table. We'd pass the dust joint, and the gun, take a hit—and then pass the joint and the gun back across the table, until it was gone. I'm not sure if the experiment was a failure or a success, since we were both were still alive afterwards. Although I don't really recall ever seeing Cliff again, after that evening. But I read somewhere about Cliff going to jail and his dick getting cut off.

D.J. BONEBRAKE   I'd already played on a session with the Eyes for Chris Ashford of What Records when I got the call that the Germs needed a drummer for another of Chris' recordings. What I remember most about the "Round and Round" session was Bobby Pyn interrogating me. "Why are you playing this music?" He knew I had had formal schooling in music. He asked me, "Why aren't you playing with a band like Yes or something?" Ha ha. I said, "Well, 'cause I don't like that type of music." We did what we had to do pretty quickly and he goes, "Do you know 'Round and Round'?" And they played a second of it. And I said, "Oh, the Chuck Berry thing?" I'll never know if they really knew whether they were covering David Bowie or Chuck Berry or what. I'm sure he must have known. I was a little bit older. I was about 22, 23. They asked me to do a gig with them, which never happened. They were at the Starwood and said, "Hey, you wanna play this gig, we're gonna rehearse tomorrow." And I said, "What time?" "12 o'clock." I walked from there to the beach and slept in the sand, walked to their house, another three miles and I got there and Nicky Beat was there already. and I said "Oh shit." They were really kind of flaky.

BOBBY PYN   I don't like rock and roll myself, but it's fun to do sometimes, like we do a cover version of "Round and Round" and that's what I consider rock and roll. You know, like Chuck Berry and stuff. But mostly there was a change back in the '60s or early '70s from "rock and roll" to just like "rock," when Cooper and Bowie and those people came out. Of course we have roots there and stuff but why should we go back?

D.J. BONEBRAKE   There were a lot of people who could really play their asses off, but it was the trend to pretend that you couldn't play, that you'd just picked up your instrument last week. Like Pat Smear … he could play, he would just forget to put strings on his guitar … but he could play all the Yes songs … you name it, he could play it note for note. I noticed it, watching him goof around and stuff. I did a recording with the Germs once and you could tell by their ease of playing, the way they held their instruments, they weren't looking at their fingers, they're just playing. My wife went to school with Pat and apparently he knew all the Queen licks … all the Brian May licks…

CHRIS ASHFORD Where did the Germs belong? They were already banned for life from the only three venues they'd played! I was working at Peaches Records and somebody came by with flyers for the first show at the Masque and so I went down that night … I thought it would be a good place to do a photo shoot … it had a great alley…

BRENDAN MULLEN I met Chris Ashford around June, 1977, when he was working as a clerk at Peaches Records on Hollywood Boulevard, right around the corner from the Masque. He came down and introduced himself one afternoon and said "This place is great! Would you let this band I manage come down here for a photo shoot? It's for the cover of a record." I said, "What band is that?" He said, "The Germs." I froze. The Germs!? Oh, no! Their rep from the Orpheum and the Whisky preceded them. I said, "The Germs?! You're their manager? The Germs actually have a 'manager'? Aye-ee! Well, fine—so long as it's only a photo shoot and it doesn't interfere with the other bands practicing here. And NO food fights! Is that a deal? I have your word?"

CHRIS ASHFORD I remember Brendan saying "What's the point, Chris, if they can't even play? Do I have to clean it up afterwards or do you?"

BRENDAN MULLEN The Germs showed up for the photo shoot the next day and Bobby Pyn seemed eerily sweet-natured and charming, the opposite of this scary notion I had of him as some snarling crazed out-of-control half-man, half-monster. If anything, the high-energy live-wire of the day was Cliff Hanger; Pat was also immediately likeable with his own cool elegant style, while Lorna just stood there smiling beatifically throughout … totally erasing the hearsay image I had of them as these shit-faced lunatic droogs. Everything was quiet at the Masque in the middle of the afternoon. Everyone seemed stone cold sober and rational. It was too early to be all fucked up.

There were no drugs or alcohol that I was aware of, although I'm sure there was a beer or two floating. There was no one else around while we discussed setting up a Germs show after they gave their word they wouldn't just schlep a bunch of food around. Bobby made a point of saying that they were finished with the goop-slinging … they'd been there, done that already, they needed to move on, he said. Okay, fair enough. He also said they weren't treating the band like a joke, but they were treating the Orpheum and the Kim Fowley gigs as a joke, there was a big difference, he said, and the band was really practicing pretty hard. How could you say no to these thoroughly charming eager-to-please people who seemed really sincere about what they were trying to do? I just knew I wanted this energy—whatever it was—in the club somehow.

Somebody—I think it was Chris—had the idea to do it over the Labor Day holiday weekend. He said there was never anything going on over long weekends because most people left the city, but there were always tons of kids left behind with nothing to do who couldn't afford to just take off. The Masque was about four or five gigs into it at that point; it had gone from 20 people showing up for the Controllers to double that for the Skulls; then the Bags were pretty crazy—and then that Labor Day weekend when the Germs played, 150 people showed up!

CHRIS ASHFORD   We had garnered a lot of press like, "This is the worst band ever." The buzz was like … you had to go see the Germs … just to see, are they really that bad?

CLAUDE BESSY   The first time I heard about Bobby Pyn had something to do with Brendan Mullen … he was putting some punk bands on at the Masque and one of them was the Germs. I was told they were probably the most untogether band ever conceived in the universe … they were literally a joke band.

CHRIS ASHFORD   I think that was one of the first gigs where money was charged—$2.50 for four bands; this was our first "organized" gig after the place got raided and shut down by cops the first of many times. We got the Alley Cats to headline, 'cause they'd played at Gazzarri's, a "real" club—so we thought, that's it, they're the shit—they must be happening, let's get 'em on the bill.
  I drove them all to the Masque, except Cliff … the first song they did was a trashed-out version of "Rock and Roll All Nite" by Kiss … and the crowd was bouncing off the walls and the floor for the rest of the set which ended with Cliff's drum set collapsing.

BRENDAN MULLEN   By the time the Germs went on, I think I'd sunk a few Guinnesses down me belt and they did this ridiculous punked-out cover of Kiss' "Rock and Roll All Nite" as the opening song, I cracked up laughing and the stout sprayed through my nose! Then Pat trashed a Yes song! Sacrilege! An outrage to the prog-heads I knew! Cliff Hanger didn't have the floor spikes down on his bass drum, and his whole kit kept rolling all over the place, confetti was being thrown—they were trying to get through these songs, and it didn't matter if they finished them, and it didn't matter if they were in key or in time. Nobody cared what they sounded like, neither did they, but everybody was going nuts anyway. I think it was Geza's first night as the in-house sound guy. I had never seen a 'rock band' that really just didn't give a toss … other bands said they didn't, but this one was the real thing. Not caring to such a degree was fascinating. They unleashed the same kind of energy that the Bags had a couple of weeks previously, but the Germs were even more intense because there was triple the number of people in the audience. The Bags were great, too, but even the Bags seemed to care.

JOE NOLTE   The first show I ever saw at the Masque was the Germs; I think it was the second or third show there. I was never moved by any L.A. bands more than the Germs and the Screamers, and the best time I ever saw the Germs was still that first Masque show, that was so beautiful…

BRENDAN MULLEN   The Germs brought in an interesting mix of so-alive young people that night. I met Will Amato and was impressed with his intellect and his artwork, and Paul Roessler, who said he was a classically trained musician, and his sister Kira, a hot young tomboy siren who was also studying bass. Dinky and Michelle. Gerber. It turned out many of these kids were from Uni High, a school I'd never even heard of.

The Germs had also attracted the attention of the *Slash* people. The Skulls begged me to open up the show. Some of the Screamers and the Weirdos showed up, too … and I met the original *Flipside* fanzine kids, too, like Al, Gabi, and X-8.

CLAUDE BESSY   The first day I was down in the Masque when the Germs were playing I knew I was facing genius. I was amazed, amazed. This man Bobby Pyn didn't give a shit [breaks up with wheezing laughter]. The first time I met him up close was in the Masque a few days later. He was puking in the bathroom and I was puking and I think somebody was trying to puke on top of the other. There was a particular girl in the Masque at that time, she was a rich girl, and the punkettes had slashed her fur coat and had totally destroyed it. Darby and I were trying to flush the fucking fur coat down the loo.

BRENDAN MULLEN   The Germs didn't throw food around the stage—they kept to their word—but the Masque got trashed out that night anyway. Perhaps they told their friends to make a mess, but then the next day it occurred to me, what was there to trash? There was nothing breakable or combustible in the entire basement! It took us a good few hours to clean up afterwards, but those who helped out thought it was worth it, and nobody had been hurt. The gig had been a complete exhilarating gas for all concerned. It was a magical, life-altering night for me when absolutely the right band played at the right venue at precisely the right moment.

NICKY BEAT   By the time Cliff Hanger was out of the band, I was starting to be a kind of "punk-rock session guy," sitting in with this band or that band, mostly for gigs and some recording. I liked the Germs, and was on speaking terms with them, so it felt natural to sit in. Cliff Roman said he thought it was weird that I was playing with the Germs. He said, "I thought you were in the Weirdos." I told him, "I am in the fucking Weirdos, I'm just sitting in with these guys, you don't actually fucking think the Germs are going to get anywhere, do ya? I'm just having some fun here!"

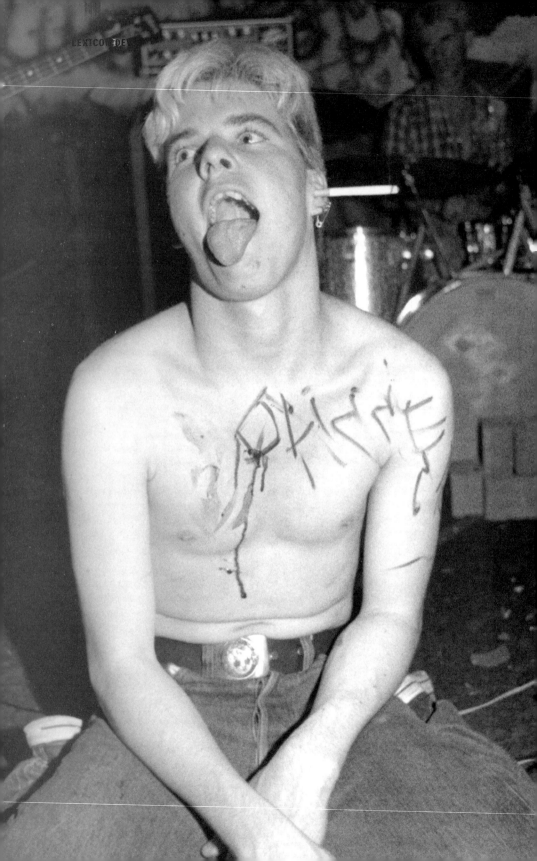

WE MUST BLEED

O

CHRIS ASHFORD   We drove all night up to San Francisco in some battered old vehicle Cliff Hanger came up with and somehow found our way to the Mabuhay Gardens. We got very drunk hanging out on Broadway before the Germs played. On the first of two nights when they opened up for the Weirdos, the Mab's more laid-back old hippie-punk crowd just sat there and gawked in astonishment. It was like a full house, and they just sat and stared. It was really bizarre. For the first couple of songs when the Weirdos came on, same thing, they were all just sitting there! So Pat and I, and a couple of other people started pogoing up front, or whatever, and all of a sudden the whole place erupted. Everybody just jumped into it—tables were flying. After that first set, people seemed to take to the Germs pretty well; I think it was all sort of new to them yet, 'cause in San Francisco it seemed like it was still much more of an art-school crowd.

BOBBY PYN   I don't think there's anything to get across to them [in San Francisco]. If they're not going to like us, they're not going to like us. They were calling us an art school band because that's all they knew how to say. Go back to art school, ha ha ha. They said I had "a Rod Stewart haircut." Middle Class got tear-gassed when they played there. It's ridiculous. Penelope was going to art school all the time she's been in the Avengers. And she admits it. It's just that we weren't from San Francisco. Maybe they thought we were faking; that we really could play, and that we were acting like that.

NICKY BEAT   The Germs went up to San Francisco [a second time] with the Weirdos, and so I wound up playing in both bands at Mabuhay Gardens—it was the night after the Sex Pistols played Winterland. We started the set with "Circle One"—I think Sid Vicious was watching from the wings. Between the first beat of the drum intro and the roll that leads into the vocal, Darby struts onto the stage, grabs Lorna's beer off her amp, walks across the stage, drinks the beer, breaks the glass over his head, carves a gigantic, bloody circle in his chest with the broken glass, then comes in right on cue with, "I'm Darby Crash, a social blast."

HELLIN KILLER   I had a thing for putting my fists and feet through plate glass. I've got a lotta scars to prove it, too! I had stitches on several occasions. One day, me, Darby, Jello Biafra, and some other people were running around Chinatown in San Francisco and there was this huge antique store with these 6x12 plate glass windows. We all wore boots, me, Darby, everybody, we all had big-ass fuckin' boots on except for Jello who had on a pair of Converse All Stars, and he chose this particular antique store as the place where he was going to kick in a window. We all yelled "Nooo!" as he put his foot through it and fucking sliced his Achilles tendon! We had to carry Jello to this beat-up Volkswagen and drive him to the hospital with all six of us in the car. They immediately took him into surgery, and we all split up into pairs, grabbed some wheelchairs, and just wreaked havoc. We'd

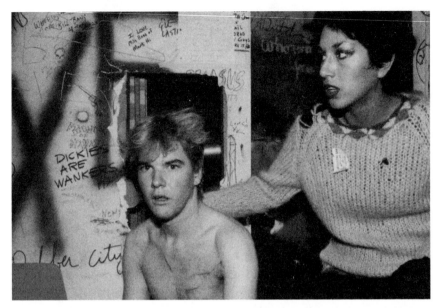

Darby and Alice Bag. The King and Queen of L.A. proto-hardcore backstage at the Mabuhay Gardens in San Francisco during the same weekend the Sex Pistols played at Winterland, their final show. Sid was in the audience for one of the shows. Photo: Ruby Ray.

be in the elevator, see the security guard, close the elevator and go to the next floor; we trashed the cafeteria—we caused so much shit, until they finally kicked us all out. That was pretty fun. It took Jello a while to recover from that one. I don't think he ever kicked in a fucking window again! Afterwards, we all laughed about how totally weird it was that Jello felt he needed to do this, what made him go that far out—literally on a fuckin' limb—just to win Darby's approval.

JELLO BIAFRA   I will never forget the image of Darby Crash in his leather jacket being chased down the hall by orderlies on the fourth floor of this hospital, with this crazed look in his eyes, carrying an unopened loaf of Wonder Bread pirate-style in his teeth!

HELLIN KILLER   All those early Germs gigs were fun, all that trash and blood and cliché punk, which no punks even really did. The Germs started cliché!

BOBBY PYN   I was into Iggy a little, but that wasn't why I got cut up. I didn't know what else to do on stage. So, you know, you do anything to get people to watch. I had like 12 stitches right here and 30 on my foot once when I came running down the stairs at the Whisky and I jumped on the glass. I thought it was a little cut, and I looked and I said, "Aw, a couple of stitches." And then I sat down and looked again, and I said, "Aw, shit," so I finished the song and just went off to the hospital.

HELLIN KILLER   The Plungers came together when we were just sort of hanging out at each other's houses. Mary Rat, Trudie and I got dressed up in these weird men's

shirts and put dirt on our faces and stuck out our hair all weird and took a bunch of pictures of us in wraparound sunglasses, holding plungers. We were one of those "fantasy" bands that never played 'cause we couldn't be bothered to learn to play anything, but we lived together and had one of the the biggest party houses. The Plunger Pit was a single apartment across the street from the Starwood. There were constant people sleeping everywhere. Food was spaghetti or instant mashed potatoes or whatever you could get. We'd wake up at three in the afternoon when somebody would show up at the door and we'd say, "Go buy a bottle of alcohol … and let's start getting drunk now." And people would do it. When bands came to town to play the Starwood we'd go "Party at the Plunger Pit!" after their gig, and everybody would literally just stumble across the street. Sometimes cops would break up these huge out-of-control parties.

TRUDIE'S DIARY (10/30/77) Tonight the show is The Dickies, Germs and Deadbeats. Pat Smear had a cold and he was blowing huge long rubber bands of snot out of his nose as he played guitar, and it was hanging out of his nostril down to his waist before it would fall off on to the stage. So disgusting! Bobby was playing with glass on stage, cutting himself up, wearing only his underwear. At the end of the show he ran down the stairs and jumped on to the stage right onto the glass and cut his foot badly. It was a bloody mess!

GERBER Pat and I went down to the Masque one afternoon when we were fucking around in Hollywood and drinking. We were both roaring drunk. We took this girl from school, Nickie Rickles, down there and we were waiting for Bobby to show up. Bobby and Pat loved to beat the shit out of Nickie. She was an earthy, dirty, unbathed hippie type. So Pat and I were beating the shit out of poor her. We just fucked her up and down that weird "stairway to nowhere." When Bobby showed up, Nickie was trying to run away. We had really beaten the shit out of her with belts and fists; we had her on the ground and we were kicking her and then we did something fucked up to her hair, we were gonna chop it off 'cause it was really long. You know that stuff that came in a can, it was called, like, "Party Slime" or something, and it said you could put it on your skin and hands but never put it in your hair? Well—we dumped a can of it in her hair. So she ran off with her hair full of slime. Pat's favorite story to talk about is beating the shit out of Nickie Rickles. Why? I think Pat just really wanted to grow up and be Cleopatra but it didn't happen.

TONY KINMAN This horrible New York band that wore all stripes, The Fast, was playing the Whisky. They were coming off like, "We're rough and tough and from CBGB's in New York," and they were playing this godawful pop garbage. There were like a dozen or so punks heckling them. The singer, who had long curly hair, leaned way out over the crowd, and Pat just grabbed the guy's hair. We were all cracking up at the sight of this hapless New York clown bending way over, right off the edge of the stage, desperately trying to keep his balance and stay onstage, sort of hanging there the way you'd hang off monkey bars. The guy was in such a precarious position he couldn't move. Pat was just standing there holding onto the guy's hair with one hand and holding a cigarette in the other, snickering with this evil grin from ear to ear.

The Stairway to Nowhere at the Masque. Photo: Ladd Mc Partland.

THE GERMS SPREAD

O

CLAUDE BESSY   The Germs became our darlings, our babies, you know? They're totally out of their heads, they're totally insane, but they are the Germs.

TRUDIE'S DIARY   (12/2/77) The Germs are my favorite band. People say they're lame but I like something about them, I think the chaos. You never know what will happen. They're such a fun sloppy mess and I like their songs. Bobby is painful to watch, he's like a tragicomedy. You can't decipher one word he sings, only the talk between songs.

NICKY BEAT   Somewhere along the line the Germs started coming up with songs; I thought, "Wow! Where the fuck did these guys get songs? These guys don't have any talent, they've got shtick! That's it! What the fuck? They can't play, they can't do anything, and yet they're doing something that sounds good." They added a different dimension that was completely unexpected; it was as unexpected as if you were caught up in a hurricane or something, and a pothole opened up and a waiter came out and said, "So, what would you like for dinner, sir?" Who could have imagined? It was barely even a real band! They began as just some people with nerve enough to get up on stage and make fools of themselves—and now they were coming up with songs! Fuck ... how weird is that?

JEFF MCDONALD   The Germs had all these "Dracula's Daughters"—about 10 or so girls who were devotees; they were kind of like under the spell, and would do anything their leaders asked them to.

JENA CARDWELL   There wasn't any money being a Germ; but there was always a girl that would buy Darby or Pat anything they wanted—there was always a group of girls that had jobs, like me, that would always foot the bill, just to hang around with them. I would basically work all week at an answering service, get paid, and go out on the weekends and spend every penny on them.

NICOLE PANTER   Malissa Hutton, the Germs hairdresser, was always possessive of Darby. Malissa didn't like anyone, especially other girls. There was a lot of competition between the girls; she was incredibly combative about me. Malissa might have known that Michelle [Baer] was too formidable to get rid of, so there was toleration. Malissa was very very very proprietary; she always made a point of calling Lorna Terri, which established inside knowledge. She called Darby Paul too, or Bobby at the very least, even when he became Darby. I didn't really hang out with Darby too much because there was too much jockeying for position among all the little girls, I was a year or two older and had been self-sufficient since I was 14. Many of them were brats who would come and be a punk for a day and then go back home to Beverly Hills or Encino to sleep in their canopy beds. Darby and my relationship was a little more mature than that, as mature as he was capable of being at that point, because there was a big façade, like a cool-sarcastic-mother-fucker-brat façade that he had a really hard time letting drop.

JENA CARDWELL   There were also the drivers, those girls who had a car, like Jill Ash, Michelle Baer, and Hellin Killer. There was a little group of girls that called themselves "Crash Trash." They'd do anything for Darby. I remember some extremely pretty girl with long blonde hair trying to grab Darby onstage, and we all jumped on her and started kicking her and hitting her. We were like, "How dare you touch our Darby!" They were a pretty hardassed little group of girls. There was the core group, and there were people that floated in and out during the years, staying around until their parents sent them away to boarding school.

HELLIN KILLER   I was the one who took care of him ... as long as I was around, he'd be all right, and that's really what it came down to ... after we separated, he latched onto a lot of the wrong people.

CASEY COLA   "Oh no ... Darby you can't do this. Oh no ... Darby you should never own a motorcycle. Oh no ... Darby you're gonna come with me right now." Most of the time it was like girls always protecting him. "Oh, no Darby, you can't have that knife." And I never did that. And he didn't tell me what to do either, he just sort of made sure nothing happened to me.

HELLIN KILLER   People *really* liked to be around Darby. Even the people who hated him sort of gravitated to him. Everyone just wanted to be around him. I have no idea why. I really hated him, and then I turned around and became his "girlfriend"/surrogate mom. We were really comfortable together; it was cool, there was absolutely no weirdness between us. It was good—go out, party, get fucked up, whatever. Malissa and Lorna and all those girls would say "Why don't you just rip his clothes off and rape him?" I told them "Look, I really wouldn't be comfortable doing that; I really don't see any reason to destroy this perfect relationship!" I really, really loved him.

CHELSEA HOTEL—WEST

O

BLACK RANDY [Around early 1978] the Canterbury apartments located a block away from the Masque became a nest of punks. It was so like Haight-Ashbury going on around Hollywood Boulevard and Cherokee, and that was when there was the first heat on the Masque, and then it folded up except for private parties and special events, but by this time it had caught on and there were all sorts of new bands.

TERRY GRAHAM The Canterbury was a classic rambling old Hollywood apartment building whose proximity to the Masque was the sole reason it flourished as this tiny punk colony. The pioneer of moving in was Rod Donahue, but then Debbie Dub and Jane Drano [née Wiedlin] also set up crib in there and I just kind of like inserted myself in their apartment. Then Debbie moved out because I was with Jane and things got uncomfortable. Punks were continually moving in.

BOBBY PYN Like the day the first person moved in, Rod Donahue, the manager said some pimp was throwing one of his girls out the window, so he shot him, or something. The police said that building's got the highest crime rate in the whole city. In the last year there's been five murders there and stuff.

KIM FOWLEY Most of the Canterbury punks were over 18 but they stayed eternally junior high. Even 20-somethings were trying for that perennial teen high school popularity crap. Consequently the Germs and the Go-Go's could flourish as local celebrities in that community.

ANDY SEVEN The high school aspect of it delighted some because before that nobody could be very cliquey 'cause there was no scene. Once people moved into the same building you had the Maicol Sinatra section, him and Chase Holiday and the West L.A. Bowie people … and then you had the Belinda Carlisle people, and the other gals who became the Go-Go's lived there, too … Jane Drano and Margot … they were rehearsing at the Masque … they used to split the rent on one of the monthly rooms with the Motels.

MARGOT OLAVERRA The Canterbury was so run down and the rents were so cheap it became a haven for underclass marginals like punk rockers with no income. Rod Donahue was the first to move in. He said 'I found this place right near the Masque … let's go.' I had no income, but I was creative in my self-support.

ALLAN MACDONELL Craig Lee lived at the Canterbury, too. Lance Loud from the Mumps, Howie Pyro from the Blessed, and Tomata's big pals, Cherie the Penguin and Tony the Hustler, lived at the St. Francis on Sunset, a dump that was even

The Canterbury, today. Photo: Jim Carberry

worse. Man, early punk in L.A. was a rough, hardcore street-hustlin' scene. Blank Frank moved from there to the Canterbury; he was in the Plugz for a minute—then after that he was just turning tricks.

MARGOT OLAVERRA   The building had a really big hallway with staircases on both sides, and these rickety elevators that smelled of mildew and petrified soggy mattresses and this red carpet that wasn't shag and wasn't flat, in between. Perfect to capture dust and dirt. There were many Vietnamese refugees and you could smell the rice cooking. There were many people living there who played in bands like the Deadbeats, Black Randy, the Screamers, the Bags, the Germs, the Weirdos ... and Rod, who also played in a bunch of bands. Some of the Plungers lived there, too ... Hellin Killer had an apartment there, K.K. and Trudie moved in together ... Alice Bag and Nicky Beat had a place ... Belinda roomed with Lorna Doom from the Germs ... Darby used to hang out there all the time. This crazy girl from Detroit, Sheila Edwards, was there ... we used to get into all kinds of trouble.

BARBARA JAMES   There were like two different cliques going on [at the Canterbury]: Belinda Carlisle and her gang—they were the Poodles—and Shannon Wilhelm's was the Piranhas. I didn't want to be a Poodle, that's for sure, but I didn't want to be a Piranha either, because Shannon's a little scary, and being a Piranha was too much of an extremist man-hating feminist thing.

TERRY GRAHAM   The apartment on the first floor, just to the right of the front gate where Allison Buckles and Shannon Wilhelm lived, was sort of like the central front desk for the Canterbury. Out in the courtyard was where everyone found out about everything that was going on ... who was coming, who was going, what was happening in the building. Their window was the first one you passed when you walked through the gate ... it was always open with people crawling in and out who couldn't be bothered entering or leaving the building through the front lobby. Somebody was always perched there at that window. There was always music and constantly shifting people 24 hours a day.

HELLIN KILLER   I was close friends with Lorna Doom who lived at the Canterbury. Her roommate Belinda Carlisle always struck me as this weird kind of '60s-style New Wave fashion chick who dressed in day-glo colors which we Plungers thought was really lame. She got into the Go-Go's and we were like "Oh, God!" But it was okay. They did good.

MARGOT OLAVERRA   The first time I met Belinda Carlisle was backstage at the Whisky. It was a Dickies show, I think, and she was wearing this black priest's tunic with a pink bowtie and had really, really short hair and a big head, and we proceeded to call her "Big Head." She told me she wanted to sing in a band ... I knew she was part of that clique ... the Germs' Circle One contingent. We met and made noise. Jane [Drano, née Wiedlin] was on the first floor, I was on the third floor. We started a rehearsal room in the basement right next door to this black Muslim organization.

Terry Bag (Graham) and Jane Drano (Wiedlin) at the Canterbury. Photo: Michael Yampolsky.

TERRY GRAHAM   Every single night something was going on at the Canterbury. You slept all day 'cause you were up all night. A lot of people were on SSI. Some had part-time jobs. I didn't want to be on the outside [of the punk rock scene]. I wanted to be in the dead center of it. I didn't want to watch it happen from a distance, even if I was just a fan.

ALLAN MACDONELL   The first time I was [at the Canterbury], some pimp was beating the shit out of a woman in the hall; another time there was a guy down in the courtyard, calling someone out—then you hear the guy come out, you hear them talking, then you hear this gun shot—POW! Then you don't hear anything else—it was fucking terrifying! Rod Donahue was the first guy that moved in there—and the first night he was there, the manager shot someone to death in the foyer! I remember when they were showing us apartments, we came to one, and the manager opened the door and said, "And this is a two-bedroom ..." and we heard someone inside going, "Get the fuck outta here—GET THE FUCK OUTTA HERE!!" Then we find out later that he's a pimp and he'd just thrown a chick out the window two days earlier, I guess he was a little tense, 'cause he wasn't sure if he was gonna get away with it ... there was all kinds of fucking shit going on there! I remember when Randy was in my apartment, and Wild Man Fischer was out in the courtyard looking for Nicky Beat, going "Nicky—Nicky Beat!" And Black Randy had this pot of water, and he was going, "Over here! Over here!" and he just poured the water on him, and Wild Man goes, "Niiiick-yyyyy!!!" all dejected-like!

DON BOLLES   On the fourth floor overlooking the courtyard was Ygar Ygarrist, the guitar player for this New Wave space-themed band called Zolar X, the "house-band" at Rodney's English Disco. I was lucky enough to see what must have been one of their last shows, at a club on La Cienega and San Vicente, when I was visiting L.A. from Phoenix. They wore Spock ears and had futuristic pointy Eddie Munster haircuts, and had those little microphones that receptionists used before anyone else. They did the whole bit—the shiny leotards with triangular metallic Klaus Nomi collars, the chrome donut things around the shoulders and wrists; they even painted themselves silver. And that was just to go to the 7-11! Their manager, Charlie, who looked like an overinflated version of Martin Mull's sidekick on *Fernwood 2nite*, lived a couple of floors down from Ygar's place. Every night he'd drink a pint or so of Southern Comfort and howl at the moon like a crazed werewolf for hours. The echoes in the courtyard made it seem even scarier.

MARGOT OLAVERRA   I remember Black Randy howling right on the edge of the roof, just howling, and that was normal … that was so normal, that when this girl got raped one night and she was screaming, screaming these bloodcurdling screams, I just didn't think anything was going on. People screamed in the night all the time. It was that kind of environment. Very crazy.

TRUDIE'S DIARY   (12/11/77) People have complained about being stopped by police after leaving our apartment. That happened to Bobby Pyn. He's been having bad luck lately. One day he came over and said he had just been beaten up by someone from the bar across the street.

BOBBY PYN/DARBY CRASH   I couldn't live there [at the Canterbury]. Too much everything. Lorna lives there, but Pat lives down in my neighborhood in West L.A. The Canterbury's in a really horrible neighborhood, too. One of my friends got hit in the head with a champagne bottle thrown by somebody going by on a motorcycle. Belinda just walked in the building and somebody threw a knife at her. A lot of people are moving out.

JIMMY WILSEY   I would go down to L.A. [from San Francisco] and hang out with Darby. He had his finger on the Canterbury scene and the whole underground. It was when he became real nihilistic that he became popular, but he was actually a real nice guy. He would get some girl to drive us to his mom's house in the middle of the night and make us huge sandwiches. I think as he got accepted for being weird, it just sort of took over.[8]

ALLAN MACDONELL   One night Rick Wilder, Sheila and I were in Rod Donahue's kitchen, shooting up pills or something, and Sheila starts banging on the glass panes in the connective door, and breaks one; so then Rod grabs her and throws her out, just hustles her out of the room. About three minutes later, there's a bang on the door, so I go and open it and there's a Negro there, in bikini underwear, with a gun, saying, "You mothafuckas ..." And I said, "Oh, no, no, no—we threw that bitch out—she's gone!" Then he goes, "Y'all sure?" We said, "C'mon in, man, look for yourself, check it out," so he lowers the gun and comes in and then he starts hangin' out with us, so then Rick Wilder looking like this sick-faced scarecrow from hell comes crawling out from hiding in this weird U-shaped space by the window ... and totally spooks the fucking guy out.

BOBBY PYN/DARBY CRASH   The Canterbury is such an in-group thing. The only way I define "in-crowd" is just by who's there whenever like we say, "Let's go to Lauren's party tonight," or something, you know. Just who's there, not because they look alike or think the same that we do or anything. And of course there's safety in numbers. If you have blue hair you're going to hang around with people like that. I mean when some girl gets hit with a bottle, you know, her head gets cracked open because she has pink hair or something, you know, it makes a good target. But when you dye your hair or something like that, you expect that reaction.

TRUDIE'S DIARY   (5/21/78) Someone said Pat Delaney and Pat Smear were goofing around at the Canterbury. Pat D. was spray painting a swastika and a peace sign on a door when Pat Smear opened it and threw boiling hot water on Pat D.'s face. Then Pat D. comes in crying. He is hurt. A bunch of guys are after Pat Smear now.

BRENDAN MULLEN   "The Reverend," so-called because he was a clergyman from some Muslim sect for spiritualized reformed Crips, was last seen dressed in bikini briefs chasing away punk types with a loaded semi saying he was fed up to the teeth with "muthafuckin' punk rocks."

TRUDIE'S DIARY   (6/24/78) Mary Rat told me in the unused room that Don Bolles admitted he's had a crush on her for such a long time, and so she's been fucking him; but she's got a crush on David Consumer, and Don told him she wants to fuck him. Mary says he's bisexual.

GERBER   When someone passed out at a party I'd take a straw, fill it with vodka and just blow it down their throat. I did that to a lot of people when they were passed out. It was very not cool to pass out at a punk rock party. I made people throw up a lot doing that—Darby loved it, he thought it was one of my greatest special Gerber stunts.

BLACK RANDY   My drummer Joe Nanini told me, "The first time I ever saw you, you were with your best friend John Doe drinking beer, and you were supposed to be getting a ride in his car, but John was passed out drunk and you were pissing on him." I said, "Listen up, man ... everybody knows it's not cool to pass out at a punk rock party..."

ALLAN MACDONELL Black Randy was already a legend for his party-destroying antics. So many of them seemed to involve poop that he could've called himself "Brown Randy." Poop-filled baggies were placed in the snoring mouths of passed-out revelers; guests' purses were removed from the hostess' closet and pooped in. Sometimes he'd call the cops on parties, just for fun. But what really impressed me was when Randy drew an enormous swastika with what must have been an equally enormous turd, on the floor-to-ceiling mirror in the foyer of the Canterbury.

JENA CARDWELL During Germs' rehearsals at the Canterbury or in Pat's garage girls like me would be just fading into the woodwork, but I don't remember them ever having private summits that we would be excluded from. Darby was doing his thing, and we were just there, not participating in it. We'd be totally ignored, sitting there like lap dogs, just waiting, until it was time to go buy some beer or drive them somewhere. Darby was always very, very nice to me; very kind, very considerate. But he was the type of person where you always knew your place. I don't think there would ever be a girl who would step out of those bounds, because the relationship was defined from minute one.

TRUDIE'S DIARY (5/5/78) Bobby bought a Scientology book for K.K. Bobby's really into Scientology and says he'd go through it if he had the money. The story he tells everyone is that he was solicited off the street to take their I.Q. test and his score was so high that they were in awe of him. Thought he was a genius, he says.

K.K. BARRETT I had a lot of one on one conversations at the Canterbury with Darby about religion as a business … the whole idea that you could start your own religion and make money off of it, which carries an obvious L. Ron Hubbard reference … and the fact that religion was just basically a funnel for lost souls…

BOBBY PYN Scientology is the biggest rip-off there is but it's also worth the money, their philosophy's unbelievable. The government's been suppressing them … everything they say works. If I had ten thousand dollars I'd go back and do it … it does work … it's gonna save the world.

MARGOT OLAVERRA I had to move out of the Canterbury after a fire when the ceiling collapsed and drenched all my belongings … the whole apartment above burned out and caved into mine. They wanted to renovate the building and so they started driving out all the punks by starting fires in the hallways…

K.K. BARRETT Finally the owner of the building hired a group of thugs to get the punks out.

TERRY GRAHAM I remember at one point somebody saying, "Well, maybe it's time to go." We'd been there a year. It's just inevitable.

GERMS BURNS AND THE CULT
THAT RULED THE WORLD

O

CIRCLE ONE

I'm Darby Crash
A social blast
Chaotic master

I'm Darby Crash
Your mecca's gash
Prophetic Stature

I'm Darby Crash
A one way match
Demonic flasher

Deep, deep, deep in my eyes
There's a round, round, round, circle of lives
It's a tame, tame, tame, sort of world
Where you're caught, bought, taught, as it twirls

I'm Darby Crash
A social blast
Chaotic master

Snap, crackle, pop
Snap, crackle, pop
Snap, crackle, pop—out there

Lyrics by Darby Crash; published by Crash Course Music (BMI).

PLEASANT GEHMAN   I reported in my column on the scene in *New York Rocker* that Bobby Pyn showed up at this hideous punk fashion show thing at the Palladium [September 23, 1977] in a jock-strap to announce he was changing his name from Bobby Pyn to Darby Crash, but nobody seemed to pay it any mind for a while afterwards.

RIK L. RIK   He started off as Bobby Pyn before I knew him. Very Britpunk-sounding, wouldn't you say? After a while he obviously recognized the limitations of Bobby Pyn, that it was too cute, not heavy enough.

PAT SMEAR   We were playing the song "Circle One" during some show, and Paul just announced that he was changing his name from Bobby Pyn to Darby Crash. Up 'til then we had thought "Darby Crash" was just another storytelling character, like "Richie Dagger."

RIK L. RIK   Darby was seriously considering renaming himself Richie Dagger at the time he was divesting himself of "Bobby Pyn."

TRUDIE'S DIARY   (9/30/78) Birthday party at the Masque for Bobby Pyn, who has now changed his name to Darby Crash.

BRENDAN MULLEN   Darby was the ultimate passive-aggressive. One time at the Masque he kept rushing the stage while the bands were playing, so I grabbed him expecting him to resist. My mind and body were braced for physical struggle, but instead he just sort of melted softly into my arms. I wasn't going to beat him up, or hurt him, or anything, I just wanted to remove him, but instead of some minor scuffle, I ended up carrying a small child in my arms out of the club—much to the amusement of the crowd.

RIK L. RIK   Darby completely re-socialized me. He taught me to question everything, and to totally look at reality, not to accept everything, and to make up my own mind. [He taught me to] evaluate reality and to make my own conclusions, rather than just accepting the way society wants you to accept it. He did it for everybody he came in contact with. Sometimes Michelle Baer and I would talk about Darby when he wasn't there, and Michelle would wonder aloud if he knew what we were saying about him—whether he had some sort of telepathic powers, because the power of his mind was so overwhelming. I once thought, "Maybe he really does know what we're thinking."

GEZA X   I liked the social magnetism of the Germs … this alien presence about them … like Darby had some kind of hypnotic power and he used to love wielding it. It seemed out-of-whack that this messed-up little kid could have that much power over people. He seemed to have an intuitive grasp of fairly advanced behavioral psychology. I discovered later that he'd apparently read up on that stuff. I used to say the Germs were like five-year-old kids with the atom bomb … and they didn't think twice about setting it off…

TONY MONTESION   Darby definitely wanted to make his presence known—he wanted to be the guy. He wanted to tear the whole structure down, point a finger at a guilty nation, and then for him to be the new main man—he was narcissistic like that.

ALICE BAG   It used to really bother me that Darby enjoyed trying to control people. I felt it was demeaning not only to his followers but to himself. It used to bother Darby that I treated my fans as equals. He would lecture me on what people expect in a leader. We had very, very different views on this subject. I think we had both really thought long and hard about the responsibilities that went along with having a bunch of kids look up to you. We were both committed to our beliefs. Anyway, we took ourselves very seriously, and we were very drunk [one night at the Canterbury], so we started arguing, then shouting at each other and

finally throwing punches. Although I can't say for sure, I'm willing to say I probably started the fight. I was quite a hothead in those days. Did he hit back? Of course he did. It was a good scrap!

TONY MONTESION He had disciples wearing the black and blue armbands, getting the Germs burns. I have a burn—he did it himself—and Courtney my wife got one, too.

X-8 Darby wanted to give me a Germs burn. He said, "Everybody's doing it." And I said, "I don't think so."

DARBY CRASH Cigarette burns are tied-in because of circles. If you do a cigarette burn right here, right on the bone, you get a circle scar and a lot of us have them. Jimmy the bass player from the Avengers has the first one. Over 200 people have them, even in San Francisco. You can only get them from a person who already has one. It all has to do with circles.

PAT SMEAR The burn was the circle, it was a circular thing, but I didn't know what the circle meant. It was his idea of something permanent, so that in ten years you'd be at the supermarket, and some lady would give you change, and you'd see the burn and make a connection. I gave my first burn to a 15-year-old girl. The rule was once you got yours, you could give it to other people.

TRIXIE Hellin could hypnotize people into letting her pierce them with safety pins, it wouldn't bleed or leave a scar. We Plungers preferred razor slashes to burns, though.

Trixie and Donnie Rose at the Masque, early '78. Photo: Michael Yampolsky.

IRIS BERRY   Darby wanted to give me a Germs burn but someone stopped him. I was going for it. I was like, "Yeah, gimme one." He had the lit cigarette ready. I know people who had Germs burns and later covered them with tattoos and now they're sorry about it.

BILLY ZOOM   I said, "If you put that cigarette near me, I'll tear your fucking arm off."

GEZA X   I avoided the cigarette burn thing … I thought it was icky.

PHRANC   Darby gave me my Germs burn outside of Club 88.

TOP JIMMY   He never tried to give me a Germs burn … he knew I wouldn't do that shit.

CLAUDE BESSY   He was so full of shit. I said, "Darby, what are you talking about? He said, "Bessy, the Germs burn?" I said, "Okay, give me the fucking Germs burn, but cut out the fucking pseudo-philosophy crap."

DARBY CRASH   You've seen our circle on our armbands and stuff. Everything works in circles. Sometimes you're doing something and then like a year later, it seems like you're doing something else, but you're back at that same point. It's really hard to explain.

TERRY GRAHAM   I have no Germs burn personally administered by Darby Crash. I am not the victim of any mind control. I didn't swallow the whole Germs thing. I could never quite understand what the deal was with this Darby Crash guy. Sheep-like people, the followers, wanted to think that he was something that he wasn't … maybe the blind seek out the blind, who the fuck knows?

DONNIE ROSE   Darby's obsession with circles was simply that everything goes in circles and you're always completing cycles and starting new ones, small cycles, big cycles, always.

RIK L. RIK   He liked the idea of cyclical things, although the blue circle idea probably came from some Zen thing he'd copped from an Alan Watts pamphlet.

NICOLE PANTER   Darby had the circle insignia, and when people would ask him about it, he'd say, "Well, you know—Hitler had the swastika." People would mistakenly make that jump: well, because you have this symbol, then you must therefore have a fascist agenda. But the Germs did not have a political agenda. Their agenda was, "Have fun, get fucked up." Darby just came up with a good symbol, and made a bad analogy—an analogy that stuck in people's minds, like Hitler and his swastika.

JENA CARDWELL   Darby's circle thing was a theory like, seven degrees of separation— everybody that you know knows somebody else that you know; it's some

Nicole-Elena Olivieri, prior to her marriage to renowned punk artist Gary Panter.
Photo: courtesy Richard Meltzer.

philosophical thing—the "connectedness" between everybody. The blue and black was from this group of people from back in the days of Nazi Germany that were fighting against the Nazis, and they had taken on blue and black as their colors, maybe it was the Poles, I don't know. But these were his "anti-Nazi" colors, and the circle was where he took the fashion sense of Hitler and the fascists because he thought Hitler was a pretty stylin' guy.

DARBY CRASH What we're going to do is get lots of—what do you call them? … allies—in key positions and um, if you get somebody that works for the post office … I mean somebody that's just even a mail clerk, you can really screw the post office up bad. If you go to the newspapers and they have those big machines, you know, that print them and you shoot a rubber band into it … it rips the paper; it ruins the whole day's edition. So if you can get enough people to do that, you can go to the government and say, "Well, you've got the armies, but we can just stop this country from working." We're trying to get Reverend Moon to back us to go over to China … so he'll just say, "I'll show them how decadent America is, we'll put these people up here to play on this wall and they'll make fools out of themselves." And after that we're going to play the Berlin Wall, right? Is that the next one? Any more walls we can play?

NICOLE PANTER I thought he was troubled, talented, bright, but certainly no genius—I still don't think he was a genius, but he was smart enough to die before anyone could figure that out. Lots of people on the scene really disliked him and maybe even feared him a bit and with good reason, he was very much a pest.

THE COMING OF CACTUS HEAD

○

DON BOLLES Rob Graves and I had been planning to go to L.A. for a Dils show at the Whisky that we saw advertised in an L.A. paper. When the day finally arrived, we grabbed some punky clothes, and gassed up the Chrysler. I was eating Desoxyns—pure, pharmaceutical methamphetamine in a handy tablet—and guzzling beer the whole way, so I was in top form by the time I made Hollywood.

It turned out that the Dils had canceled, and when the MC for the evening, Rodney Bingenheimer, introduced the band that was actually playing, the Quick—a sort of New Wave Sparks clone band—I got a little upset. According to Pat (I don't remember much of this myself), I started heckling Rodney; a lot. Rodney got angrier and angrier, and I got more and more obnoxious. Finally, Rodney got so pissed off he hocked a giant loogie right at me, which amused Pat and Jena to no end. About six months later, when I moved to Los Angeles for real, Pat and Jena saw me out somewhere and Pat said to Jena, "Oh my God—it's that guy! The guy that was at the Quick show heckling Rodney!" Pat told me that he and Jena remembered me because in all the years they had known Rodney, I was the only person to ever make him so mad that he actually spit! I was pleased to have earned my new bandmate's respect, although had I a choice I suppose I might have done it differently...

JENA CARDWELL The first time I saw Don Bolles was at the Whisky when Rodney was on stage. Don was wearing a white jacket and spiked-up black hair—cliché punk rock—and giant, round sunglasses. I don't remember what he said, but he mouthed off at Rodney. That was like slapping God in the face! Then we find out that this is the guy who had heard the Germs while he was living in Phoenix, and decided, "I'm coming to L.A. and I'm going to be the drummer for that band."

JOHN DOE Don Bolles became known as Cactus Head because he came from Arizona. He was just a wide-eyed ... a what-kind-of-trouble-can-I-get-into guy.

DON BOLLES I first heard the Germs when the Consumers' singer David Wiley brought a copy of the "Forming" single back from Los Angeles. I was transfixed; this was either the best or worst thing I had ever heard. The A-side was this amazingly low-tech approach to "stereo"—vocals in one channel, music (or three-chord sludge, as it were) in the other, with the singer matter-of-factly pointing out that "whoever would buy this shit is a fucking jerk," and then itemizing everything that he and his accompanists were doing wrong, finally ending his oddly understated rant with a fairly believable "Aww, I quit," punctuated by the thunk sound of the mic hitting the floor! Now THIS, I thought to myself, is PUNK! I'd heard that these guys needed a drummer, and even though I had only been playing drums for about two weeks and didn't even own a pair of sticks, let alone a drum kit, I was their man.

I got Darby and Pat's phone numbers and when I got Pat on the phone I started running down my favorite Krautrock, avant-noise and punk bands. Every name met with the same response; "Who?" "No, never heard of that." I finally asked, "Well, what music do you like?" "Well, I really like Queen and David Bowie." My jaw dropped. "You are, of course, putting me on, right?" I asked, incredulously. "Oh … and I really like Yes, too!" he giggled. I thought this person must be fucking with me. I figured these L.A. punk rock folks are probably the most sarcastic people on the planet. I said I'd heard they needed a drummer, and that I was going to somehow get a drum set and move to L.A. and join their band. This merely caused a few more giggles, followed by a polite, "Uh … okay!"

Darby was even stranger than Pat. First, he rattled off a seemingly endless litany of really juicy gossip that was pretty entertaining, detailing every sexual indiscretion of a bunch of people I not only did not know, but had never even heard of. I ran down my favorite band list only to strike out once again. Giving up, I popped the same question, "So, what do you like?" It still seemed mighty odd when he said, "I'm really into Bowie and Queen." I told Darby the same thing I told Pat—that I'd only just started playing drums, and was going to somehow acquire a kit and move to L.A. to join their group. "Whatever," said Darby and he told me that the Germs were scheduled to play a benefit for the Masque at the Elks Lodge in a couple of weeks, with Nicky Beat from the Weirdos filling in on drums.

On the day of the Masque Benefit [February, 1978], Rob Graves and I loaded stuff into this old Chrysler including our punkiest threads and sunglasses and drove to L.A., where our first stop was the Plunger Pit before we headed down to the Elks Building at MacArthur Park [now the Park Plaza Hotel]. The day after, Rob and I drove straight over to the Canterbury to see about getting rooms. It was cheap—I think it was like $125 a month for my "bachelor" on the third floor.

ANDY SEVEN It was a mistake to move into the Canterbury. People got too familiar with each other … people went from being really civil to totally hating each other … it divided a lot of people … everybody got into each other's business and it reached a point where people were expecting too much from everyone else and they wanted everyone to conform to what they were doing. Then you had Don Bolles and those other obnoxious Arizona guys moving in … they were pretty over-assertive, they were way too needy, too pushy … the Hollywood in-crowd, who were in their own little box, didn't really dig it … they didn't want too many strangers coming in.

GEZA X I was at the Masque when Don Bolles auditioned for the Germs. There was a bunch of pounding, then Darby came out of the bathroom, and sat down next to me in the big room and said, "So what do you think?" I said, "Dude, he came all the way from Arizona to join your band—that's gotta count for bonus points, you know?"

DON BOLLES   I set up my drums in three inches of beer and urine in the over-flowing Masque toilet and banged out some noise. Lorna, Darby and Pat watched horrified but amused. "Uh...." Pat politely interrupted, "Can you play, like, a song?" I played "Life of Crime," the Weirdos song Nicky had shown me a couple of weeks prior—and they went out into the other room, out of earshot, to deliberate. Later Pat replayed the conversation for me: "What do you think? I dunno ... what do you think? Well, he did come all the way from Phoenix." A long, tense moment later ... imagine being turned down to drum for the biggest joke-band in L.A. ... Darby came back in the bathroom and said, with a characteristic nod to some vague, perceived audience somewhere just above his head and off to one side, "Well, you're a Germ!"

NICKY BEAT   When Don Bolles came around in early '78 I gave him lessons. I taught him how all the songs went. I stopped the lessons when he said punk rock is supposed to be sloppy and it's supposed to have mistakes.

MARGOT OLAVERRA   The Go-Go's first gig was a private guest-list only party at the Masque. I remember getting to the Whisky parking lot and Darby said, "Hey, I hear you're playing at the Masque tonight." I said, "What?" So we just got there and played I think one or two songs ... we played one song over twice. Living at the Canterbury ... da da da ... fighting off the roaches ... da da da ... that was one of them.

CLAUDE BESSY   Darby and I were sitting one Sunday afternoon on the stairs in the Masque ... and there was this girl band practicing. I asked, "how are you doing, Darby?" He said, "I've got a hangover." Then he said, "What do you think?" And I said, "Man, they sound like shit!" He said, "I think they sound like shit, too." So we just shook our heads and listened for a few more minutes, then I said, "Darby, this band is going nowhere, nowhere!" Darby said, "Of course they're going nowhere, they haven't got a clue! They've got no lyrics, they've got nothing." I asked, "What's their name?" He replied, "Ah, you know ... it's what's-her-face and what's-her-face and they call themselves the Go-Go's." About a year and a half later the Go-Go's had the number one summer pop hit in America, and Darby was dead ... [breaks up laughing]

"I want to have complete control over everything."
—Darby Crash, '78. Photo: Jill Ash.

GIMME GIMME THIS, GIMME GIMME THAT

O

BRENDAN MULLEN Whereas Bobby Pyn seemed to me a much more innocent, goofy, carefree character, Darby Crash became much more demonic, complex, intense, intoxicated, as he gradually began to exude a much darker persona. Once he became Darby Crash his compulsive manipulation and panhandling seemed to increase. The dreaded "Gimme two dollars . . . gimme a bee-ah ... gimme a ride home" was the Klaxon From Hell around the scene which witnessed a series of socially ostracized, overweight women, many of them easy-pickings mind-suggestibles with absent or disapproving father complexes; of more or less the same psychological type preyed upon by people like Charlie Manson. Such women openly competed for the attention of this emotionally unavailable alcohol-besotted LSD guru while picking up his tab for booze, drugs, gas, food and clothing.

DARBY CRASH Kickboy [Claude Bessy] from *Slash* was supposed to be managing us, but he didn't want to be called a manager because you think of things like Robbie Fields and Malcolm McLaren, so he was going to be our "advisor." But he hasn't done anything. We aren't playing anywhere. The one time we've played since we've gotten him was just something that we set up on our own. So now I think Nicole and Bruce are going to be doing something.

NICOLE PANTER By mid-'78 I started getting them gigs and stuff. We became friends and I was the good mom who got the band shows and talked to them. The night I met him I was sitting in front of some club, and he said, "Buy me a beer!"—a classic Darby line, and I just looked at him and said, "Fuck you, you can talk all those kids into that shit, but not me, you idiot!" That started our bond. I still hadn't seen the Germs play; I had just heard that they were really stupid and bratty.

WILL AMATO I always think of [Darby] saying one thing: "Gimme a beer!" He'd say, "Gimme a dollar—Gimme—Hey, gimme that shirt!" Gimme gimme this, gimme gimme that. That's really one of the earliest things that little kids say— "Gimme that!" Whenever he says, "Gimme a dollar," he's not saying why he needs it, or that he'll pay you back.

NICOLE PANTER Darby used to make people do things, like he'd make one girl take off a bracelet and give it to another girl, just because he could, or he'd say, "Gimme that button," "Gimme that shirt" or "Gimme a beer," and five little girls from Beverly Hills would run and get it.

WILL AMATO   It must have been endlessly amusing to him every time he said "Gimme" and someone actually gave him whatever it was. He found the irreducible nugget of rhetoric for himself right in that word "gimme." He'd never say "Gimme a beer or I'll beat your fucking brains in," it was "I'm pathetic and I just want a beer." There was a plaintive quality to it that was so kind of Paul Beahm to me.

LEXICON DEVIL

I'm a Lexicon Devil with a battered brain
I'm lookin' for a future—the world's my aim
So gimme gimme your hands—gimme gimme your minds
Gimme gimme this, gimme gimme thaaaat

I want toy tin soldiers that can push and shove
I want gunboy rovers that'll wreck this club
I'll build you up and level your heads
We'll run it my way coldmen and politics dead

I'll get silver guns to drip old blood
Let's give this established joke a shove
We're gonna wreak havoc on the rancid mill
I'm searchin' for something even if I'm killed

Empty out your pockets—you don't need their change
I'm giving you the power to rearrange
Together we'll run to the highest prop
Tear it down and let it drop ... away

Lyrics by Darby Crash; published by Crash Course Music (BMI).

BOB BIGGS   The major record companies did not want to know about punk. No critic wanted to view it as a legitimate expression. New York had much more of an avant-garde tradition, and L.A. had produced the Eagles. Nobody was willing to take the leap from A to Z, from the Eagles to the Germs. So in the beginning, it was easy pickings. Every band wanted to do something, and we already had the credibility of the magazine.

JOHN DOE   In Los Angeles, the truer definition of punk was always more about music than politics. It was more about: "Don't tell me about it, just do it."

BOB BIGGS   We [at Slash] had a bit more of a foundation in terms of what we were doing because we came from a background in the arts ... rather than any kind of rock background. It just made it easier to do. I didn't want the burden of knowing these people so closely that I was gonna have to change how I did things. And they wanted it that way, too. My stake in punk was more intellectual and financial.

Biggs with Bessy (Kickboy Face). Photo: Chris D.

CLAUDE BESSY Biggs had no idea. Biggs told me the magazine has got a certain importance, I wanna put some money into a record company. Biggs said, "Who do you think?" I said, "Well, you've got two bands; one of them's gonna cost you a lot, which is X, and one of them's gonna cost you nothing, which is the Germs."

BOB BIGGS I heard some Germs recording that Steve Samiof had, it might have been "Forming," and I wasn't sure whether I liked it at all, but then it stuck in my mind. Then Samiof said, "Look, I'd like to do an ep," and asked if I'd finance it. So I said sure, I'll put up because 600 bucks didn't sound like such a big risk.

CLAUDE BESSY Biggs paid for them to do "Lexicon Devil/No God/Circle One" with Geza X producing. I thought it was the most insane single I'd ever heard. I still play it when I want to send friends out of my house.

GEZA X I'd been spreading the word at the Masque that I was a producer and Darby just came up to me one night and said, "So, you're a producer? Then produce us." And that was Slash's first record, "Lexicon Devil." It was my first record too, and technically their second record … but the first that they didn't do on a little cassette by themselves. We recorded it underneath some bank building on Hollywood Boulevard. They didn't have a regular drummer so Nicky Beat played. Pat didn't even have an amp so I just rigged this chain of pedals and that's why it has this tubular guitar sound.

DARBY CRASH   I think [the "Lexicon Devil" sessions] could have been better. Things got screwed up and stuff. Like on "Circle One," there's half of the vocals missing and we just had to make it like a lead and turn up the guitar and stuff because we didn't know what happened, and it just disappeared. [The vocals] were all repeated in there so it didn't matter, we just said, "Well, turn off what's there, turn up the guitar." And Pat couldn't show up and he's the one that knows the most about music, so me and Lorna had to tell [Geza X] what to do, you know .. you can hardly hear the drums. We did it in like two or three days in some studio on Hollywood Boulevard.

BOB BIGGS   I gave Samiof the money, and a couple of days later he brought me back a 7 1/2" reel-to-reel tape. It was the best thing I'd ever heard. It was sort of analogous to seeing a DeKooning or some painting that was just so absolutely out there. There was just no comparison, no way of even assessing it to be able to make a comparison. We pressed about a thousand copies, and that was it. It was mostly available through mail order from the magazine, which of course gave it a rave review, and we shipped a couple over to Jem Records, a big indie distributor at the time. The marketing campaign for our artists was: put an ad in our paper and give it a great review. That was it. The ethics didn't bother me.

DARBY CRASH   A lot of those Nazi things on Lorna's wall are from this ad for [the "Lexicon Devil" ep], but they said they couldn't print it. Slash wouldn't print our ad because of the cover artwork which can be taken either way. [The ad copy] said "Six million Jews can't be wrong," and we had Hitler on the cover. The Lexicon Devil part doesn't make sense unless you know about Hitler and his speeches. The image on the front was a German propaganda painting, and the one on the back was American propaganda.[9]

DON BOLLES   When I walked into this tiny studio, Nicky Beat was sitting behind his trademark metallic gold Alligator-finish asymmetrical Vox drum kit, headphones on and a cigarette dangling from his mouth. He counted off another take of "Circle One," which he executed perfectly, as always. Although I had just recently been accepted into the group, I was still a spectator at these sessions. Nicky had been rehearsing for a while and had already put the drum parts together. He was an amazing drummer, and I was mighty glad he was so fully committed to the Weirdos! I still managed to appear, if uncredited, on the record. Pat Delaney and I helped out with some handclaps, while chanting "Non Deus" during the bridge in "No God."

Geza X. Masque house soundman, guitarist in the Deadbeats, the Mommymen, Arthur J and the Gold Cups. Produced the "Lexicon Devil" ep. Photo: Michael Yampolsky.

Slash ad for the "Lexicon Devil" 7-inch ep, circa early '78.

NICKY BEAT   I stole the opening drum lick for "Circle One" from the Allman Brothers' "In Memory of Elizabeth Reed." It was just the perfect thing...

JEFF MCDONALD   I think the "Lexicon Devil" record has one of the most unique guitar sounds I've ever heard. It kinda sounds like a banjo being played through a wah-wah pedal.

PAT SMEAR   I didn't even own an amp. Geza was supposed to bring me one for the session, but he forgot. So we had to record the guitar directly into the soundboard. Also known as: "It was an accident."

NICKY BEAT   You know what I don't like about "Lexicon Devil"? On "No God," in the instrumental middle part, when Darby comes back in, Geza had Darby come in too soon—I told him when, but I wasn't there that day. I didn't know he was going to fuck up like that—to me it fucking ruined it, you know?

DON BOLLES   Darby's singing on the "Lexicon Devil" record was the best of all his recorded output—it was all downhill from there. You could compare his vocal decline to that of his L.A. rock wordsmith predecessor, Jim Morrison. By the time the Doors were recording *L.A. Woman*, Jimbo's voice was gone, as much as his ability to use it. It sounded uglier, dumber, lower in pitch. Sort of like someone on downers. Just like Darby from "Lexicon Devil" to the *G.I.* lp.

Flyer by Don Bolles.

GEZA X The Germs were like, "Wow! A recording studio!" They were like kids in a toy store; there was an innocence to it that disappeared later. I tried to get him to sing intelligibly into the mic, maybe double a few things, and then I tried to get Pat to try some different effects and a couple of overdubs. Nicky was playing drums, and he was kind of in my corner already. Darby hadn't really become the "Creature from Hell" yet; he hadn't quite finished cutting himself in stone as this premeditated death-trip guy.

JOHN DOE You didn't know the words because it was all like "Warrrrrrrrwarrrwarr," when Darby'd sing them live, so everyone was just astounded when they got that first Slash record and actually read the lyrics. They were great! I know that he cheated a lot. He used a thesaurus. He'd take Nietzsche books and pick stuff out that sounded cool and reflected his feelings, and he was able to put those words together really well, but he'd never use those words in conversation.

CHRIS D. I loved to read his lyrics. You couldn't always make them out when he sang them. It didn't matter if he hardly ever got near the mic or was so fucked up he'd leave out words. Darby was one of the only performers I know of who literally used the English language as a weapon.

GEZA X I couldn't believe that Darby who was just this weird little goofus had written these spectacular, poetic lyrics.

HELLIN KILLER You couldn't understand a single word he said, but it didn't even fucking matter.

GEZA X I got a lot of flak for that record; people said I made them too bubblegum. I was just trying to do what I've always tried to do, before and since—make a little pop masterpiece with whatever kind of music comes my way, you know? 'Cause I love singles!

DARBY CRASH All they gave us was $150. Slash is going under. They've got like $65 in their bank account and they're $1,600 in debt, so we figure they took the money from our records and just put it in there. We could've never gotten it out any other way. We didn't have the money to do it ourselves. It's a hassle to distribute it yourself. People all say, "Well, we're going to start Dangerhouse Records, we're going to start Slash Records. You won't have to go to the big labels," and on and on. Then they rip you off. But the contracts are really easy to get out of. Most of these people don't know what they're doing. We don't have a contract with Slash at all, so we could easily just tell them we don't want to record [for them] any more.

LOBOTOMY #6
LEXICON DEVIL/CIRCLE ONE/NO GOD (Slash)
For anyone who dismissed the Germs as crap—WAKE UP! this is one hot record. they not only play at the speed of light, they do it well. pat smear's lickety-split guitar work will have you going in two seconds—and darby crash practically vomits out the vocals. LEXICON DEVIL's great, but my fave is CIRCLE ONE—musical poison—it'll have you shaking violently from the intro: "ready, aim, fire" down to the last chord. be careful when you play this record—it may burn right through your turntable.
   Pleasant

PAT SMEAR   The Germs music changed just because we eventually got better. We couldn't help it. We started out with nothing so we had no choice but to change. In the beginning we were playing so slow because that's all we were capable of. We speeded up when we could. It was funner to play fast.

DARBY CRASH   I never really did [want to shock people], but you have to do something when there's all these bands. When we first started, we couldn't really play and neither could anybody else so you have to do something to draw more attention to your band, so that was an easy way. But when people said, "Ah … let's go see the Germs, they'll probably bleed a little this time," we stopped doing that. Then we started to learn to play better …

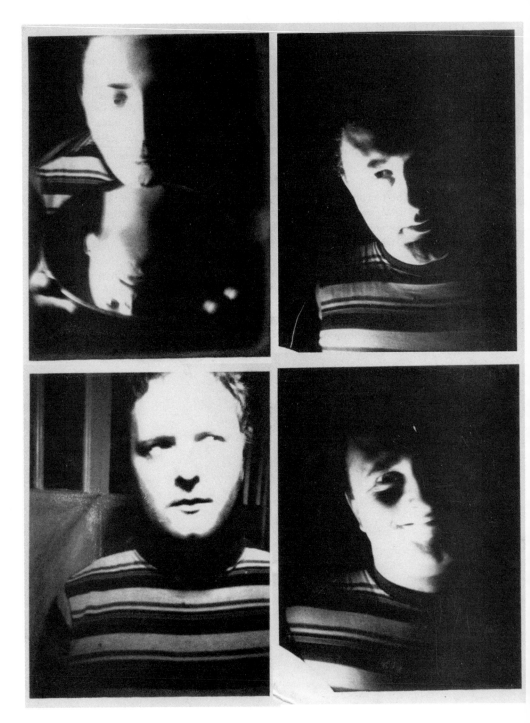

RIFT AMONG THE RIFFS

O

DON BOLLES Darby believed in the old Hollywood punk scene as a real community. He was extremely family-oriented, and he was intuitive in a lot of ways, but he was also loyal to a fault.

DARBY CRASH At first everybody said, "Oh, punk rock, we're all going to be together." Now everybody will step on anybody. Lorna called her roommate in the Go-Go's yesterday and was told, "We can't put you on the guest list because we have more important people to put on."

BLACK RANDY David Brown, the guy who played keyboards in my band the Metro Squad, and I, started Dangerhouse Records about the same time that we started the band, and we made 14 singles and two albums. We did X, we did the Dils, the Weirdos, the Alley Cats ... the Deadbeats, which was sort of avant-garde jazz, and the Eyes and the Bags.

David worked late as a typesetter and I worked a day job in telemarketing so we could make these damn records, but as soon as we put the record out with X they started talking to Biggs and decided they didn't want to work with us anymore. Now they were going with Slash. And they were going to control this and own that and we were ripping them off and this and that. We didn't make any goddamn money with Dangerhouse and that's God's truth. David wasn't a drug dealer. The money came from him putting half his paycheck in every week.

We spent a lot on packaging. We had real unusual packaging ... plastic sleeves, with the slip jackets, in color, and they were done by good artists, local artists from the scene. And they were printed up on clear vinyl and colored vinyl, some runs would be in one color and some in another, so they would be collector's items. We were real experimental without regard to cost. We literally stuffed the records into the sleeves by hand.

Just as soon as we finally got this damn Dangerhouse thing set up, then the Weirdos and X called up and bailed, and that was the end of that. So David completely lost it. He and my drummer Joe Nanini would spend every night calling these people's answering machines and leaving torrents of hate. There was ill will in a big way ... they got used tampons and dead fish and wrapped 'em all up in old Slashes, the one with Exene on the cover, and left these stinky packages on her porch.

DARBY SPENGLER

"Fate is who one is, where one is born, in which year, in which nation, in which class, with which body and soul, with which character traits. The tragedy of the individual lies in the conflict between these internal and external circumstances. His manner of dealing with them marks his rank, whether proud, craven, common, great, law unto himself, lawless."

○○○○○

"The great man lives in such a way that his existence is a sacrifice to his idea."

—Oswald Spengler, *The Decline of Western Civilization*

RIK L. RIK   Darby found Spengler's *Decline of the West* interesting because of his theory that there is no *ad infinitum* chronological progression with cultures. In the West people think of culture in terms of each century building on the last and becoming more and more advanced, but Spengler disagreed. He saw each culture living a cycle and then dying. Then the next culture comes along and has exactly the same kind of cycle and dies. Each culture has three phases … where it starts out primitive followed by a glorious epoch … then it goes into decline and finally dies after a period of crazed decadence and general degeneracy of the masses.

DARBY CRASH   Everybody's talking about politics and what's going to work and what's not going to work. None of it's going to work. You've got to throw it all away and start over. There's other ways besides overthrowing the government. Work from the inside and sort of just slowly take over and then throw it away. There's lots of people around you who're doing what we're doing.

PAUL ROESSLER   I saw him write a religion. Not like Hitler writing *Mein Kampf*; Darby was writing a New Testament, the Gospel according to Jan Paul Beahm; later, he dropped it, but I saw him working on it.

DARBY CRASH   It's just a big game … either you play my game or you get to play their game, and if you play their game … their game's going out. We're not into military. We're not into industrialism. We're not into anything except for me, and I speak for me.

PAT SMEAR   Darby was intrigued by the concept of fascism. He was such a leader that people would follow him around and do what he asked. Whatever it is people like that have in them that enables them to attract a following, he had it in him. I'm not talking about the hate part. I'm talking about some guy coming from a log cabin and ending up being president of the USA.[10]

DAVID BOWIE Adolf Hitler was one of the first rock stars. Look at some of his films and see how he moved. I think he was quite as good as Jagger. It's astounding. And, boy, when he hit that stage, he worked an audience. Good God! He was no politician, he was a media artist himself. He used politics and theatrics and created this thing that governed and controlled the show for those 12 years. The world will never see his like. He staged a country.[11]

DARBY CRASH People associate us too much with the Nazi thing. Yeah, we're fascists, but we're not Nazis—there's a difference. We don't believe in killing off races. I can respect Hitler for being a genius in doing what he did, but not for killing off innocent people. [His genius] lies in his speech. What he could do with words. There's films of him giving speeches in Germany. A lot of it's just an emotion—the energy you can get up. Fascism—it's just we've tried [other forms of government] and none of them are going to work. The only one that will work is a complete fascism. A complete fascist state, but you have to have the right person to lead it. If you get everybody to believe in one person, then it'll work. Communism can never work.

DAVID BOWIE I believe very strongly in fascism. The only way we can speed up the sort of liberalism that's hanging foul in the air at the moment is to speed up the progress of a right-wing, totally dictatorial tyranny and get it over as fast as possible. People have always responded with greater efficiency under a regimental leadership.[12]

PAUL ROESSLER Darby thought that fascism was the best possible situation, as long as the leader, whether it was Hitler, Stalin, or Abe Lincoln, was actually the true embodiment of the people in whatever land. That was the only stipulation. What could be wrong with one guy running everything with absolute authority? It just made sense. A word like "fascism"—Darby would never bandy that about lightly. He knew what fascism was. When Darby talked about fascism, like anything, you could bet that he knew exactly what it meant.

DON BOLLES Darby would announce stupid rock platitudes like, "We want to take over the world." He loved the Nazis' style and look, but didn't know who Albert Speer was. Darby was full of little inconsistencies like that. All the details didn't concern him.

NICOLE PANTER Darby wasn't that politically sophisticated.

DARBY CRASH [Fascism] could happen in a positive way … that everybody believes in one person. It doesn't matter who the person is or what they're saying. The ideal leader would be … me.

HELLIN KILLER He had weird aspirations of fascist rule world domination, but at the same time, he was really afraid of anybody knowing him at all.

ALICE BAG   When I was younger I knew a lot of people who thought that most other people were basically stupid and required a benevolent dictatorship to keep them in line. I agreed with that for about ten minutes until I realized that in the long term nothing much good can come from absolving people from thinking and making their own choices. I don't know if Darby aspired to be a benevolent dictator, but he did tell me he felt that people who could be controlled, should be controlled. I am sure he would have been flattered if someone had compared him to Manson, or Hubbard or Hitler. We got drunk. We got in an argument. We duked it out. And, of course I won!

TONY KINMAN   In San Francisco people were always trying to create these little "collectives" based around some punk rock bands or some vague sort of punk rockish idea, but it always had so much more to do with these dumb-ass leftist politics than it did punk rock that it just became stupid.

PAT SMEAR   I think maybe the Clash was into Communism, or at least flirting with it, and so the Dils jumped on that. Just like we were going to out-punk the Sex Pistols, the Dils were like, "Yeah, we're gonna out-Commie the Clash!"

NICOLE PANTER   The Dils said the Germs were fascist and anti-Semitic, but the entire Germs support system was made up of big Jewish girls from the Westside. I'm half-Jewish myself.

> DARBY   We're gonna make the Jews into wallets. (laughter) No, we don't have anything against the Jews.
> LORNA   They're some of our best friends.
> DARBY   We're doing a song about them, too. It's called "Altars and Ovens." Do you notice I know a lot of Jewish people? That's because they have money. Whoops!… There was no reason [for Hitler] to kill all those Jews. [He should have] just got them to move back to Israel.
> (From *NO* magazine interview, 1979)

DARBY CRASH   People get bothered by racial slurs and stuff. I happen to know lots of them. I say them because they're funny. I guess it's funny because they bother people.

Don Bolles holds one of Rudolf Schwarzkogler's rare photo books depicting the Mysteries Orgies Theater. Photo: Michael Yampolsky.

ART DAMAGE

O

CLAUDE BESSY   Darby didn't even know how to spell the fucking word art.

DARBY CRASH   If the Bags said, "Yeah, sure I'm an artist," everyone would give these odd looks.

CLAUDE BESSY   Chris Burden once came to the Masque. Maybe he wasn't there the night Burden came by, or whatever, but I doubt Darby even knew who Burden was.

DARBY CRASH   What's the guy that nails himself to the Volkswagen and stuff? I don't like it, can't understand it.

DON BOLLES   One day I was hanging out in the office at the Masque when Brendan got a phone call asking if he knew any musicians who'd play in an impromptu orchestra for a Hermann Nitsch performance at some warehouse in Venice. Nitsch is one of the "Wiener Aktionists" (AKA the "Vienna Suicide School" of perfomance art), a group of extreme performance artists.

BRENDAN MULLEN   I asked what kind of musicians … Jazz? Classical? Rock? What do you mean by that? How do you define a musician … formally schooled in theory, or primitive self-taught? Would they need to be able to sight-read charts? I was told it didn't matter … any kind of musician, any kind of instrumentation, any kind of experience. This sounded great, something that I could get in on. I immediately called the guys from the LAFMS [the L.A. Free Music Society] and a few music people at the Otis Arts Institute. Don Bolles rounded up a bunch of punks from the Canterbury, and we got a great turnout of about 30, the perfect number … many of them were actual real musicians mixed in with people who were just wailing away free form while Nitsch conducted his hyperreal Mysteries Orgies Blood Theater, a relentlessly grisly sort of interactive animal/human alchemy purification ritual.

DARBY CRASH   One time in Venice they like sliced these cows up and stuffed them with internal organs and people were pouring blood in people's mouths and stuff. What's that guy? He had a couple of books out, and albums and stuff. I heard his record. It's just noise. I don't see the art in it myself. The only painters I'm into are Picasso, DaVinci, the really old stuff … I don't understand how you can compare that to cutting up a cow.

DON BOLLES   There were a lot of people crammed into this smallish warehouse in Venice the night of the Hermann Nitsch show. It was an insane and messy event. There was a lot of pouring blood into crucified naked guys' mouths, people running in place in piles of guts, and what looked like "reanimation" attempts, where people were putting the guts and blood back into the flayed and splayed sheep carcasses. One of the naked guys flipped out, and started yelling and screaming and crying, then took off. It wasn't part of the show—he was on acid, and after blood got poured in his mouth, he just snapped.

DARBY CRASH   I don't like to go see somebody milk a cow like what they did at the Masque. There's got to be something I'm missing.

BOB BIGGS   At the Masque I had a video shoot that was going on television. The idea was to get a cow into the Masque, and I was going to hit a triangle or a bell or something, and that was going to be the indicator for me to milk the cow and give everyone in the audience milk. But the cow couldn't get down the elevator because it was too big. I didn't realize that it was a 1500-pound animal, so I decided to take it down the stairs. I got it to the first landing and that was it, I couldn't get it around the corner. So when my commercial came on, there was no cow.

BRENDAN MULLEN   Nobody knew what the fuck Biggs was on about. The small crowd, which included Darby Crash, was dumbfounded. I'll never forget people laughing in the alley outside the Masque at the sight of Biggs pleading with the agitated cow handler. It was drawing close to when Biggs' time-encoded performance piece was supposed to trigger. The cow wouldn't fit in the elevator after several hilarious attempts to jam its butt in. Biggs was frantic, and in desperation he tried to convince the handler to slide the cow down to the basement on its knees. But the handler insisted, "No way, pal! That's a movie cow! You understand that? A valuable movie cow. No way you're slidin' no movie cow down those stairs!"

DARBY CRASH   The only people I know around here who are into art are from Phoenix.

F-WORD

O

GERBER   I had a thing with Rik, and Darby and I were always attracted to the same boys.

RIK L. RIK   My band F-Word made our big debut at the Masque. Darby was there and he said we were the most suburban band he'd ever seen. I was 16, a teenager and suddenly "in" with the happening thing! The next show, Darby was there again; he was riveted ... that's when I think he first noticed me. Then we started hanging out at the Masque and the Canterbury—it was just a friendly thing. He kept saying "F-Word's a pretty good band!"

One time I needed a place to stay, so Darby said, "Stay at my house." The next day, we got up and he made up these huge sandwiches. We were waiting for the bus back to Hollywood, and we weren't saying much, 'cause we still hadn't quite broken the ice yet. The bus was really overloaded and passed us by; Darby made a comment about how we were punk rockers, and that people hated us, and the buses weren't gonna pick us up. We didn't say much when we were around each other, but around Michelle it became sort of a pissing contest; like putting each other down. I said to Michelle, "Darby and I seem to get along when we're alone, but whenever you or anyone else is around, Darby starts pulling this shit, and it's weird." Well, she told Darby that, and he was kind of sensitive, so from then on he never put me down, and was wanting me to come over all the time. He would talk for hours, and I could never get him off the phone.

In '78 I was either with him or on the phone with him almost every day for a six-month period. He was one of the happiest, most well-adjusted people that I knew. There was a happy-go-lucky slumber-party time, there was no talk of suicide then.

We'd get up, and talk on the phone all day long, listen to records, then somebody would come by, pick us up and go out. He never had a steady job. We'd go to bed around five in the morning, then we'd get up around one in the afternoon. Darby had foil on his windows so it was pitch black all day. And his mother worked nights so she wasn't around in the daytime, she'd come home and sleep all day, so we were never bothered by her. I was overwhelmed by the way his mind worked, and the way he would design the conversation around whatever group of people he happened to be with. You'd hear that he would have this spell on everybody.

He'd call and just tell me about the most mundane stuff; it wasn't like he was discussing Nietzsche; it would be more like *The Warhol Diaries*—he got off on catty homosexual gossip. He developed this attachment to me, and was always wanting to be around me. It was the type of thing where he couldn't say he had a crush on me because of social pressure at the time. This went on for like four months 'til summer of '78. By that time, everybody was beginning to talk about Darby's sexuality. Darby propagated this image of a superman who didn't need

Rik L. Rik at the Masque, circa Fall, '77. Photo: Michael Yampolsky.

sex—like, "I am an asexual person, who has developed to a point where I am beyond sex." I was buying the whole thing, very naively, I guess, but I'm not the only one that fell for it. He kept paying more and more attention to me, until one day Michelle Baer called me and said, "You know, Darby called me just to tell me that you had called him." It turned out that he was just fucking crazy about me.

We'd go to a club and then we'd usually go back to his mom's house. I was just drinking, but as the weeks went on, Darby was doing more and more pills. And then he would try to get me to do pills, too, but I was 17, and I just didn't want to get involved with drugs. One night when we'd come back from the Whisky at like three in the morning, he tried to shove these downers on me. He put some in my hand and said, "Here, take these," but I wasn't into drugs, and I'd say, "I'm not going to fucking take 'em." I stood my ground every fucking time, and said no. Then he'd put the phone over on the other side of the bed from where he was, on my side, so that every time the phone would ring he'd have to reach over me, put his arm like over me, to answer it. I was starting to wonder, "What the fuck is going on here?" That was the very first time he ever did anything even the least bit physically overt. He did that all morning and all afternoon. And his phone rang a lot.

GERBER Rik L. Rik idolized Darby as an older platonic mentor, but I think Rik kind of rejected him so Darby cut him off. Darby pulled this godawful ultimatum thing on Rik, he was, like, saying, "If you don't wanna fuck me, baby, then, baby …fuck off!" Y'know the old Jayne County tune? Poor Rik. Darby could be very cruel sometimes.

RIK L. RIK He lectured about the Greeks and the Romans, about how every advanced civilization was basically homosexual. I was starting to get a little bit freaked out. If I had been 21 I would've had no problem dealing with him—I probably would've just laughed at him, and given him some more back, you know? Then he started turning the lights off and on—which, I guess, was some psychological thing to disorient me—some sort of pathetic mind-control technique that he'd read about. His current driver was Jill Ash and she was coming over at five, and this was the big day he was finally going to do it. It seemed like he was desperately trying to get this thing done! He'd read me Rimbaud, the homosexual parts of *Season In Hell*—he'd done the whole everybody's-basically-at-least-bisexual Greek propaganda thing. Now, all of a sudden, my best friend was trying to make a move on me. As the afternoon went on, he became more and more desperate—and I was getting more and more freaked out. He never came right out and said, "I wanna fuck you." But it was pretty obvious this guy was trying everything he knew to seduce me. But as the time for Jill to arrive got closer, he started noticeably bumming—he went really silent. He knew that the game was up, that I knew what was going on with his sexuality. He couldn't help it anymore, and so he finally lifted the façade. I don't know if it was the first time he'd lifted it, but I just felt sorry for him.

GERBER   I freaked Rik L. Rik out very badly, really badly; he had a big party at his house and Bambi, his girlfriend, was there; she hated me, just hated me, because I didn't give a fuck that she was there and I was just like on his dick in front of her. As always, I was the girl in the room that was the most loaded and did too much drugs, now I was taking a kitchen knife out of Rik's mom's kitchen and I started sticking it up my pussy in front of Bambi and Rik saying, "Look at this!" This was in West Covina and it freaked everybody out really badly. Bambi flipped out and left. I got many, very intense, very dark romantic love letters from Rik L. Rik for a long time.

RIK L. RIK   I was very freaked out over Darby's big pass at me and I was talking to this girl about it, and she got right up in Darby's face a few days later and asked him point-blank, "Are you trying to fuck my boyfriend?" A couple of days later in front of the Whisky, he never even looked at me, and we have never had any relationship since. I was devastated. He made up some kind of catty sex scenario to tell people a couple of years later, and told people, "I'm usually a bottom, but with Rik L. Rik I was a top." Man, when I heard that, I was pissed! I was so angry I even called Michelle. I said, "Listen, if you talk to your fucking faggot friend Darby again, just tell him to keep his fucking mouth shut, and stop telling lies about me!"

GORILLA ROSE   I thought Darby Crash was just a whining little brat. Oh, he was such a snob. That must've been the gay part. He was just this precious, precious little blonde thing. If it had been a strictly gay scene rather than a young enthusiastic, excitable punk scene, a wild bunch of extremists—gay and straight hanging out together—who were open to almost anything, Darby would've been seen as just some obnoxious pretentious little blond scenemaker in tight jeans. Any typical gay gathering would've probably just thought he was real hot but brainless. I just didn't dig his style. Darby couldn't hang with Tomata du Plenty or Black Randy. Oh no, no, no. He was a kitten compared to those guys.

CLAUDE BESSY   Fear was homophobic … fuck, basically we were all homophobic.

LEE VING   We did the "fag shtick" 'cause we thought we'd found a source of humor. I thought everybody would get the joke pretty easy, 'cause there was Philo Cramer, our guitar player, wearing a dress. It was strictly a joke, a confrontational tack to get all these big boneheaded jocks all riled up. We decided it was our job to throw these bozos into states of mass homosexual panic, but it was not meanspirited … not meant to be taken personally by anyone. I don't know what image people had of us … I was going to the gym and my arms were big but we weren't into beating anybody, or having people be intimidated us. We just wanted to play this music and maybe sell some fuckin' records.

DO DAMAGE

O

JENA CARDWELL The Germs played at the Roosevelt Hotel—the first and last time they had a punk show there, and Darby had these handcuffs, and just went out into the ballroom and trashed the whole place, smashing all the mirrors on these columns with his handcuffs and spiked wristbands. One night we were driving with Hellin in West Hollywood, and Darby was being really obnoxious, so Hellin said, "Get out of my car," and threw Darby out. Next thing you know, he was smashing all these plate-glass store windows, so we just drove off and left him there, smashing everything in sight. We sat watching cop cars go flying by while we sat waiting for him at Tiny Naylor's restaurant...

PAT SMEAR Darby and I weren't really regular vandals, we were nowhere near as bad as has been made out, but sometimes that's just what the evening called for.

JENA CARDWELL Vandalism was an ongoing theme. It was pretty much an ongoing art project. That was why nobody ever wanted the Germs to play at their clubs.

DARBY CRASH They always blame it on the Germs...

PAT SMEAR Whether it was us, the music, the kids banging into each other, or whatever—the show would start and then security would try and stop us. At the Roosevelt Hotel show [Halloween '78] we played a couple of songs, and they said, "That's it!" and they shut off the power. But Darby said, "Okay they're gonna stop the show—let's fuck this place up! Do damage!"

DON BOLLES There were mirror shards falling everywhere, like some kind of Fortean glass hail, reflecting the chaos in a million flying facets; it was completely psychedelic. It was sort of like we were in one of those "snow dome" things, and somebody had just shaken it.

TRUDIE'S DIARY (12/2/78) Hellin tells me she has a crush on Darby Crash. Strange, why would she like him of all people? Such a little whiny guy, and you can't call him good looking either. He's nice and I really like him, but I just don't see the attraction. She's been hanging out with him and his bunch of Germites. They all have circle burns, wear long trench coats and have short hair with just one long thin strand of hair down their foreheads or the back of their necks. Only the Darby clones have that strand. K.K. calls it a leech.

GERBER I fell in love with Hellin Killer, how about that? She was horned in trying to be Darby's girlfriend, and I was really close to her, so I didn't really want to tell her, "Chick, don't even, you're wasting your time."

HELLIN KILLER   Darby was so like Sid in a lot of ways; really self-destructive—but, unlike Sid, Darby was really smart.

DON BOLLES   We were driving down Santa Monica Boulevard and I had a bunch of those fireworks that spin around really fast on the ground and make this huge dome of flames and sparks; they're called "Ground Bloom Flowers." There was a big, fat, hairy-chested bear of a guy sitting at a bus stop with no shirt on. Pat thought he looked like Black Randy, and, as we drove by, Pat lit one of the squibs and threw it at him, and it stuck to his chest. This poor guy's just sitting there at the bus stop one minute, and then the next, there's all these flames and sparks shooting out of his chest hair. Darby was trying not to let anybody know he was laughing about it that much. Pat and I thought it was hysterical, and Lorna just sort of giggled.

Livin' in a fury
Life's kinda blurry
Dyin' in a hurry
Story's kinda lurid

(*Not All Right*, '79)

BOB BIGGS   The Germs played at the Second Masque, the Hong Kong Café, Blackies or the Whisky and various other independent promotions throughout 1979 and early 1980, and he'd get a little money for that, but mainly he had women friends who'd feed him. He lived hand to mouth. You'd invite him over for a barbeque and he'd make fun of you the whole time. It seemed that he was acting out a lot of what people expected him to be doing. If you read his lyrics he was obviously a lot more sensitive than he was allowed to let on because of this image as a tough guy ... a punk. He'd never allow you to see what was there. It was masked behind the punk trip.

PHILOMENA WINSTANLEY   He talked about death and bleak depressive states of utter hopelessness in his lyrics which made frightening sense on the printed page but were generally incomprehensible during performance.

FAITH BAKER   Paul and I lived here a long time, just the two of us, after Faith Junior wasn't at home any more. That's why he moved out—the last year he was alive he lived over in Hollywood, or West Hollywood or something...

ALLAN MACDONELL   My favorite punk rock story is when Malissa saved my life. It was the day Sid Vicious died [February 2, 1979], and there was a requiem party at Joan Jett's house, right across the street from the Licorice Pizza parking lot. So I see these stocky hairy guys in the bottom level and Exene is screaming at them, "Fuck you!" So now this means poor old John Doe has to go in and get his ass kicked on her behalf! John goes down and he's groveling on the ground in like a fetal position, and these guys are whupping his ass, and Chris D. is standing beside him with a sweater in his mouth. So I stroll down there, and the guy says, "Who's next? Who's next?" So I said, "Well, how about me?" So now this sick-faced putz

A newly made-over Hellin Killer at the Masque, circa '78. Photo: Al Flipside.

ST PATRICK'S
DANCE
SPRING TRAINING

X ALLEY CATS
GOGOS PLUGZ
ZEROES AND ANOTHER
GROUP
SATURDAY MARCH 17
ELKS HALL AUDITORIUM 730 PM
607 SOUTH PARKVIEW LA
ACROSS FROM MACARTHUR PK
ALL AGES WELCOME 5 00
REAL LIFE RECORDS

with a big fat butt comes up after me, and he's really short, so I just put my beer down and like kept poppin' him on the top of the head, so he couldn't get to me, right? Then I realized he was slowly backing me up toward the cliff edge! Then Malissa stepped up and screeched at this fuckhead—and she could really screech, more than Exene, even, if that was possible—she screeched at this fat little shit so loud, he freaked out, grabbed his head and ran and jumped in his car—just to get away from her screeching! Exene was still shrieking full blast, too, the two of them going at it. Between the two of 'em they scared the piss out of this fuckin' guy ... man, those two crazy broads woulda scared the shit out of anyone! Just as they're jammin' outta the parking lot with brakes squealing, I throw my empty beer bottle and it arced over everybody and comes down right on the guy's windshield and shattered it all over his ugly face! This was like the Super Bowl of my life—everything was downhill from there!

ST. PATRICK'S DAY, WHEN RAMPART GOES RAMPANT

DON BOLLES   The riot squad from LAPD's infamous Rampart Division went up both sides of the ultra-wide staircase in the foyer of the Park Plaza Elks' Lodge single file, formed a line on top, then descended the stairs and closed in from the sides on the surprised Go-Go's fans unlucky enough to be in their path, with billy clubs swinging. Little 15-year-old girls from the Valley and OC suburbs whose parents had just dropped them off to see the Go-Go's were getting their heads bashed in by these helmeted Terminators with no provocation or warning! Cops in full riot gear running amok, chasing after a bunch of scared, freaked-out little kids.

CRAIG LEE   I was sitting next to Jeff Atta from the Middle Class and his girlfriend Dorothy James when the cop charge came. The next time I saw him he had a huge wound in the middle of his forehead, and Dorothy had a black eye and cuts all over his face. Her sister, furious at this brutality was seen swinging a board at a cop. Other kids put bricks through police car windows.[13]

MARGOT OLAVERRA   We'd already finished our set ... we were offstage when the cops arrived. Mayhem broke loose, helicopters were flying really low ... the cops came storming up the stairs with their batons.

KEITH MORRIS   Suddenly these cops flew through the front doors in full riot gear with shields and batons swinging. They were cracking skulls, anybody who was in their way. Three or four dozen people got hurt, half a dozen seriously. I hid in the men's room. All of a sudden Donnie Rose comes flying through the door, bleeding from the head, and he said, "Just stay where you are."

GINGER CANZONERI   When we [the Go-Go's] were leaving the cops were behind us and they had their batons and they were poking me in my butt. I really resented that. They thought it was hysterically funny and they were laughing and there was nothing I could do about it. I had on these really tight pants and these like high stiletto shoes and they thought it was amusing.

Flyer for the Saint Patrick's Day Massacre by Michael Friend and Paul Sanoian.

The well-publicized punk martyrs, Jeff Atta and Dorothy James, show off their victimization from St. Paddy's Day Massacre. Photo: Ann Summa.

DON BOLLES   Local news bulletins showed a police car with a broken windshield and some footage of police chasing kids, while calling it a "punk rock riot" that the police were called in to stop.

CRAIG LEE   The Masque basement became a temporary center for helping victims of what was called "The St. Patrick's Day Massacre." It set a precedent. In the old days cops might have shown up when the Plunger parties got too wild, or when a show spilled out onto the street, but basically the cops left punks alone. Who cared if a bunch of weird-looking kids were drinking, fake-fight dancing and listening to ear-shattering music? After the Elks Riot the police became a genuine menace and started appearing at shows with increasing regularity.

DEZ CADENA   Cops chased everyone out of the building. Then, when we all got outside, they charged everyone with their billyclubs, forcing everyone to run away around the block. It was chaos; I remember Darby trying to scale a church fence. He was just too fucked up to make it over, and he got stuck on it—a spike through each sleeve of his leather jacket. People were trying to help him, but the cops were running by hitting people and Darby was stuck hanging there like he was crucified. We ran by him, and saw the cops hitting him, and then we came back around again and he was still hanging there, helpless, so we just kind of pushed him over and ran for it.

HELLIN KILLER   Germs shows were like a complete meltdown! It was complete, "Take it all down and rip it to shreds" chaos, until you couldn't even stand up at the end.

BOB CLARK   (in a letter to the editor, *L.A. Reader,* March 30, 1979): I've been reading about police action against punks (*"New Wave of Police Brutality,"* Reader, *March 23rd*), I think your readers should be advised that there is another side of the coin when considering what happened on St. Patrick's Day at the Elks Club. I am an artist downtown, with a 5000 square foot studio, [who] arranged to throw a party/concert here on March 31. [My friend] Buzz put out about $300 for a professional sound system, mixing board and engineer, in addition to a large selection of drinks. The 80s were up first and finished their set without a hitch. They were followed by Cotton, which unfortunately set up their equipment in the same area as the Germettes (the cute little Germs groupies) wanted to dance and play in. And of course, Cotton's bass player kept walking into the beer bottles lofted by the Germettes, which made his playing very spotty. While the next band, Holly and the Italians, played, the Germettes amused themselves with little games like "Cut yourself and pass the blood around" and "Poke holes in the walls." They spent so much time in the restroom making themselves pretty that they wore the door clean off its hinges. Later they did me the service of editing my art collection, removing from the walls those paintings that were improperly hung and throwing them on the floor. Meanwhile, I was talking to this real cute one, who was about 15 years old, five foot one inch. The plan was to dismantle the space piece by piece while the band was playing, and then when everything was in a pile of rubbish on the floor, they'd throw up and pee all over it. I agreed that it sounded like great fun. As I drifted back toward the band area I ran into a friend who said that the Germs were getting ready to go on and had discovered that they had forgotten their instruments. Well, imagine our disappointment! He and Buzz got on the mic and made some lame excuse about how the person who worked here was upset about the damage and everyone had to leave. Well, the crowd was understandably upset but kept cool and managed to leave quietly, breaking only small things like chairs and beer bottles. When the crowd had thinned out, a group of maybe a dozen Germettes remained in front of my studio, shooting the breeze about the old days.

As they chatted, I became aware of a strange force in their midst ... a force that was whisking beer bottles from their hands and, to their utter amazement, was sending them through my windows. This continued until $250 worth of windows were destroyed at which point they got bored and left. This night cost in the neighborhood of $1,200 and we never got to hear the Germs. There must be readers out there willing to put up $5,000 to $10,000 to hear this group. Would you please refer these people to me?

143

MMMAILLL

FLIPSIDE
P. O. Box 363
Whittier, Calif. 90608

RIVERSIDE POLICE RAID

AL,

No doubt in the coming days you will be hearing about what did or did not happen on March 13 when Rhino 39, the Germs and I were scheduled to play 'The Squeeze' in Riverside, the following is a play-by-play description of the event as I saw it:

Rhino 39 opens and turns in a competent but tight set. They get polite applause from the audience but no dance activity. Toward the end of their set, they draw some boos from a segment of the audience getting impatient to see the Germs.

The Germs begin to play their standard set. In other words they did nothing out of the ordinary (for them) to incite the audience. But the Germs fans came to dance and proceeded to do so at a level of intensity never before seen in Riverside. It's apparent at this time that 'The Squeeze' is not set up to handle activity of this type. For one thing the PA columns on either side of the stage are just stacked on top of each other and are in danger of being knocked over. There are actually some PA amps located at the foot of the stage where they are obviously in the way. The club owner gets paranoid about his equipment and tells the Germs to stop playing and eventually shuts off the power to the stage. The Germs refuse to leave the stage until they get an explanation of why they are being asked to stop or at least some assurances that they will get paid. In the eyes of the owner, the situation involving the audience and the group is out of hand and he calls the Riverside Police Department to bail him out of a predicament he got himself into.

About four cops arrive to disperse the crowd. Some members of the audience take this as a challenge and confront the police as they begin to us not-so-gentle methods. An officer gets kicked and a number of people are handcuffed and taken away.

In the past. The Department has recently been hassling the Squeeze even during their standard Rock nights so you can imagine what went went through their minds when they saw a new wave audience. They never seen anything like what they say Tuesday night and they weren't prepered to react to what they saw.

I hope this isolated incident doesn't damage the chances for LA bands playing in our area but I'm not overly optimistic. In the recent past bands such as the Alleycats, Fear, the Tremors and the Rotters have played the Squeeze with no incident. I am afraid we have a 'Madame Wong' type of situation developing in that the future may find nothing but wimpy pop bands being booked for new wave night.

Armando Castro, Colton

That's about what happened but let me add th the only reaction the punks gave the police a verbal one. When they randomly grabed one from the audience (Tar, a skinhead) and star abusing him, what could he do but react-- to which he got a headlock stranglehold and a b on his head while they hadcuffed him. Melisa (Germs fan club) was the other arrest, she sp in the cops face as they attacked the audien and was also roughly thrown to the floor and handcuffed.

While in jail with a $300 bail, they question her saying 'They don't like cults', tore off armband and badges and insisted she was a li and 'Did not believe in God'.

As far a payment, I did get a few dollars, th Germs got nothing but I gave them $5 for gas.

For the rest of the evening the Germs and I (who didn't get to play) argue with the owner of the club that they should get paid for the gig because they are not responsible for what happened in front of the stage.

My conclusions: The Squeeze should not book acts that they are not equipped to handle. By this I am refering to the audience activity. The Germs should be paid in full for their abbreviated performance but they probably won't. I who had a verbal agreement wiht the club should also be paid in full. or at the very least I should be given expense money fo their time and traveling expense to Riverside A few additional points should be made: The San Bernardino-Riverside area is still'redne city' and the 'strong arm tactics' of the Riverside Police Dept. have been well documen

san diego

P.S. ROVER FUCKED UP DOWN HERE, WHEN MIDDLE CLASS PLAYED SHE TRASHED THE BATHROOM SO ME & MIKE TOOK OUT OF OUR OWN POCKETS TO PAY THE DAMAGES. BECAUSE THE PROFITS WENT TO PAY THE HALL ANY MORE, SO AN I HAD TO GET CANCELLED - I HATE THAT FUCKIN WITH THE ZERO CUNT. SHE'S BAD

Excerpted from *Flipside*, March 1979.

THE RIVERSIDE CONTINGENT

O

DON BOLLES   The "Riverside contingent" spawned somebody for everyone in the Germs. There was Gary Moss, who ended up marrying Lorna and moving to New York after the Germs broke up. Gary became full-time bass player for Joan Jett's Blackhearts; Donnie Rose, who was Darby's true love; Rene, who got killed on the freeway on the way back from a Queen concert, right in front of Pat; and then, weirdest of all, I got my own personal stalker, Pat Fear [AKA Bill Bartell].

BRENDAN MULLEN   The Germs, X and Rhino 39 were scheduled to play the Squeeze, some failing hard rock dive in Riverside on March 13, 1979, but cops busted up the show allegedly because of the behavior of the Germs' Circle One contingent, and X didn't get to play at all. A fight ensued with management when X demanded to be paid, maintaining that the cops' interception was not their fault.

DONNIE ROSE   The owner of the Squeeze just totally freaked out. He thought people were killing each other and so the cops came—yeah, to join in. Malissa got arrested, Tara got arrested, and the rest of us all went over to my house and had a really wonderful party.

> "There is an extreme political end of new wave, which is punk rock. Some groups are really trying to be revolutionary, like the Germs. Bands like that engage in non-entertainment," [the club manager said]. "When I told them they weren't going to get paid, they told me they were going to play until they wanted to stop," he said. "There are very few bands like the Germs who intimidate and mean it."
> —*San Bernardino Sun*, April, 1979

DON BOLLES   Although Darby knew Donnie long before this night, it seemed that it was around this time that they became a secret item.

DONNIE ROSE   I'd first gone to Hollywood with Gary in late 1977 where we hung out at the Masque a little, but I hadn't run away yet—it took a little longer for Hollywood to get its hooks into me.

JENA CARDWELL   Donnie Rose was one of the Riverside guys, who came up to L.A. with Pat Fear. Pat Fear was a big fan, and was always around. He just wouldn't go away. He was a conduit for the Riverside scene, and Donnie Rose was part of that. I was naive and didn't really realize just what was going on with Donnie and Darby. I knew they were close, but not that close. Pat S. was friends with Donnie, too, so there was never any sort of rivalry. It was not cool to be gay; unlike nowadays, it was really underground.

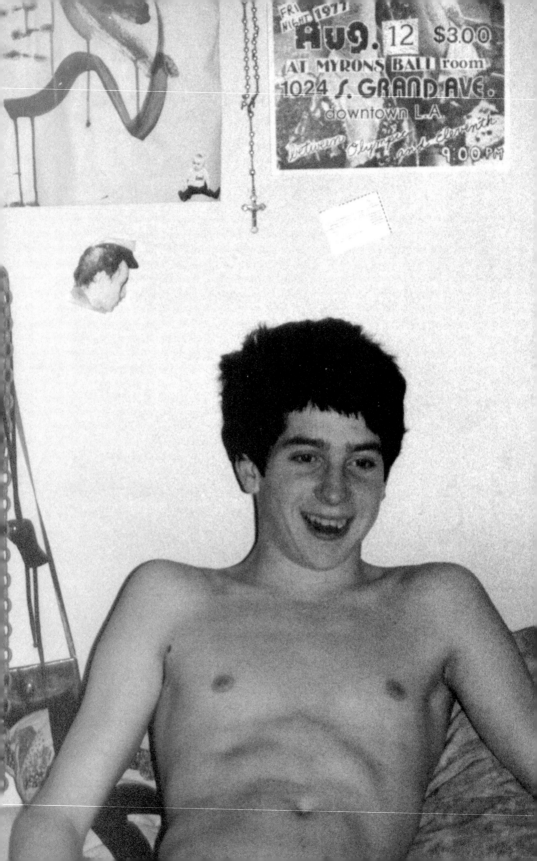

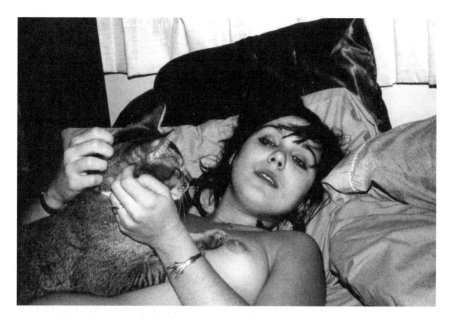

Gerber photographed by Donnie.

GERBER Darby's first relationship had been with Donnie, and it fucked him up a lot in the head, probably because we shared him. There's no real way for me to describe our relationship other than saying we shared a lot of great times, and we loved each other and it was okay, but the other half of the time there was jealousy and the love-hate stuff. Definitely, always, we competed, we competed ...

DONNIE ROSE I remember hanging out at Lorna and Malissa's apartment, right across from John and Exene's little house on Genesee—sleeping all day and going out all night; getting fucked up and drinking. I was 14, I guess.

JENA CARDWELL Just down the street from Lorna and Malissa's apartment on Santa Monica Boulevard there was this hardcore leather bar called the Spike, and we'd all try to get in there, but they'd never let any girls in. I thought it was just his fascination with some sort of strange underworld, but I didn't realize until later that maybe Darby had a different interest in it, beyond "Isn't this weird? Let's check out this bizarre place!"

DONNIE ROSE Darby didn't hang around the bars in West Hollywood, he was different. When we first had sex we were over at his mom's house, and he really, really wanted to, and I really, really didn't want to ... but I loved him a lot, so ... it's personal, I don't want to talk about it anymore. We loved each other a lot, but I couldn't give him what he wanted; I'm a pretty heterosexual kind of guy.

Donnie photographed by Gerber.

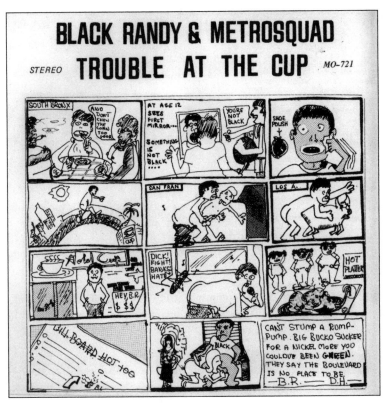

Black Randy's "Trouble at the Cup" single. Dangerhouse Records. Cover by K.K. Barrett. Released late '77.

TROUBLE AT THE CUP

O

BLACK RANDY   The Gold Cup was a restaurant on Hollywood Boulevard at Las Palmas, a block away from the Masque where all these sleazy male prostitutes hung out, who I admired and fraternized with. I was closer to them than most of the punk rockers walking around in their punk army suits. If you want to talk about who was close to the lumpenproletariat, I thought I'd gotten pretty close, closer than, say, Chris Desjardins.

TITO LARRIVA   I'd pick up Blank Frank for rehearsals with the early Plugz while he was turning tricks on Santa Monica Boulevard. That was how he got his junk … he'd just suck a few cocks and then go off and get high. I'd pick him up there 'cause I knew that's where he was. I'd pull up to the corner and say "Hey, Frank, you wanna rehearse?"

BLACK RANDY   My record "Trouble at the Cup" is about this fantasy I had that all the male prostitutes in Hollywood would become punks and overthrow the LAPD. That's what that record was about, and it went: "They say the boulevard is no place for me/Pinball and coffee is all right with me/I can't live at home, I gotta be free/I hate my parents more than they hate me/Schools and factories make me sick/I'd rather just stand here and sell my dick/Trouble at the Cup, trouble at the Cup."

GERBER   I met Donnie Rose at the Masque. He was running around with Darby, and we all ended up taking acid, doing dope and drinking. Right when I was coming onto the acid, Donnie said, "Do you wanna come with me?" I said, "Yeah. Let's go," and that's when I met A…… R…… the chicken-hawk. One entire wall of A. R.'s apartment was this huge mural-size, kiddie porno picture, it was a wall-size photo of Donnie, who had just turned 14, naked with just this huge cock. Donnie easily had the biggest cock on the entire punk scene, and he was still only a growing boy! It was massive. Basically he had been tricking with A. R. Donnie and I had a long acid trip, and we fucked away and just kind of clicked.

DARBY CRASH   Tommy Gear gets 25 on Selma for 10 minutes! [from *Flipside*, '79.]

GERBER   Donnie Rose and a bunch of other very young kids could usually be found tricking around the corner at the Gold Cup on the corner of Las Palmas and Hollywood Boulevard, or at the big Cahuenga newsstand. A. R. cruised that whole corner, and then up Yucca and Las Palmas, that whole little bit right there, from the liquor store down to the newsstand, because that's where all the very young runaways looking to trick would hang. Later on, they started calling 'em "gutterpunks." I was so grossed-out by A. R., because he was fucking this one boy named Roy, who was about nine. He was a sweet kid, and he was neglected badly and who knows where his parents were … yeah, A. R. was just a little too perverted, even for me; he just really freaked me out.

THE PRIVATEER

YOUNG BOY!
I Want YOU for Sodomy
Pay: $2,500,000. Join a
Patriotic Armed Robbery

Volume 2   August 1978   50¢

A classic example of vitriol from the Dangerhouse crowd. Photo: Scott Lindgren.

DONNIE ROSE   From A. R., I met Tar.

GERBER   Tar was a boys' youth counselor, at some place in Silverlake. Tar had a bigger place at the Hollywood Towers, so Donnie and I moved in there. A bunch of these little trickin' kids, like Animal Cracker, followed me in, and Tar loved it. There was a whole procession of gorgeous very, very fucking young boys, and they all decided Gerber's so cool, and would follow me everywhere. Very young, they weren't even punk rock boys yet; they were just like little Hollywood boys whose mommies were not around, kids who lived up by Playboy Liquor and that whole pimp 'n' dope strip from Yucca to Selma.

Darby hated A. R., and I know that he didn't like Tar. Darby hated going to the Hollywood Towers because we were living with Tar. You might speculate that he feared that that's who he would become—because he was going for those exact same fuckin' boys, you know? But he just wasn't as old as these sick fuck chickenhawks ... fuckin' short-eyed needle-dick ass-fuckers.

U. B. was a herpetologist and another gay pedophile who lived with the Roesslers until they had a baby boy and thought better of their living arrangement. There would almost always be a few kids between eight and 16 hanging around, with their skateboards leaning up against the apartment walls next to them. And this was nothing compared to Tar's place. And there was that Steve guy in Manhattan Beach that was even creepier.

Booklets like this were openly distributed on Hollywood Boulevard while Scientology street   151
barkers nearby tried to hook passers-by with free IQ tests. Teenage prostitution was rampant
in a two-block area bounded by the Gold Cup coffee shop, the Masque, and the Canterbury.

MIDDLE CLASS

U.X.A.

NEGATIVE TREND

GERMS (GI)

TOOTH
AND
NAIL

CONTROLLER
FLESH EATER
U.X.A.
NEGATIVE TRE
MIDDLE CLA
GERMS (GI)

TOOTH AND NAIL

O

DON BOLLES   Chris D. from *Slash* was putting together a compilation for his Upsetter record label, and asked the Germs to participate. It seemed like a good idea, and we knew most of the other bands—U.X.A., the Middle Class, Chris' band the Flesheaters, and Negative Trend from San Francisco, who now had Rik L. Rik on vocals. Chris wanted us to record three songs at a little 8-track studio called Program, on the corner of Selma and McCadden in Hollywood. The album was eventually called *Tooth and Nail*.

JEFF MCDONALD   John and Exene were the only people that Darby would admit to admiring, publicly, besides Iggy and Bowie. He would always say that he hated all bands except for X.

CHRIS D.   X were trying to do something raw, but at the same time it was more polished than a lot of the other bands. A lot of the other bands didn't give a shit but X really cared about how they sounded. They rehearsed and really tried to hone it into a sound that was recognizable and unique. They were writing about having an artistic temperament but living in this urban jungle that didn't encourage that kind of thing. They vented a lot of frustration at the ugliness around Los Angeles at the time. The repressive atmosphere from the police and the political atmosphere in the U.S. at the time. I hate to use the word political but X were really political in a personal way, not in an anarchic way but right from the heart.

GERBER   I always loved Exene's writing. When I think of her and John they always seemed like these mature adults who had it all together. Like they had that pad on Genesee and some kind of committed relationship. They always seemed like parent role figures, definitely to Donnie, and later to Rob Henley. I know that John and Exene let Rob stay there, and they were trying to get him to go back to school. They were already great musicians, whereas everybody else was just starting out. I was close with Exene, spent a lot of time in the bathroom with her, doing MDA and coke … but they still seemed so straight—very responsible. That's why I always viewed them as, like, my parents or something.

Rob Henley. Photo: Unknown.

Rob Henley. Photo: Unknown.

SOUTH BAY

O

DEZ CADENA   Some people I hung with from the South Bay were cruising by this party where the Germs were supposed to play, and Darby and Pat came up to our car. They knew we were looking for the party, 'cause there just weren't very many punk rock types in L.A. at that point, and they said, "Where are you guys going?" We said, "We came here to see you guys—you're the Germs, right?" They said, "Yeah, but don't go see us—we suck, we can't play; we're horrible!" so we kinda just hung out with them and drank a bunch of beer. That was my first Germs experience.

JEFF MCDONALD   I was in Hawthorne and I was probably 15 … my brother Steve was 11. We were listening to Rodney and reading *Rock Scene* and *Creem*. Then we found *Slash* which somehow made it to this liquor store in our neighborhood, and that's where we first read about The Masque and bands like the Germs. There was absolutely no punk rock where we lived whatsoever … nothing … and so we found out about shows in Hollywood and we talked our parents into driving us there in early 1978. Anything that was happening was happening in Hollywood, and when you're a teen in the South Bay, 15 miles from Hollywood, and you don't drive and there's no rapid transit, you're basically just stuck there.

JOE NOLTE   The Church got started in Hermosa Beach in early '79, probably January or February. It was just after the New Masque closed in Hollywood. Greg Ginn and Chuck Dukowski had rooms at The Church. It was an old Baptist church and there were rumors about Satanic rituals from a long time ago. The basement was the perfect place for parties; it was huge, it was soundproofed—in the *Decline* movie that was the room where Black Flag did their interview.

JEFF MCDONALD   The Church didn't exist that long. My band Redd Kross would rehearse there and we'd occasionally have parties there; the first two were pretty small. It was a really fun place to hang out in the summer of '79 and then it was over. The neighbors hassled everyone. Hermosa Beach is a tight-knit community and really uptight. The cops would hassle you … just awful, really bad news. It was only a matter of time before everybody was run out of town.

JOE NOLTE   Anybody who was into things in the South Bay was hanging out at the Church because it was the only place to go. I would be lucky if I only got ten cat-calls walking down the street; I didn't look outrageous or anything, I had short hair that maybe wasn't combed nice and I wore a black T-shirt and straight leg pants. Once The Church was happening, it was like we could go to Hollywood or we could stay and do our own thing right there in Hermosa. But there was always so many great shows going on in Hollywood, or at the Hong Kong, in downtown, so the tendency was to go up there for shows and then come back and party at The Church all night.

EXENE CERVENKA   When the South Bay scene first started happening I really liked the new bands like Black Flag, then there became this divide between Hollywood and the Beach scene. Greg Ginn said they wouldn't let those bands play in Hollywood so they had to create their own scene and it kind of became anti-Hollywood. I would reject this because everybody I knew wanted to see those bands play. Fuck Hollywood was what we were saying, too! Somehow, the South Bay punk scene opposed the old Hollywood scene and the audiences started becoming anti-rock star, anti-whatever, and if you were signed to *Slash* then you were a rock star traitor. The South Bay girls didn't like me very much. So I stopped going to the hardcore shows because I was threatened too much. They'd shove me and push me and tell me they hated me, they'd tell me I thought I was a rock star. They'd spit and hiss "Fuck you, Exene, you suck" ... that kind of stuff. I couldn't even go in the bathroom at those shows...

JOE NOLTE   I think it was sort of a mock perception thing [with Greg Ginn and Chuck Dukowski] that only people who were in the "in" crowd in Hollywood could play [at the Masque] but they couldn't because they were from the South Bay. I'm sure that they played this myth up to help create a regional niche for themselves. There was a natural kindred spirit just because we were geographically distant from Hollywood.

MUGGER   Rob Henley was from Lakewood and I was from Cerritos. We were like 16-year-olds when we first started hearing about these all-night parties at The Church in Hermosa Beach so we just started hanging out there.

JEFF MCDONALD   Rob Henley came from Edison High School; he was one of the first HBs. Mugger also went to Edison, I think.

MUGGER   Robbie and I began hanging out with the Germs and Malissa and their circle of disciples and we got our Germs burns and then Henley and Darby just started seeing each other. He and Darby were at my house sleeping together in my bed ... but not with me in it! They spent the night there a couple of times. At first the three of us would hang out ... then Rob started going with Darby alone to places more and more and I was like, "What about me?" Not about the gay thing, I mean, but "Why aren't you guys taking me? Am I not cool enough any more?"

GERBER   Rob Henley was one of the first little skater guys from Huntington Beach. Darby and I went nose to nose on that one. He told me, "Just don't fuckin' touch him," and told Robbie the same thing about me, and so the chase was on, but Robbie was such a dirty boy ... and that's quite a statement coming from a jizzpot like me ... he was actually physically dirty, like contagious and stuff. I was like, wait a minute now, somebody sleazier than me? No, thanks!

MUGGER   Robbie was also going out with Michelle Bell, Gerber ... I don't know if Darby was bummin' on that or not. What ended up happening was that Robbie

Gerber and Henley. Photo: Al Flipside.

went with the Germs and the Hollywood scene and I started hanging out with Black Flag and the SST guys in Hermosa, and ... we split our ways. It was really weird, Rob Henley was my best friend who I hung out at the beach with, who I poked chicks with ... under the pier and in the water ... and for him to turn gay was kind of odd ... the gayness is not a big thing, it's just that it's your best friend, you know ... like, "What was he thinking all this time?"

GERBER Robbie was living at this guy's house, a total pervert who lived right on the beach in Manhattan Beach, and tuned pianos for a living. Darby and I used to go down and stay there for the weekend, 'cause he'd buy us anything we wanted: he'd buy us food, he'd buy us drugs; he'd buy us fuckin' heroin; anything. But he was a real sick fuck—he would buy all these young boys dope, and when they were just completely fuckin' nodded out, he'd make these videos of himself butt-fucking them or shooting off in their mouths while they're passed out! He even made one with Robbie. At some point this all came out; Darby knew about it. The dude eventually committed suicide. He ate the exhaust pipe in his garage.

JENA CARDWELL One day I acccidentally came across this handwritten message from Darby to Rob Henley, and it was really personal. That's when it finally hit me there was some sort of relationship between these two guys. But Robbie was also going out with Gerber...

157

THE HB PSYCHO SKINHEAD SCENE

O

BRENDAN MULLEN   The arrival of the HB's was basically the invasion of the yahoos. By early 1980 female attendance fell off at Germs and other hardcore shows which had degenerated into bizarre post-pubescent all-male warrior bonding rituals with frequent interventions by S.W.A.T. teams and helicopters. Apart from the committed wrist-burned Germs cultists, most of the original Hollywood punkers either OD'd, went back to school or got jobs with their families' businesses. Many turned to rockabilly and other U.S. roots music from the '40s and '50s, while others opted for experimental art music, post-disco early dance club music, Goth rock, and even proto-hip hop R&B funk. Three years later, L.A. punk rock was looking like the exclusive domain of sweaty acne-scarred sexually frustrated teen boys with bashed-in faces. In other words, Hardcore.

DARBY CRASH   I don't want the surfers hanging out at the beach. I don't respect those people, I don't want their respect.

JEFF MCDONALD   Black Flag had this big party and they got some of these lesser-known thrash bands from Edison High [the epicenter/nucleus of the Orange County hardcore movement] to play. It was instant violence, immediate stupidity. Hardcore came into its own later as a more positive energy ... but it began as a suburban So Cal thing when suburban high school kids were into hanging out in packs and were starting to present themselves in big numbers for the first time in that area ... the South Bay and Huntington Beach. Most of the first wave of So Cal hardcore bands were awful and many of the people were horrible.

JOE NOLTE   There were maybe a few surfers-turned-skins around The Church, but it wasn't like what it would become after the invasion of the HB's. Punk really started to get going in HB [Huntington Beach] in early '79, and I believe that the Skinhead Army kids from there started coming up to The Church after Greg Ginn invited them to party there [sometime around spring-summer of '79].

EUGENE   Around that time there were a lot of kids from the beaches who were getting seriously fucked up by these longhaired redneck hicks in their 4x4 vehicles, real Lynyrd Skynyrd kind of guys. They were going to punk shows and hiding out in the parking lot and ambushing us, and I think a couple of people died, a couple got put in wheelchairs fucking forever, and nobody was doing anything about it. No disrespect against the old Hollywood party punks who'd been around longer, but they just weren't prepared to defend us out in the 'burbs where kids were getting beaten on all the time. So my friend Dana who was in a lot of heat with the cops and whatnot in Huntington Beach, came up with this idea: "How about making a fight-back skinhead army?" And so we made this insular group of like maybe 20 to 25 guys. We were called the Wayward Caines—that was the inside inner circle, the fucking SS of the Skinhead Army, and Dana controlled the whole thing. He called up all these guys from Huntington and Long Beach and just hammered out the big "Skinhead Army" plan. Originally, it comprised of skins, crewcuts, flattops, and we decided we were going to eradicate this fucking hippie threat by any means necessary. And within a couple of weeks, Dana had control of, fuck, maybe a hundred guys. Most of them went to Edison High, and then there was an extra amount of kids who just wanted to associate with it … and that's where the hardcore shit really started. It was just a self-defense thing at the beginning and then we totally fucking took over.

JEFF MCDONALD Suburban hardcore definitely started at Edison. A girl I knew said, "There's this high school, and there's like 250 punk rockers!" So I ditched class and went there with her—but it was really this big ugly nightmare. We were shocked and bummed 'cause we were expecting it to be cool, but here were all the exact same surfer jocks who'd been harassing us for liking punk a few months ago … now they're huge punkers, emulating the secondhand media version of punk. This new scene was created by upper-middle-class suburban kids with bad coke habits who were always being chased down by the cops 'cause they'd break into their friend's parents' houses and steal jewelry to keep them in blow. It was a major bummer of a scene, a lame high school jock scene with a punk rock look. It wasn't very exciting, and it definitely wasn't anything I could relate to.

MUGGER Edison High is just this one school. There were a lot of schools in the Huntington Beach and Costa Mesa area that attracted kids whose families didn't care about them, or whatever, and they just got crazy. "Those goddamned fucked-up HB's" was the popular term for them, but it was all over OC … it was basically a full-on white suburbanite rebellion. Kids were saying "fuck you" not only to these people that were trying to tell us what to do but to the establishment in general … the hippies did their thing and now the punkers were doing their thing. I don't think it was one particular club or one particular band that had a big effect on these people, it was just sort of a gradual build-up.

JEFF MCDONALD Up until the scene exploded at Edison High, there were only like 15 punk rockers in the entire South Bay, and I knew every one of them. Suddenly there was this new crowd of punks hanging around the Church. One day Greg and Chuck invited all these crappy little HB bands to come up and play, and suddenly there were like 500 kids! There was the Skrewz, the Slashers, the Gestapo, the Klan who sang with bad English accents—in fact, all HB bands sang with fake English accents, and worshipped Sid Vicious. There was the godawful China White … now *that* was a homophobic scene.

KEITH MORRIS I don't think they were calling it hardcore yet. A lot of the OC, South Bay, Huntington Beach bands, the more aggressive, athletic, surfer skating kids, were just starting to get into it.

RIK L. RIK The music was very quickly dumbed down to this one sound, this one generic thrash style with moronic lyrics. Hardcore meant there was no more free interpretation of punk. All of a sudden there were all these rules, a complete 360 flip on what punk was originally all about. I think that, plus the mindless violence and dumb witless jocks being drawn to punk depressed Darby.

TONY MONTESION I once asked him why he continued to use a vehicle like punk for his art. A lot of the new beach punks who were comin' out were just goons, you know? He couldn't take it any further, and I think he realized that.

JEFF MCDONALD We rejected it as an invasion of lunatics because these were our peers and they were people we didn't get along with in the first place, you know ... part of the reason we'd got into punk in the first place ... to get away from jerks like this, but now, it was like ... oh, no ... now they're coming in on our territory! But Black Flag immediately saw this as an opportunity to expand and they desperately needed the numbers to have this rock career, and so they actively pandered to that crowd. That's where it split off for me.

RIK L. RIK Everyone on the scene would show up to whoever was playing all the time, but some of the older people gradually began to shun Germs shows because they weren't that musical, but they could still draw pretty well from the younger end of the scene. So the Germs started playing Orange County, and because they were perceived as kinda hardcore extreme, all these psychotic jock surfer types started coming to the shows, and then the crowd got really violent. The Hollywood people wouldn't drive down there anymore.

MIKE PATTON The new kids thought the Germs were cool because they were so extreme ... they had this mystique of being so dissolute, they had to be cool. I always thought the Germs were a mess live. When Darby was sober, he was a real nice guy. Musically they were atrocious ... they made some great records, but I saw them live all the time and they were just this mess, but they had this mystique, so when the new kids showed up, the Germs were always cooler than the crowd. I don't know if they liked the music ... but it didn't matter, they were The Germs ... you know? He was Darby Crash.

KEITH MORRIS Yes, there was violence at some of these shows, but it was basically a friendly kind of violence. These guys pushing each other around on the floor or leaping off the stage, they knew what they were getting into. They were like 15, 16-year-old kids. If they hurt themselves, they were gonna spring back from that in a few weeks.

JANE WIEDLIN The whole scene began to change. It started as a scene of girls and gays and stuff ... it had been taken over by all those real angry young white boys. Black Flag. We were like, "What is this all about? It's really gross." We got lumped in with all those bands but we never even knew those guys.

JOHN DOE   Kids from the beaches were coming to punk rock shows with the idea that to be really "punk," they should hurt somebody, which was never anybody's idea from the old Hollywood scene that we knew. Fights may have broken out in the earlier days but it was because somebody was acting like an asshole, but no one came to the gigs with the specific intent of kicking somebody's ass. You just went 'cause that's what was going on. The idea of physically menacing punk took over which was more inspired by media attention than the music.

KEITH MORRIS   The Go-Go's were playing pop music. They weren't a punk band. It was a female vocal harmony group with rock guitars and drums. Of course they're gonna be taken aback playing a show where it's 95 percent sweaty guys jumpin' around and a little blood flowing here and there.

CLAUDE BESSY   It was just 50 or 70 friends running around behaving like maniacs, and suddenly "Punk Rock" was on the news. The Germs were one of the original events, but as the scene expanded the Germs kind of disappeared.

HELLIN KILLER   The new kids were in it for all the wrong reasons, for what they heard on the news, that punk was violent. Then there were all these skinhead Nazi psychos … it was ugly, it wasn't fun anymore … they'd be out there just beating the shit out of everybody.

BLACK RANDY   Black Flag was much more extreme in directly provoking the shit out of the South Bay establishment. They really shocked and frightened the right-wing. Anti-Christian hardcore bands like them shocked people of common decency right out of their minds. You just cannot live with people who cut half their hair off and wear an upside down cross with a syringe on it … with tattoos, Mohawks and bones through their noses, and big boots.

> RODNEY BINGENHEIMER   You were there before Black Flag … you started it!
> DARBY CRASH   Someone's gotta finish it!
> RODNEY BINGENHEIMER   The Plasmatics might finish it, I don't know…
> DARBY CRASH   No—they won't.
> RODNEY BINGENHEIMER   'Cause they destroy … uh…
> DARBY CRASH   Yeah, I know what they do, but it's like—it's theater; it's nothing.
> (From "Rodney on the ROQ," circa '80.)

G.I.

O

JEFF MCDONALD The Hong Kong Café was a great time, it was just like one six month period; I saw the Go-Go's do two nights there, the first time they ever played with Gina and the first time they did "We Got the Beat." I saw the Germs and X up close. I remember that courtyard and the weird Chinese gangs that would beat people up like when they jumped Tom—he was this six-foot-something musclebound leather guy straight outta that Screamers logo, but he was really quiet. He was just walking down the street with this other Marine-looking guy, and suddenly this car pulled up and these Chinese guys jumped out and started whaling on him!

DEZ CADENA Pat would come running up to us at the Hong Kong Café and go, "Darby's fighting a Chinese gang up the street—we have to save him!" And a bunch of us would go to deal with this Chinese gang! I don't know what he did; probably said some smartass thing—but this happened more than once.

DARBY CRASH Records are only a medium to get something else done ... I want to die when I'm done.

LORNA DOOM My fondest memories of the Germs are right after the beginning and up to recording *G.I.* ... which was a thrilling experience for me.

BOB BIGGS We were pretty much winding down *Slash* as a regular magazine at the time we did the *G.I.* album.

DON BOLLES For a couple of months before we recorded the *G.I.* album, we rehearsed more than ever, mostly in Pat's garage. We'd spend at least four hours a day, three, maybe four days a week.

BOB BIGGS When Steve [Samiof] left *Slash* to do a magazine called *Stuff* I was stuck with the magazine, which was not making a lot of money, so I decided to do a record label. I wanted to take making records more seriously than just putting out an odd single here and there. Making a record for a couple of thousand dollars was better in the long run than trying to put a magazine on the stands that got yellow in two weeks.

PENELOPE SPHEERIS Bob raised the money to run Slash Records from dealing coke—he raised a *lot* of money from dealing coke, the whole time the magazine was going. People used to line up around the building at Slash. He sold it all from his office on Beverly; yeah, he was dealing coke down there big time!

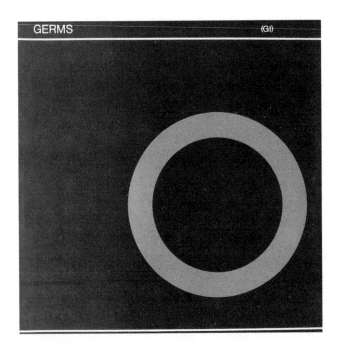

G.I. lp, front and back. Photos: Melanie Nissen.

BOB BIGGS I was never a drug dealer, and I defy anyone to find proof. It was in a party context. There was never any wholesale dealing going on. I wasn't any more deeply involved with cocaine than anybody else. It was the '70s!

PENELOPE SPHEERIS When Bob was still deciding if he really wanted to do a Germs album—Bob, Joan Jett and I all went to this tiny garage in West L.A. to hear them. It was so small you could barely even fit a car in there. They had all this equipment jammed into this tiny, tiny space. While they were playing, I was thinking, "Putting the words 'lexicon' and 'devil' together? This is *truly* an evil force." My brain just shut down! Bob had that interest in the evil forces, too. One of the last things he'd done as an artist was a piece where he had a goat and a stripper on stage with him while he sat and read poetry. This topless stripper in a G-string played around with the goat in weird ways—that piece had an undercurrent to the whole dark evil-devil shit that was going on in the punk scene.

BOB BIGGS Darby was standoffish … sarcastic. He was like a wise-ass teenager. Pat was a lot more willing to engage you and to talk straight without making fun of you, so I dealt with him more than with Darby. The very first thing that Darby did whenever he saw me was ask for money. I'd say, "Darby, would you cool it, you idiot? I'm not giving you any money." This had nothing to do with royalties or legitimate means of income. He wanted a dollar to get a beer! He never had a job. I can't imagine him ever having a job. He was a smartass punk which was what the scene was all about and he was right on the money. Claude thought the album was a great idea, if a little crazy, and a few other people were baffled. They'd say, "Why are you doing these guys? The live show will never come across on record." Many people thought they were too rough, too raw, they didn't know how to play or write or sing. The consensus was that the Germs were 100 percent uncommercial.

DARBY CRASH They keep printing that we're unsignable.

NICOLE PANTER I gave them the name *G.I.*

BOB BIGGS Darby said, "I wanna call it *G.I.*" He told me what it meant but I can't remember.

NICOLE PANTER Darby was like, "What are we gonna do? No one'll book us any more." I said, "Germs Incognito, G.I.," and that's what he wanted for the album cover.

DON BOLLES Now there seems to be some dispute as to who actually came up with it, but that's when the off-center blue-circle-on-black-field cover was designed. The blue circle on the black field was just a given. I wonder to this day how the Germs legend would have fared if we had let Biggs do the "jelly beans and meat" cover.

BOB BIGGS   I had an artistic background so I said, "I'll put the cover together." Darby said, "Well, what are you gonna do?" I said, "I'm just gonna put this blue circle on the front and call it a day." And he said, "Okay."

NICOLE PANTER   Biggs wanted the cover to have GERMS spelled out in rotting meat and jelly beans and I said no—it's going to have a blue circle and a black background with white letters.

DON BOLLES   Nicole called an emergency band meeting over Bob's "concept" for the cover. Biggs wanted it to be "The Germs"—spelled out in a mosaic of jelly beans and rotting meat! I guess it was a cool idea, but I think it was absolutely the last thing that anybody, even the Germs, would want for their album cover!

BOB BIGGS   But Slash still wasn't even a real label, although I called it a label. I admit it now, I didn't know what I was doing—we didn't even have a distributor … I was so out to lunch I didn't even know you had to have promo people, y'know? It was learn from scratch on the job.

DARBY CRASH   Why should [major record companies] go with us when they know we're going to fight them, when they can get what they want from other people? And they think they know what they're doing and they don't. They're just screwing it all up. They'll never figure it out. I don't really want to [make any more records] unless someone will give us money and a new gig.

BOB BIGGS   Everyone was looking for that "crossover" into mainstream record companies, and we all knew the Germs were not that. They were looked at as Iggy rips, or something. I didn't care about all that—I just wanted to make the best possible record I could. It wasn't musical. It wasn't about musicality. It was about sheer aggression … a feeling that what you were hearing was not complicated by any poetic relationships. The only way to deal with that was to just record it. To get it down and solid and as sharp as you could.

CLAUDE BESSY   It was not music, it was noise. The Germs were fucking primitive abstract expressionist. X knew what they were doing; X had a singer, X had a lead guitar, X had a fucking rhythm guitar, X had a bass guitar, they had John, they had Exene, Billy Zoom, DJ the drummer. X were playing music, the Germs were making organized noise. The Germs were experimental, X was a great rock band.

DARBY CRASH   A lot of people outside of L.A. are like ah, they'd sign anybody just 'cause they're from L.A. You know, "They're so close to the record companies," but the record companies don't sign people here. And then there's New York record companies like Sire who just sign everybody in sight and let them rot.

EXENE CERVENKA   It definitely helped the scene that there was no major label involvement. I think an artist working in a vacuum has got to be the healthiest thing. The five percent who do it in a vacuum are the ones who create the lasting art.

DARBY CRASH   There was this big thing [where] record companies like Sire tried to stamp out punk rock and stuff, and I thought maybe these people were just paranoid, but it really starts to look that way when they close down the Masque for not having the right fire exits, and we can't play the Whisky. All the Whisky would need is a word from the record companies and they would start booking new bands.

SEYMOUR STEIN   (From an open letter to the nation's FM programmers in 1977): One of the most significant trends in recent years has been "New Wave" rock, all-too-often wrongly referred to as "punk rock." The term "punk" is as offensive as "race" and "hillbilly" were when they were used to describe "rhythm & blues" and "country & western" music 30 years ago.[14]

GREG SHAW   At some point in '77, Warner Bros acquired distribution of Sire, with all of Seymour Stein's new bands, including the Ramones, Dead Boys, Richard Hell & the Voidoids, and Talking Heads. Warners was signing the Pistols as well, so they had made a corporate decision to get into punk. I was invited to give an orientation talk to the Warners creative people. I went over the ways this "New Wave" music differed from the "album rock" they were more familiar with and discussed the politics. They went on to market "punk" under the name "New Wave" and quietly forced Sire to drop the rest of its punk roster.

PAT SMEAR   We wanted a big-name producer.

DARBY CRASH   Eno is great at what he does. He worked good with Bowie, but I wouldn't let him touch us.

PAT SMEAR   Darby was set on Mark Lindsay, from Paul Revere and the Raiders for some reason, but he was too expensive. We thought, "Who's our most famous friend?" and we came up with Joan.

DON BOLLES   One of the things that made the Germs work musically, to the improbable degree that it did, was the fact that we always played at the very top of our abilities, mentally and physically. But at the same time, we were still trying to raise the ability ceiling. We rehearsed a lot before we went in to record. It had been more than two years of playing live constantly. We just wanted to do an album and not get completely fucked. We thought it was going to be the shit. We didn't get any advance from Slash on the signing of the contract, maybe we got some beer, but that was it.

ADAM PARFREY   While the contract between Slash Records and the Germs is not quite the worst one ever entered into—at least Darby and Pat were not forced to turn over their publishing rights—it is typical of a big label "take it or leave it" type deal in which the artist is 100 percent committed to the company, but the company has very little obligation to the artist. This document is as draconian as any recording agreement I've ever seen. With no advance to speak of, Slash included four yearly options to renew the contract, or they could drop the Germs after the first record at will, with the Germs having no say in the matter.

BOB BIGGS   Nicole Panter was their management. She didn't know a thing about business but she was trying hard. When people don't know what they're doing they overcompensate by getting hysterical over some two-cent issue. Most of the discussions about the contract and producer were between me and Nicole; she looked out for their rights as best she could, and set up Crash Course Music, Darby and Pat's publishing company.

NICOLE PANTER   It was my idea to set up Crash Course Music. I wanted Darby to have his own publishing company. I have seen nothing from the Germs, ever.

FAITH BAKER   Honey, it's provided my family with an extra ten grand a year ever since.

DON BOLLES   We were so laissez-faire about all the business stuff. That's why we had Nicole. We trusted her. She was a really smart girl with a little legal acumen who supposedly had knowledge of the music industry, although from what angle we had no idea ... insane in the brain as this woman may be, that's what makes her so loveable. Darby and Pat probably listened to her a little more because they had publishing interests but I didn't. As a musician I had nothing, no real financial stake in the Germs whatsoever, although I was giving it everything I got...

BOB BIGGS   For the first record, the "Lexicon Devil" ep, we'd just kind of written up a two- or three-page agreement, so when I came up to them with a 30-pager for an album deal it was kind of shocking. It was shocking for me, too. Nobody, including myself, fully understood the terms of this contract. I just had a lawyer draw up an industry standard, and after going back and forth over it with Nicole they quietly signed—it wasn't a big thing, no big fanfare, no signing party like with X, but everybody seemed happy.

BRENDAN MULLEN   The contract was signed during May, 1979, by Jan Paul Beahm (p/k/a "Darby Crash"), Georg Ruthenberg (p/k/a "Pat"), Jimmie Giorsetti (p/k/a "Don Bolles"), and Ms. Teresa Ryan (p/k/a "Lorna Doom"), c/o Nicole-Elena Olivier, 2012 Beachwood Drive, Hollywood, California 90064.

JENA CARDWELL   Nicole was there for a brief period and has been living off the glory of whatever legacy the Germs left behind for the last 20 years. They were

Darby, Lorna and Pat at a small party celebrating Slash's signing of the Germs.
Photo: Philomena Winstanley.

really unhappy with her and this guy Bruce that was supposedly managing them. They were going to come in and do some great business things, but nothing ever panned out.

BOB BIGGS Darby violently needed to have an authority figure to rebel against and I was that. Fine, I accepted that role. I never went to his in-crowd things because they were a bunch of scary young people who were very tight and exclusive and I really didn't give a shit to be a part of their scene anyway. Like I was gonna line up to get my wrist burned with a cigarette and shoot up a bunch of smack to show I was cool enough to hang out with Darby's little entourage? No thank you, sir. My experience with Darby was that he was a total brat, he was difficult ...

BOB BIGGS The Germs cut the *G.I.* record at a place called Quad Tech on 6th and Western. It took about three weeks and cost me about six grand. I was a glorified babysitter, trying to get the sessions going. Giving them a ride there, driving them home. I had a big International truck. Typically, I'd go over to Joan's house first and there'd be naked girls all over the place doing each other. Then I'd pick up Pat at his house over in West L.A. We'd get to the studio and Joan would pass out at the console and I'd have to wake her up and get her going.

RODNEY BINGENHEIMER What does "G.I." stand for?
DARBY CRASH Germs Incognito.
RODNEY BINGENHEIMER Germs incognito?

DARBY CRASH   Well, we have a list, actually, of about 25 different things that it stands for, and you can pick it out.

RODNEY BINGENHEIMER   Did Joan Jett really produce the *G.I.* album?

DARBY CRASH   No, she slept on the couch! Listen to "Shut Down" and you can hear where she's asleep on the couch...

DON BOLLES   The extent of her art isn't really evident on the album itself, but she was great. She was really good.

RODNEY BINGENHEIMER   What's the line that you say in "Shut Down" where you mention Joan Jett's name, and Cherie's mentioned in there?

DARBY CRASH   Just something like ... Cherie!!?? You've been hearing things! Something about Joan being passed out on the couch because, uh, she was ... at the time.

(From "Rodney on the ROQ," circa late '79.)

JOAN JETT   We were really on the ball most of the time, not drinking, and trying not to party while we were doing the record. There was one day I got drunk, and I probably did pass out; that was the day that we recorded "Shut Down," live in the studio, and Darby made that joke about me being passed out or whatever. But that was just one song, and one day.

PENELOPE SPHEERIS   I was there, and that bitch was asleep on the set, all right?

DON BOLLES   Quad-Tech was a very utilitarian studio which had all the good workhorse analog shit. Pat Burnette the engineer was a young guy. He was a descendent of the famous musical Burnette family. He was like only about 30, but he seemed really old to us. Although he was really into the Germs as a band he wasn't into wearing spiked wristbands or wanting to get drunk with us or any of that punk shit stuff. Pat [Burnette] was more than just the engineer, he was really the uncredited co-producer with Joan, although Pat [Smear] knew exactly what he wanted his guitar to sound like. So everybody was pitching in at one point ... and Joan was very cool and open to all suggestions. Joan is a rock goddess because she understood rock 'n' roll. Darby knew he could never capture what he had onstage.

NICOLE PANTER   The guy that engineered it was a fuckin' loser, Joan Jett was useless, she was asleep.

JOAN JETT   The Germs were great. I had a lot of fun doing that album, and I really took it seriously. Since I had seen the Germs live so many times, I knew that there were great songs. I thought we had the potential to just really make a classic record, and I think we did. It's still in print. I think the record captures the energy really well. It was really pretty straightforward—there wasn't the time or the budget or the technology for it to be anything else other than the way it came out. Sure, I doubled tracks here and there and had them do things they'd never done before. I had Darby doing harmonies. Darby took it pretty seriously.

We didn't have to do a lot of takes. He was certainly not out of control in the studio. He respected me. Did what I asked him to do. They were trying to get something done and they were very serious about it. It was a controlled nuttiness at that point.

NICOLE PANTER   During the *G.I.* sessions I was the one saying: "Darby do this, do that. A little more, a little less. Come on honey, sing into the microphone, you can do it. No, don't get mad at Don; is that really the way you want it to sound?"

DON BOLLES   We all drank a little but we stayed incredibly focused. We were a hard-working little unit determined not to fuck it up.

PAT SMEAR   If anybody was the producer, it was Pat Burnette, the engineer. He was really, really good, super nice—he was great! Didn't try and be like "I'm the producer!" He just took over the role, because he knew he needed to fill those shoes to get the job done, and he never said a word about it afterwards. It was just us rehearsing our asses off, and then going in and playing what we rehearsed.

DON BOLLES   I wanted the drums to sound like some sort of cross between the first Fall album and the power-drama drum sound of the early King Crimson or Van Der Graaf Generator albums. And this was supposed to happen with my limited playing abilities and a hodgepodge of borrowed drums. But with Pat Burnette's console skills, Joan's ear, Carla Maddog's drums, and my chutzpah, I think it did.

DEZ CADENA   I remember arguing with a lot of people who were *positive* that Lorna didn't really play on the album. That Joan or Pat played the bass parts. Bullshit! I could recognize her bass plunking anywhere.

DON BOLLES   Absolute insulting nonsense about Lorna not playing on the record. Her bass sound was huge, like reggae, like Jah Wobble—Lorna's trademark "wall-of-whump." She was the perfect bassist for this music. She was never so chop-heavy as to get bored and overplay, but once she learned a pattern, she never forgot it. Lorna was our secret weapon, for sure.

PAT SMEAR   I liked the way Don Bolles played drums—the best parts of the Germs album are the drums and the lyrics. I loved the lyrics, I always thought they were great, although sometimes they got a bit pretentious. But it was the first shit he wrote!

DON BOLLES   Pat suggested I come up with a concrete media-collage for the middle part of "Media Blitz." So I threw together some random soundbites: "We're pullin' a high price, boy," "The observations of ..." "... the pimple!" "Comin' in the side door!"
  Pat's guitar sound was extremely problematic, but somehow, between Pat Bur-

nette and Joan it became a worthy vehicle for Mr. Smear's frighteningly intense musical jihad of angst and distortion. As much as he hated playing solos, Pat ripped a couple of the most insane leads this side of the Stooges' *Raw Power* on "Let's Pretend" and "Strange Notes." Where the hell did that come from? I'd rehearsed with this guy almost every day for months, played a bunch of shows with him, but I'd never heard him play anything like this.

PAT SMEAR My problem with playing leads is that I don't know any scales, or how to improvise, or any of the other stuff you're supposed to learn. I only know how to practice with a band. I could never just sit at home and practice by myself. There are two ways I can play lead—either I think about what I want to play in my head and then learn it on guitar, or the other way is just random playing. When I play a lead randomly, it might sound really cool, but it usually ends up sounding like "Shut Down." When I hear somebody that plays great leads, I always think that person has no life; they must just sit in their room and practice for five hours a day. You may go, "Wow, impressive," or you may go, "So what? You practice for five hours a day!" Some people told me they were inspired by the guitar on the *G.I.* album ... but I always thought of the Germs as a T-shirt band. People have the T-shirts, and they say they love the Germs, but they don't listen to the record—maybe they even have the record, but they don't really play it. "We Must Bleed" is my favorite. It's the only one that, if I were to listen to the record now, I would listen to, or if I was going to play someone a song, someone who had never heard of the Germs. Just that or "Forming," depending on what way I want them to think the band sounded.

BOB BIGGS I'm more proud of the Germs album than any other thing I've ever done. To me, that album was it, for a lot of reasons. In my life I've had a lot of success, I've been blessed, but the Germs experience was one of the most authentic experiences. I still feel to this day that that's the single most important thing I've ever done.

DON BOLLES We got good reviews here and there, but outside L.A. County people would just say, "Who?" We didn't even think about tours. Nicole didn't get us an agent to set that stuff up and, face it, we just didn't have that brutal Calvinistic Black Flag work attitude anyway. Black Flag had this paleolithic work ethic thing happenin' ... they worked their asses off, night and day, 24/7. The Germs barely even liked getting up in the morning.

BRENDAN MULLEN As the "world's most volatile band" according to Kickboy [Claude Bessy], the Germs didn't have a snowball's chance from day one. There was absolutely no possibility for widespread success no matter how the deck was stacked. It was still the dark ages of the great American underground rock renaissance of the '80s which reaped all the benefits of the radical L.A. punk scene at the same time as it eclipsed it. Forget not that at the time of the Germs there were no corporate-financed "alterna/cutting edge" national networks of cool labels,

John Doe and Exene of X, the only punk band Darby expressed admiration for. Photo: Scott Lindgren.

agents, bookers, promoters, and trust-funded careerist CMJ radio interns. No MTV. No Internet. No digital technology whatsoever. When the Germs were first coming up having a basic answering or fax machine was a big deal. Phones didn't even have call waiting yet.

BOB BIGGS I signed X next after the Germs because I figured they would sell records and I was trying to start a label, but I didn't see how I could ever be that emotionally involved with another band after the Germs.

GERBER One night X was playing at UCLA, so Clag, this sugar-daddy of mine, drove Darby and me over there. In some kind of parking stucture we bumped into these two Persian guys who just freaked out when they saw us! We were drunk, trying to find the concert—I don't even remember if we said anything—but these guys saw us and just immediately laid down on the ground and started to give us their wallets, like we were trying to rob them. We were laughing so hard, like when you can't stop and it hurts. I was, like, on the ground laughing—and they were going, "No, no, take the wallet!" My stomach was aching; we were all hysterical. It was like being in this incredibly bad punk gang movie, one of those cheap shit exploitation things from the '60s, or something. So we took the wallets, right, and then they were still laying there, saying, like, "Don't hurt us." They were cringing and crying and holding their heads, they thought we were going to shoot them in the back of the head, execution style, or something, but we had no weapons, not even a Swiss knife! And so we had their wallets. We had no plan whatsoever, but it was like, "Okay, this is too good—we've got to do something." So we all checked our pockets, and I was like, "Pop Rocks! I have Pop Rocks!" So we told them, "You will now snort the Pop Rocks." Sure enough, they snorted the Pop Rocks—you could actually hear them blowing off up in their sinuses, and I guess it hurt really bad; they looked like they were in agony! We took the money out and threw their wallets back at them, and left, laughing so hard.

DON BOLLES The Germs played gratis at the Hong Kong Café [July 17, 1979] in restitution for a window which Darby broke on a previous occasion, otherwise the band was under threat of being banned from the only venue who would take them.

> BAT BOY The Germs siege the stage, and it's instant party, any sense of order or meaning is gone. The crowd, now up and active, seems to be fighting more than dancing. Confusion prevails, and Darby plays host:
> DARBY CRASH Whaddaya wanna hear? Know any songs? Gimme a beer! Pretend you're at a party! Everybody onstage!
> BAT BOY Beautiful Lorna smiles coolly, Pat, relaxed and in good form, is on the floor.
> (From a review in Pleasant Gehman's *Lobotomy* 'zine.)

L.A.WEEKLY

Free

The Publication of News, People, Entertainment, Art and Imagination in Los Angeles   August 3-9, 1979   Volume 1, Number 35

Michael Ventura: Peter Weir's Genius

Big Boy Medlin: Surviving Manhattan

Who Is Darby Crash Anyway?

Critic Contest Winners Page 8

Inside: L.A.'s Biggest Guide to Movies, Music & Fun

175

The Germs new "Germs G.I." debut album: a musical strip mine of the soul.

NEW STRAIN OF GERMS

BY R. MELTZER

"GERMS G.I." The Germs. Slash SR-103.

In 1967, the year new wave could easily have made its first official penetration (true!), there were only two combos of note with eyes beyond Eastern topicalities and compulsory 20-minute solos: the Velvet Underground and the Doors. Iggy in his pre-Pop incarnation eventually picked up their combined gauntlet of brutality aboriginal form/scathing inner vision, but even at its hottest his interpretation of the Velvet/Doors heart-of-darkness was disappointingly incomplete—albeit literal as heck.

OK, time marches on. We've finally got ourselves an actual new wave and all, and with this the Germs' debut LP one high-priority inevitability has at last been delivered: a musical strip-mine-of-the-soul that doesn't miss a beat at out-Iggying the Ig, then going beyond Mr. Stooge to his above-mentioned forebears 'and leaving them closely resembling mere cofee-table poets to boot.

From first hyper-moment to last, Darby Crash's vocalizings are impossible to follow without aid of the lyric sheet, and even then you're likely to throw in the towel. Words—as utterances, meanings, triggers —are just multi-edged touchstones in the rapid-fire excess of interactive human ritual, units of unedited inscription on the toilet paper of this here life. Out of this unrelenting stream of consciousness emerges a landscape of 24-hour fever dreams with non-sequitur dialectical twists that none of your serious writers (so-called) would ever submit to public scrutiny without embarrassment.

And because everything is so open-ended, you don't see Darby tripping over his metaphors as inescapable repositories of commitment the way Jim Morrison did: Every night is *not* an endless one-lane highway, a scenario of total-loss-or-nothing. Unrelieved anguish is still plenty rampant, but it's only one non-sacred station-of-his-cross among many, to be visited at one's biological whim before, during and after TV.

This valuable piece of vinyl is (1) the album of the year, (2) the most staggering recorded statement so far from the American branch of new wave, (3) the most remarkable L.A. studio achievement at least since "L.A. Woman" (1971). It's *that* great! ☐

Richard Meltzer, not Kim Fowley, forces bourgeois So Cal readers to reckon with the "new wave" release of the Germs ' G.I. lp, December '79.

CRITICS ASTOUNDED

O

Slash, Volume 2, Number 7, August 1979.
The Germs (hurray! groan!) have completed their studio sessions for the upcoming, eagerly awaited lp. Produced by ex-Runaway part time Pistolette Joan Jett, this awesome monument (cool it! Ed.) to the genuine insanity of some of us should be available in late August. Throughout the proceedings the Germs proved to be the tireless dedicated workers we all know they really were. The package will include around 17 songs, the complete lyrics (worthy of a hardcover numbered edition all by themselves) and the definitive version of "Shut Down." Following this shimmering offering to world culture, we all feel an unlimited grant from the National Endowment of the Arts is the least this country should present us with. Of course, we will no doubt be seriously disappointed very soon.
   (*Slash*, Volume 2, Number 7, August 1979.)

TONY MONTESION   When the *G.I.* album came out the *L.A. Times* said they were the next Doors. Then it seemed like at every show after that they couldn't get through three songs without cops showing up with dogs on short leashes, and they'd unplug the equipment in the middle of a song. He tried to inspire us to ignite a riot—trash the place, fuck up the place; but we were too outnumbered, or just too frightened to do that ... and so they were eventually banned from every club in Southern California.

DARBY CRASH   If we did what we were doing then now there's no way we could get away with it. As it is we can't get booked anymore. They won't let us play the Whisky because they said me and Lorna tried to start a riot. The guy that's [booking] it doesn't like the people. He doesn't mind the music; he just doesn't like the people. So he doesn't want us to hang around. People don't drink there, that's part of it. And none of us have money to pay to get in.

AMBER   Darby would say, "I hate The Doors!" and he did hate what they were, but mostly, he didn't like to be compared, and he was compared to Jim Morrison a lot—the dark lyrics like "The Lizard King" and all. It embarrassed him to be compared.

KRISTINE MCKENNA   (writing in the *L.A. Times*, November 2, 1979): Germs *G.I.*, a superbly produced aural holocaust, is an unnervingly powerful testament to man's darker side. We've all got one, and it's frightening to recognize a bit of oneself in the demented gaze of Darby Crash. I don't like this band, but figuring out why has been an enlightening experience.

STAGGERINGLY RECKLESS

O

JEFF MCDONALD I remember an X show when Pat got up onstage and sucker-punched Billy Zoom right in front of a sold-out crowd!

JOHN DOE One time Pat Smear hit Billy when we were onstage. Billy was shooing Darby off his monitor. Billy was very particular about people getting in his space. And Pat, like the fucking chicken that he is, hit Billy and then ran out of the club. Hit and run! Darby was always getting in people's faces. He got in Billy's face a couple of times and I told him to fucking cut it out.

PAT SMEAR X were playing at the Hong Kong Café—me and Darby were watching in total worship, all jealous 'cause they were such a great band. Darby was sitting on the monitors, and I think Billy Zoom got mad and asked someone to get Darby off—so I just punched him and got thrown out, but then later Exene got me back in.

EXENE CERVENKA Doesn't Pat mean: "I punched him and then ran away?" That never got resolved. We think he ran away after he punched Billy.[15]

NICOLE PANTER The first time I quit was the night of the Masque Christmas show in December '79 at the Whisky, but they talked me into coming back.

RIK L. RIK The Germs were never the most together band to begin with, but they had a couple of months during '79 where they were fairly tight. After the *G.I.* album, The Germs practiced less and less. It was chaos. Darby was fucked up, out of his mind every show. He wasn't even trying to present himself as an artist any more; he was just trying to present his pain and his pain had become this one long scream … one long, intoxicated primal scream of despair. It was obvious by '79–'80 that nobody was ever gonna get a real record deal, nobody was gonna be rich and famous, which is what I think everybody wanted, really, if they were honest, and so he got into the drugs more, and the stage show just became like an Evel Knievel spectacle. Only Darby never made the canyon.

> RODNEY All right, Suburban Lawns on KROQ-FM in Pasadena; we just heard "Gidget Goes To Hell," then we heard the Dead Kennedys doing "California Über Alles," and they're getting a lot of press in England right now, believe it or not; we heard "Nightmare City," the Alleycats; "Eton Rifles" by the Jam, and "Babylon" by the Runts—or the Ruts, or whatever you want to call it. Okay, get back to some more music and the Germs will be here very shortly. Here's James Brown on the ROQ… (plays James Brown song "Soulful Christmas")
>
> DARBY Nicole, go get me a beer, this is the longest ad in fucking history.

RODNEY   ... and then we heard "Bleached Black" by James White and the
     Blacks; and we heard "Soulful Christmas" by James Brown...
DARBY   Awful Christmas...
RODNEY   So what does each person play?
DARBY   I play hard to get.
     (From "Rodney on the ROQ," Dec. 12, 1979.)

JOHN DOE   X and the Germs played at this place called Hope Street Hall, which was right near Morrison Hotel, the fleabag fucking hotel where they shot the Doors' album cover. Exene and I immediately went down to Morrison Hotel. They still had the same stenciled window. The Germs played, and Pat broke his guitar in half and came back to us in this little dressing room and said, "Billy, I broke my guitar, can I use yours?" Billy is so particular about his equipment and still is. And he was like, "Can you use mine? Look what you just did to yours!" We all just screamed with laughter. Pat was very quiet, very sweet. And very funny in the fact that he knew all these really terrible songs. He could pick stuff up by ear.

PAT SMEAR   The Germs had a gig with X at Hope Street Hall in downtown L.A. By the time we went onstage, we were really stupidly drunk, and, of course, I broke the guts out of my guitar. Some guy who was sitting on the side said he could fix it for me. So this guy took the guitar to fix it, and I'm up on stage, drunk and whining, "Where's Billy Zoom? Billy Zoom, I need your guitar!" Of course he had one of his fancy vintage sparkle Gretsch things for the show. He never answered me, but I heard that he was up in the sound booth or somewhere, hugging his guitar, saying "No, no, no! Keep him away from me!" Anyway, the guy that fixed my guitar turned out to be the guy that stole it later!

ooo

AMBER   I met Charles Manson when I was 16 years old, and I brought him to Rodney's house. It was great—to this day, Rodney will tell you, "Oh, Amber brought Charles Manson to my house."

NICOLE PANTER   Everybody objected to Darby hanging out with Amber.

HELLIN KILLER   Once he started doing heroin he became even more vulnerable than he already was. It became easy as kiddie play for more vampires and vultures to swoop in and circle around him. That's always an easy way to get somebody ... it was like, "Here, I'll get you dope ... just hang out with me and you'll get high." But nobody seemed able to figure that one out.

TONY MONTESION   Amber lived right downstairs from me on Franklin when Darby moved in. We quickly discovered that me, Darby, and my wife Courtney all had one thing in common—heroin—but Amber wouldn't touch it. We were a lot older, Darby was just a kid. Courtney and I had been heavy on it for about six years. To

Darby and Amber. Photo courtesy Amber.

him we were like the old pros. I don't want to say he looked up to it, but he had a bizarre excitement about it—he thought it was so cool. Amber took Darby in and supported him. Don (her husband) and Amber were really touchy as a couple, and were in and out, until it finally just dissolved, with Don leaving and Darb staying.

PAT SMEAR   I didn't believe in shooting up drugs. Way too gross. I had heard that Darby and Regi and Johnny were doing it, but didn't know whether I believed it or not.

NICKY BEAT   I couldn't understand his getting involved with heroin. It was really weird 'cause I just thought he was so much smarter than that.

JENA CARDWELL   Darby getting more and more into drugs was a gradual thing, but Pat never was into that, so that caused a distance, and everything just started falling apart.

DON BOLLES   Darby was already kind of gone because of all the bad influences, the heroin usage had started, and Amber the freak was as stupid as the heroin using was, but Darby always seemed to love being around overweight women who resembled his mom … a formidably fierce woman of wide girth.

TRUDIE   I walked into this party and I remember Darby sitting with these people going, "Trudie, Trudie, come over here. Come do some heroin." It was like a new thing on the scene. It was new for me and new for him … that's why he was bragging, "Come, do some heroin with us." And I was like, "No, I don't think so. Heroin is way too creepy." Darby always was trying to get people to do the same thing that he was doing. I don't know if it was a control thing or he just wanted this big family around him.

TONY THE HUSTLER   Amber was the latest with money prepared to pick up for him … that meant food, clothing, transportation, restaurants, drink, drugs … whatever he wanted. He never had any money of his own.

PAUL ROESSLER   Darby was over at Amber's all the time, I think he was living there part of the time, too. She was my neighbor, but nobody I wanted to be around, so I was like, "Wow—not only can he go without sleep longer than anybody, but he can stand to be around Amber!" Whether she was buying drugs, whatever the reason could have been, there was no goodness there, and I didn't respect him for it. He'd call us from her place and say, "Come on over. I don't wanna be alone," and I'd be like, "Uh-uh, I'm not going over there; maybe Hellin will come over." Amber was just way too creepy.

HELLIN KILLER   He'd call when we was over there [living with Amber] and he'd go, "Please come over here, please come over here and hang out with me." He'd beg on the phone for me to go over there so he wouldn't have to hang out with her.

GERBER   I don't hold Amber responsible for his drug addiction, but I hold her responsible for not caring whether he lived or died. She had ulterior motives, man! She wanted to be the sugar-mama. She wanted fuckin' Nicole's seat. She lusted for his idol-status, and putting enough dope in him got it for her. It's like, someone's strung out, hand them $500 worth of dope, and it's "Fuck yeah, suck my dick, I don't care." He totally used her, like he used Michelle Baer, like he used Jill Ash and Nicole, and all those other girls. I know, I was in on it with him!

HELLIN KILLER   Amber was always trying to fuck everybody! She tried to get Paul drunk and fuck him, she took him to Disneyland and bought him stuff; that was her whole trip. I don't know where she got the money from, but she had a bunch of it, and she would just, like, it was like prostitution with her—she liked to buy people. Darby sure latched onto a lot of the wrong people who rather than protecting him, which is really what he needed, they just took him down. It was like, "Here, we'll give you anything you want, just be around us."

AMBER   I put my foot down and told him that if he wanted to get high to get a hotel room, or get his friends together and have a party, but don't take it in the street, because he was going to pass out in front of the wrong person and end up in jail and *fucked*! So we agreed that when he would do drugs it would be under "thinking conditions." I knew just about every dealer of heroin and hard drugs in that area, and would go with Darby to score.

MAGGIE EHRIG   Darby was for sure a fully-blown alcoholic and drug addict ... but we didn't look at it like that back then.

FAITH BAKER   I knew he was into drugs, but not as bad as he was, from what I've read. I didn't approve of the drugs, but of course I never knew how bad 'til later—I don't think he was into them as much, or as young as they say he was—but I might be wrong, too. Georg told me that he never fooled with them—but Georg had an alcohol problem.

REGI MENTLE   Darby's room became a great place for everybody to come over to slam dope.

TONY MONTESION   We started shooting up together—just me and him and Courtney, but we definitely didn't turn him on to it—he was way past "chipping"—he had to be full-on using. I don't know who turned him on to it, but I noticed he was very sloppy. His arms were frequently covered with blood, and I had to fix him a couple of times, help him find a vein. I think he did it mostly on purpose, he had no idea how much he took, or even what he was doing, but I watched out for him on the street if anybody tried to get rough.

NICOLE PANTER   I didn't think he was strung out necessarily. He was into taking a variety of things—he was just addicted to taking drugs. Any drugs, didn't matter. I was surprised when people described Darby as a junkie. I was around him enough to know he was not a junkie, or if he was it was in such beginning stages that he hadn't started doing the typical street junkie things like burning bridges with family and stealing from friends.

JOHN DOE   We knew he was doing a lot of heroin but it was before the point where people would even consider doing an intervention ... we didn't know about N.A. or anything, we knew what alcoholism was but we didn't care. He became a bit of a gourmet, mostly doing heroin...

AMERICAN LEATHER

O

PAT SMEAR   We had a lot of gay friends that were way, openly gay—like Regi Mentle and Johnny Valium. They were full-on bathhouse poppas … they were in-your-face dick-sucking, butt-fucking, fist-fucking GAY!

JENA CARDWELL   Regi was really flamboyant but he was also really hardcore. Once I dropped him and Johnny off at the baths. They came from San Francisco, and were the first on the scene to wear spiked leather wristbands and leather pants plus those in-your-face Tom of Finland all-male porno T-shirts. Regi told me he'd run away from home and had lived with drag queens, he was even in some drag show when he was a kid. He was one of those really fun, up, flamboyant kind of gay guys that everyone loves to hang out with—especially girls.

REGI MENTLE   My friend Johnny Valium and I first met Darby at a Screamers gig. Darby was hangin' with Tony the Hustler and Cherie the Penguin, so we called 'em over and introduced ourselves. Darby just came up and put something in my mouth and said, "You are what you eat," and walked away. I was going to swallow it, but my tongue told me it wasn't a pill, so I took it out of my mouth … it was a one-inch-tall rubber baby.

JUDITH BELL   [Punk band name omitted—not the Germs] had been harboring Regi Mentle, who had killed some guy in San Francisco. He came down here and wanted to stay at their house for a while. I told [name omitted] I didn't want to participate in any of that activity. I was like, "You're covering up a murder here, kids." They liked that cool factor. That outlaw factor. Homicidal guy on the run. I realized that their audience was becoming a lot of mentally ill fucked-up people and it just wasn't that funny to me anymore. I just thought, "What am I doing here?" and started slowly separating myself.

REGI MENTLE   To make it short: I stabbed a guy with the knife he pulled on me, but I overdid it pretty much. In August, '80 I went on the lam to Long Beach and a couple of other spots. I was living with a psychic, but I didn't tell him I was a fugitive murderer, and I wondered that if he was really psychic, why the fuck would he not know that? So I asked him if he could talk to the dead. "Of course," he says. So I said, "Call up Darby Crash for me." So he puts together a Ouija board and used an upside-down plastic two-piece champagne glass without the base as the planchette. He scored on the question, "Should I come and join you?" by responding, "Not yet, shithead." That is exactly the answer I would've expected from Darby. They caught me on April 14, 1981. I was drinking tequila on the beach across from Breakers when they ran a check on me. I got life.

John E. Valium, Regi Mentle. Circa 1979-80.

HELLIN KILLER We'd get really drunk, and if we could find somebody that had something, any drug of any kind, we'd take it. We were like recreational party animal drug users; whatever was around it was like, "gimme, gimme!" One time somebody goes, "We got these pills that are just like Quaaludes—take 'em, take 'em!" It turned out they were like Librium or something, and for like two days we were total vegetables.

CLAUDE BESSY One day coming out of the Masque, this is for real man, and Darby's trying to get at some ... there's a puddle of water ... and Darby's got a syringe. He was getting two or three CCs of water out of a fucking puddle in Hollywood. I said Darby, I'm not knocking you, guy, 'cause I'm into shooting, too, but people have pissed and shit in this. I said, Darby, give me your syringe and we'll go and find some clean water. We went to Boardner's bar across the street in the bathroom. I have nothing against shooting up, but don't pull your fucking syringe water out of the street.

PAT SMEAR One day at Darby's house Regi and Johnny had this "Mystery Drug" and no one knew what it was, but they decided to shoot it up anyway. I saw people shooting up for the first time in my life, and they didn't even know what they were shooting up! They debated about how much they should do. And who did it first? Darby, of course! I just kept thinking, "Yeah, yeah, yeah—ha ha ha, right, guys," and then—WHOOA!!! Until I actually saw them do it, I didn't really believe that anybody would do that—especially not my friends! It really freaked me out. It was like, "You're shooting yourself up on purpose?!" Like, I would do anything to not have a needle in my arm! I just did not understand it all—it made no sense. We were doing MDA, dropping acid, drinking, and doing all sorts of other insane shit—but hey, what's with this creepy needle shit?

REGI MENTLE When Don Bolles shot up MDA, he said it was like "shooting up pure confusion."

JENA CARDWELL Suddenly MDA was flowing like water! But really it could be any drug, Darby wasn't too particular ... whatever was available, whatever anybody gave him ... so long as it got him fucked up. We'd be sitting at the Whisky, and Johnny or Regi would walk up and pour a bunch of MDA right into our drinks!

REGI MENTLE [In letter from prison] Johnny and I once rolled Lucky the dope dealer and got an ounce of meth, a pound of MDA, $10K in cash, and an unlabeled syringe-type bottle (with the rubber top that you poke the needle through) containing some sort of clear liquid. We went straight to Darby's to bag up the MDA for sale at the Hong Kong Café. We were throwing grams and half grams into pieces of foil to sell as nickel bags, just to get rid of it and make a little cash. After we shot up everything we wanted to it was like "So, who's gonna do the 'Mystery Drug?'" Darby said he'd do it. It turned out to be Ketamine, it's a muscle relaxer that fags use to help relax the sphincter ... it's for opening up and stretching the asshole for that special big daddy ass-fucking ... Ketamine also

186

comes in handy for forearm fisting … but Darby didn't think it was too funny … when he shot it, he sat down on the bed, cryin' out like a little kid, "It's angel dust, it's angel dust!" Everybody was falling about laughing.

TITO LARRIVA   I was in the parking lot of the Whisky one night with Joan Jett and some other people and everybody was sniffing from this bottle of amyl nitrate and Darby came up to us and I handed it to him and said, "Here, want some?" And he just took the bottle and downed it one gulp without even asking what it was and I guess he hadn't seen us sniffing it 'cause he immediately went "Ahhh! Ahhh!" Screaming and choking and puking everywhere. Everybody was laughing at him. He was fucking sick as a dog.

KID CONGO POWERS   I remember smoking angel dust with him 'til the wee hours and someone driving us out to the beach. I always sensed he half-liked who he was and half didn't like it at all.

BILL BARTELL   Henley said he saw Darby emptying out a bunch of black beauties on the dresser. He assumed Darby was going to snort them, but he just put the black gelatin caps back together, empty, and stuck them in his pocket. Later at a show, he walked up to a group of punks and asked for a drink of their beer, and when they handed it to him, he whipped out these empty capsules, threw them all in his mouth, and gulped them down with the beer. Then he thanked them, handed them back their beer, and walked off while they were left picking their jaws up off of the floor. Apparently, he did this little trick a lot.

MAGGIE EHRIG   The lengths that folks would go to cop were disgusting and at one point those lengths were taken in a very hurtful way and one of the recipients of drugs bought with money from a robbery was Darby. I didn't know the perpetrators were doing this to give drugs to Darby. I was there during that crime. It was a robbery, and with the cash these guys bought the dope … the victim was a random person, it wasn't somebody they knew and it wasn't pre-planned. It happened on the street … a spontaneous impulse crime and the result of that crime was someone was badly hurt during the process of copping drugs and those drugs were shared with Darby. When we got back Darby was already high in his room in the back of the Oxford house.

DEZ CADENA   At the Oxford House people were making a tea out of belladonna, 'cause there was a plant growing right outside. If you take a little too much, be careful—it's a poison—your breathing will get so faint that your heart will just stop.

MAGGIE EHRIG   Even the dregs, the people that would hurt somebody to get drugs, are usually people too selfish to give a fuck about the people around them and would hoard it for themselves … but even those folks were sharing dope freely with Darby, ha ha ha. They'd hog it all for themselves, but for Darby they'd be like, "Hey, Darby, look what we got for you."

Culver City Auditorium. Early '80. Photo Jenny Lens.

CLAUDE BESSY   Darby was a heavy drinker. He used to shoot up, but basically he was a drinker.

○○○

JENNY LENS   The Germs played Culver City Auditorium in 1980, the last year of Darby's life. It was awful. He was running around backstage trying to get something to get stoned with. "Do you have any drugs, Jenny? Do you have any drugs?" "No I don't, Darby." "I have to get some drugs, I have to get something because I don't perform straight." That totally blew me away, somebody who had to be on something in order to perform? Did he have stage fright? Most people perform and get an adrenaline rush and get out there and get a special high … it's typical for most performers to have stage fright and throw up, but with him, he had to get high. And it was indiscriminate, didn't matter what he took, he just had to take something, and that struck me as very sad. I was a heavy-duty drug user in those days myself … but it wasn't a crisis if I didn't have drugs, but it was for him.

TONY MONTESION   Darby would order people around, too. I remember thinking, "Why go the dictator route … why not just let the music ride, and carry the poetry, or whatever," but I don't think he ever really knew what he wanted. When you get a bit of celebrity, you get people buzzin' in your ears, everything goin' on at once—there were people always yappin' in his ear about this or that, tryin' to change his direction or whatever…

OKI DOGS

O

BRENDAN MULLEN   Danny's Oki Dogs on Santa Monica Boulevard gradually became the post-gig gathering spot for the burgeoning suburban hardcore scene. The Temple of Oki Dog became the meeting place for the consolidating of the So Cal inter-county teen punk tribes. Many of the new kids emulated Darby's classic (pre-Adam Ant Boy of London) look: a little braided pony tail with chains and tartan bandanas lashed around the ankles of military combat and flying boots. Oki Dog became the latest hot spot to get your Germs' burn and watch Darby hold court with his minions squatting open-mouthed on the ground around him as he enacted his "gimme gimme this ... gimme gimme that" mantra. This Oki Dog suburban hardcore punk look exists to the present day.

SHAWN STERN   I lived three or four houses down from Oki Dog during its heyday. Oki Dog was the place to go after a show. Sometimes there would be four or five hundred punk rockers hanging out there. If there was a show at the Palladium or the Olympic, everyone would migrate over there afterwards, but Oki Dog had its share of confrontations with the cops, too.

Boots, bandanas 'n' chains at Oki Dog, circa 1979-80. Photo: Edward Colver.

THE OTHER NEWEST ONE

O

BRENDAN MULLEN   The final nail in the coffin of L.A. punk's Naive Period can be pinpointed almost to the day. It was Christmas, 1979, at a Germs' show at the Whisky—documented on the "Caught in My Eye" video and the *Rock 'n' Rule* album. That night, Saturday, December 22, 1979, battle lines were drawn irreversibly: the Hollywood and the new HB hardcore scenes were no longer the same people—could no longer be the same people—with the same outlook or perspective. The "louder, faster" bonehead thrash aesthetic had arrived and tonight was its coming-out ball. I had booked the second annual two-nighter Masque employees' Christmas party/gig into the Whisky with the Germs on one night plus Geza X & the Mommymen and the Masque houseband Arthur J. & the Gold Cups, which featured the staff and their friends.

Having shared bills previously with the Germs, it wasn't that out of place for the Mommymen to be on the same stage. However, this time the Mommymen (I was a sideperson in this totally sick Geza X group) found ourselves playing to a packed house of suburban beach kids we had never seen before. Two or three songs into the set it was evident this crowd of angry white suburban dudes was in no mood for a freak sporting a Mephisto-length goatee dressed in a tutu over a pair of costume goat legs—complete with tail and cloven hooves. Our fearless leader wigged them out even more by shrieking bizarre anal-victim exclamations at them like: "I Want My Mommy," "Mean Mr. Mommyman Cut the Worms Out of My Head," and "No, No, No.... Not the Butt Pliers!"

The vibe in the room was *seething*. Here we were in front of this awful bunch of slithering, sweaty cretins who were becoming more restless by the minute! The club was tit-to-tit oversold. Breathing was major exertion. Management had forbidden ins and outs. A putrid, stomach-churning stench permeated like a massive collective fart—the appalling aroma of snarling, gnarly, testosterone-dripping, acne-faced, hissing reptiles with green, foam-flecked teeth, dressed in blue circle T-shirts, waving their arms around and giving the bird to Geza. Seeing the Germs was the only item on these pukes' agenda and they were the next band up, we finished our set just in the nick of time … the crowd was chanting hostility louder and louder. By the time we left the stage these putzes were ready to *kill*. Now was the moment the mob was waiting for: the Germs. But no. Not quite yet. Bolles was MIA. No one had seen or heard from him since the late afternoon.

DON BOLLES   By the time I got to the club, it was at least an hour past when we were supposed to play. I told the doorman to let me in, that I was in the Germs and he said, "Yeah, right—the Germs are already on stage! Get outta here!" So I ran by him and pushed through the crowd with a couple of huge, pissed-off bouncers right behind me. Finally I made it to the stage. Pat, Lorna and Darby were standing around while the drummer from the opening band was trying to readjust my drum set so he could play it. The bouncers were almost on me, and now there were two more coming from the wings, so I leapt onto the stage. Pat and Lorna seemed amused, if a bit stressed. Darby rolled his eyes, and continued pacing the stage.

BRENDAN MULLEN Since I was the promoter of this fiasco, I'd been summoned to this assistant manager's office. I was blitzed out of my gourd on mushrooms and Guinness when I stumbled inside this halfwit's office whereupon he demanded I get on the mic to calm the pit down with a few well-chosen punk words. "You have to be kidding," I retorted, "these fuckers are the ugliest, meanest looking crowd of yahoos I've ever seen. I have *nothing* to say to them." "They're your fucking people, man," the moron yelled at me. "You brought them ... you talk to them. You're supposed to be the big-shit king of punk." "You're the one who oversold the place ," I retorted, "you're the one who decided no ins and out. *You* go talk to them."

DON BOLLES I apologized, made up some lie about being detained by police, and crawled onto the drum riser. The other drummer, relieved that he wasn't going to have to play a bunch of songs he didn't know, happily handed me the sticks. The bouncers finally figured out that maybe I really was in the band, after all, and grudgingly went back to their posts...

BRENDAN MULLEN Suddenly Pat apparently began kicking the head of some bouncer on the floor from the stage—you can see it clearly in the video. When some other bouncer or a Whisky employee tried to stop him, Pat smacked him one hard upside the head. And again, and again. The horde of rabid suburban ignoroids in the pit took the punch-up as their cue to invade the stage, and the show came to a halt with a dozen people brawling before management killed the stage lights.

JENA CARDWELL One of these big fat bouncers threw Donnie Rose or somebody off the stage. Darby was screaming at the bouncers, and Pat took a swing at one of them and hit him with his guitar. After the show, the bouncers were going to get Pat ... they were going to get him in the back of the Whisky, beat the crap out of him, then hand him over to the sheriffs.

JEFF MCDONALD Pat used to have these huge outbursts of violence—he was always the one that would do the gnarly stuff. People don't think of him as a violent person, but I remember when the Germs were playing at the Whisky, it was this total chaos nightmare, and some huge, burly bouncer was fucking with someone in the audience, and Pat kicked him right in the back of the head.

DON BOLLES Pat was really scared—the Whisky is notorious for having mob connections, so he thought the bouncers were going to just kill him outright. To make things worse, the club had called the cops, so even if he made it past the bouncers, he would still be doomed. Finally, we managed to sneak him out the backstage door in a drum case.

JENA CARDWELL Pat took off, and actually *ran* home to Hollywood, where he was living with Rosetta just above Frederick's of Hollywood. He was running through people's backyards, all the way from the Whisky to Hollywood and Whitley. Darby and Hellin and I were driving in her car and we saw the helicopters circling around, cop cars with their lights going, searching for Pat all around the neighborhood; they were really coming down on him.

DON BOLLES Pat was so freaked out that he completely quit going out for a while; he would hardly ever leave his house, and when he did, he'd see Whisky bouncers hiding behind every shrub—this went on for like six months! I think he might have even stopped drinking for a minute.

JEFF MCDONALD The fact that he didn't get his ass kicked was pretty amazing. I wouldn't want those guys after me!

Probably at the Whisky, circa '79-'80. Photo: Jill Ash.

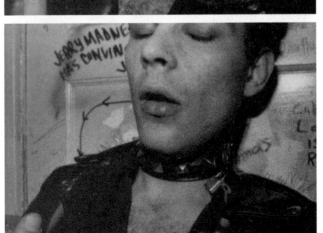

TONY THE HUSTLER

O

GERBER   In the end, Donnie basically chose me over Darby. It was kind of like Tony was a Band-Aid or whatever…

TONY THE HUSTLER   I first met Darby when he was still living at his mom's house. I would go to the Germs' shows at the Whisky, the Masque, and the Hong Kong Café, and eventually Darby and I got chummy. There would be after-hour parties at Oki Dog 'til like three or four in the morning. Then Darby would take a select few over to his mom's house. He always had his bedroom door locked with a huge padlock, and the hinges were on the inside, so you couldn't get in or out of his bedroom door from the house. So three or four of us would crawl in his bedroom window that he would leave unlocked, and sneak in there with drugs and beer and party until we passed out.

I thought he was pretty wild and sexy. One night we passed out at his house dead drunk. In the morning when we woke up, he asked me, "Is there anyone else in the room with us, or are we all alone?" I said, "No, we're all alone." He said, "Well, I want you." So that's when we became intimate. Afterwards, I thought, "Oh well, great, that kills my friendship with him. I'll never see him again." But it was totally the opposite. We became best friends and kind of, like, turned into a couple.

I think Darby was attracted to me because I was a full-on walking, talking, in-your-face leather-clad whore and I had wealthy celebrity clients who paid me well. One of them was Paul Lynde, who was on the *Hollywood Squares*, and all the sitcoms in the '60s, like *Bewitched* and *I Dream of Jeannie*. I met him through an ad in the *Advocate*. He was a freak! We'd get drunk and take his Bentley up to Fatburger, with his gigantic poodle named Alfred; he'd be so drunk, I'd have to drive. I was there with him like three days before he died; he was laying there, just saying, "This is the end!" I guess he was tricking with some other hustler a couple of days later and OD'd on one too many poppers—a heart attack in his sleep. Knocked his ass out.

Darby lived with me for about four or five months during '79 at 1775 Orchid Avenue, behind Grauman's Chinese Theater. I had this big apartment all to myself, so I said, "Darby, you really don't have to live like this, if your mom is driving you this crazy." He said, "She makes me so depressed I just want to kill myself." So I said, "If that's the way you feel, why don't you just move in with me? No rent. You can live here for free." I said, "I'm making a ton of money, I can make $500 a day easy if I wanted." I told him, "I'll buy all the food, and pick up for all the utilities, everything will be cool." How could he say no to that? And that's when he made the transition to actually move away from his mom's house. That was the first time he had ever lived away from her. Darby seemed pretty happy after he got out. It was like a great burden had been lifted. Living with him was great. He was really easygoing—but he had a problem with too many clients coming over. He would

The pink triangle of *The Hollywood Squares*, Paul Lynde, was serviced by Tony the Hustler.
Photo: Harry Benson.

hide out in the bedroom while I turned my tricks in the front room. He got so fed up with that he finally said, "Look, I'm sorry, but I don't want to live in a whorehouse."

Darby was such a sexual being, even though he was not well-endowed. He had the smallest penis you could ever imagine, but his body was completely smooth all over—no muscle fat anywhere on his entire body. He had a huge muscular back like a lion. The first time I saw him take his pants off, completely nude, he was like a hobbit, or one of those mythological creatures. It just went from completely smooth all over and fair skinned, to this thick, curly, coarse hair that ran all the way down his legs and his thighs and completely covered his butt. I mean even his toes were hairy. It was a really unique look I had never really seen on any other man. He kind of looked like Pan, the guy with the flutes … that's how hairy his legs were. He always kept them covered up. He would never wear shorts, because he was so self-conscious about how hairy his legs were, but I thought it was hot! I thought he was hot as hell.

THE DECLINE

O

I'm heading for the center of destruction
On my way down
I'm looking around
Can't spot a phase
On my way to this place
We're running out of time
                "Center of Destruction" (by Darby Crash, 1980)

BRENDAN MULLEN   Sometime around April 1980, the Germs began shooting their live segment for *The Decline of Western Civilization* at Cherrywood Rehearsal Studios on North Cherokee Avenue (through the wall to Boardner's Bar) across the street from the old Masque. The famous photo of Darby lying on his back with eyes closed looking like he's dead was used as the main poster image for *Decline*.

TONY THE HUSTLER   The Germs and a bunch of other bands in the L.A. South Bay area were asked to be in this documentary about the punk scene.

CASEY COLA   One night [when he was living with me in late 1980] Darby told me he was going to a special screening of some movie. Hours later, he burst through the door way past midnight. He hadn't been drinking. Then he threw all these damn posters on the bed. I noticed a tear on his cheek, but he didn't want to talk about it. Months later [in February '81], when I saw the premiere of this movie—it was *The Decline of Western Civilization* by Penelope Spheeris—I understood. What he saw that night devastated him. Darby was kind of a sloppy, stupid drunk and that is how he appeared in the movie. The movie made everything seem so stark, so ugly ... he thought the movie looked creepy and he was so upset he wanted to kick holes in the wall, but I held him, I rocked him to sleep.

NICOLE PANTER   I finally bailed for good on the Germs after the filming of the Decline. That was the final straw. Darby got so fucked up after I'd told him specifically not to.

CLAUDE BESSY   I approached Penelope Spheeris and said let's make a fucking film of the scene.

PENELOPE SPHEERIS   This guy Ron told me about a couple of insurance salesmen from the Valley with a few extra bucks to flash that wanted to do a porno movie. Would I be interested in directing? I said, "Absolutely not, but how about a punk rock movie?" So they wanted a look-see and I brought them to the Starwood. We saw Darby and I said, "Is this crazy or what? It's fucking nuts here."

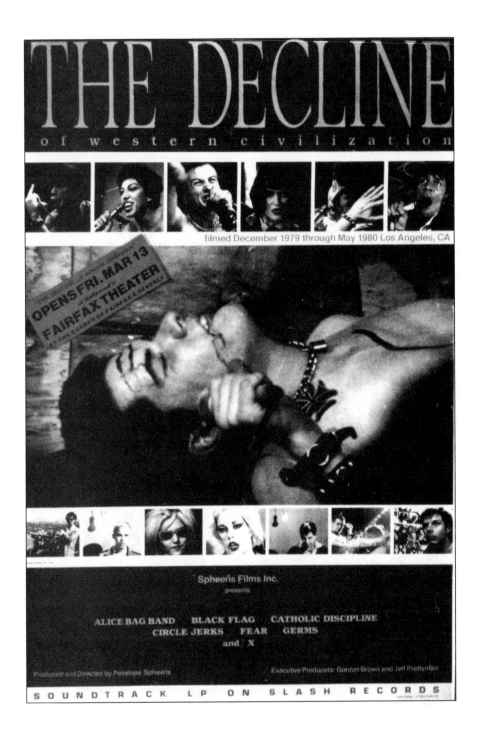

Penelope Spheeris and Bob Biggs argue over an impending divorce.
Photo: Rooh Steif.

They said they wanted to do the movie. Initially it was only going to cost around 15 grand because I was going to shoot in Super 8, but after we looked at some of the footage we agreed that the subject was more important, that it had to be shot in 16mm and blown up to 35mm. I told them the cost would go up to about 80 grand and they said, "Okay, we'll do it." It ended up costing about $120,000 altogether.

PHILOMENA WINSTANLEY   We think she did a fantastic job.

CLAUDE BESSY   The only problem is that she shoots the bands and leaves them no money.

PHILOMENA WINSTANLEY   Claude came up with the title and I talked to the bands and got them on.

EXENE CERVENKA   Everything to us was a big joke back then. It was like, "Oh, you want to put out a record, ha ha, fuck you." "Oh, you wanna manage us, ha ha, fuck you." "You wanna make a movie … fuck you."

TONY THE HUSTLER   Penelope shot a special up-close interview with Darby and another person in our apartment. But Darby didn't want me in the interview because he didn't want anybody to know he was gay, so he had asked Rob Henley to be in it. I just kind of laughed at him and said, "Oh, you don't want me to be in it, but you want this blonde-haired freak to be in it? Not only are you gonna look just as fucking gay as if I was in it—but you're gonna look like a gay dude with a hideous, acne-scarred freak for a boyfriend!"

PENELOPE SPHEERIS   I thought of Darby as the centerpiece. I ended up putting the Germs in the middle because that's where they were needed to keep the thing going. The night we shot the Germs' live segment my increasingly nervous investors were scared they were going to get sued because people were getting thrown around and stuff. It was in this really little sound stage, Cherrywood Studios. I was afraid they were going to pull the plug on me any minute now, but they hung in there.

It's possible that Darby got extra fucked up for the filming of the live segment, I don't really know. But there's a point where you say, "Oh, he's fucked up, isn't this interesting and entertaining," and then there's a point where it's "No, you can't even do this." Gary Hirstius is back there going, "Darby, the mic! Pick up the mic!" because he couldn't even pick up the microphone.

TONY THE HUSTLER   I said, "Why don't you ask one of your old girlfriends?" So that's when he called Michelle Baer in to "beard" for him. Michelle did the interview with Darby in the kitchen and they were supposedly roommates frying eggs up in a pan. Darby bought me that tarantula for my birthday. I was scared to death of the fucking thing and during the interview he picked it up and it was crawling up his arm. Some black and white stills of that are on the back cover of the *What We Do is Secret* record.

DEZ CADENA   My favorite Darby quote was at the fake show that got filmed for *The Decline*. They wouldn't allow any alcohol in the studio, so somebody said, "Oh, we'll go get a six-pack for the band," and then went out to get it. The Germs had already started playing, but were kind of stalling until the booze got there, and finally these people snuck in this six-pack of tall Buds. When that six-pack showed up, one kid in front, who looked like he was from Huntington Beach, was trying to do a "Darby" to Darby, going, "Give *me* a beer!" Darby drank one, threw it on the ground, picked up the second one, drank about half of it, and started passing it around to the rest of the band. The guy says, "Give me a beer!" again. So Darby says, "You want a beer?" And the guy goes, "Yeah, Darby; gimme a beer, gimme a beer!" Darby guzzles the rest, and goes, "How does it feel to *want*?"

EXENE CERVENKA   *The Decline* is a really important movie and I'm really glad that it happened because it's nice that it's documented but I think that the things that aren't in that movie are more important than the things that are. It makes me sad to think that you freeze a moment and that's the whole extent of the reality of it. And people believe that's what it was. It was always like that every day and those people behaved like that. And it was just so limited. Penelope had an idea of what she wanted to portray and she portrayed it. A lot of key bands were left out. It was just funny to us that people thought we were worth documenting.

TONY THE HUSTLER   Henley was also saying he's going to be the next Germs drummer, because Darby and Don weren't getting along.

At the *Decline* shoot, Cherrywood Studios, circa April, 1980. Photo: Tony Montesion.

Darby, dear to the skateboard/surfing crowd, shows off his board.
Photo: Gary Leonard.

Circle Jerks cover of Gerber's bogus wedding at Marina Skate Park.
Photo: Edward Colver.

THE SKATE CONNECTION

O

GERBER   The skate park wedding was in June or July 1980, right before Darby went to London.

JEFF MCDONALD   Tony Alva was the Elvis of skating—he revolutionized skating, and then he came out as this huge punk rock fan. Before that, surfers or skaters or whatever only listened to *Who's Next*, Led Zeppelin, and Nugent! Their big thing was "Baba O'Reilly" and *The Song Remains the Same*. Now skaters and people into extreme sports are all hardcore, but back then it wasn't like that.

STEVE OLSON   The Dogtown crew that Alva came up with were listening to *Toys in the Attic*, *Physical Graffiti*, *Cat Scratch Fever* and so forth before they got into punk rock. I had an older brother who was big on glam rock ... Bowie, Iggy, Mott the Hoople, T. Rex, Slade, all that shit. So I had no choice but to hear the music in the next room blasting out of his stereo and then all of a sudden he had a Pistols single and a Ramones album ... then I became professional and skateboarded in a pool riding contest at a skateboard park and they played some Ramones. It was just like this new sound.

GERBER   And the Dogtown Posse—that's Venice, California—Dogtown; they were so fuckin' rad! They had complete disregard for safety; they were hardcore, and that was a lot of my attraction to them—but the hair needed to go! It was like, "Oh, you're hardcore? Well come on, let's get hardcore, then!"

BRENDAN MULLEN   A feature article by Jeff Johnson in the July/August, 1979, issue of *Wet* Magazine reported on the proliferation of skateboard culture emerging from the street banks and backyard pools of Venice and Santa Monica. Mentioned were the Dogtown Boyz and one of their key luminaries Tony "Mad Dog" Alva ("the Ted Nugent of the skateboard generation"). Johnson described them as "a band of avant-garde" skaters. The article erroneously explained the "z" in boyz denoted an identification with the Zephyr Organization, a skateboard manufacturing company which had helped develop a school of "skating consciousness" by making skateboards from the same materials as surfboards. The new Z style was predominate, especially with the Dogtown posse, a gnarly but fun bunch of fucked-up stoner surfer kids who definitely were not your classic *GQ* blonde Adonis So Cal surfer types.

> "The Zephyr organization radically altered the art of skateboarding. Instead of maintaining the norm of flatland freestyle and slalom, the DT Boyz' [interpretation] insisted that pools and banks traversed with surfing lines and projections were the major media of expression. Their aggression, the lines they were finding,

their driving-but-liquid approach to riding solid curves established them as a pool-riding elite. They created the Dogtown consciousness. The D Boyz had charisma. They had style. They were crass. Their attitude was not at all sports manlike. They embodied pure cause without concern for consequence. Pool riding is dangerous. And the DT Boyz thrive on the danger, touching on the extremities of physical laws as a source of vitality. They are able to abandon thought to perfect spontaneity of reaction—on cement at high speed, radically going for it. They become so accustomed to risk that risk never occurs to them. They are irrational. You don't try out to make the cut with the DT crew, you simply have to belong."[16]

GERBER I convinced the owner of the Marina Skateboard Park to let me have a wedding reception there—I told him that Rob Henley and I just got married, which was, of course, a bare-assed motherfucking lie. I told every person I knew who had a band that I was having this party, and that everybody was playing; and they did! I think it was Social Distortion's first gig. Almost every punk rocker that I ever knew was there. If you weren't punk, you got charged; all the skaters got charged—a lot of them left without their hair, too! It was a big fucking thing. The Circle Jerks' *Group Sex* album cover is from that party. You know the photo with all the people standing in a big pool? Smack dab in the middle of that group of people is me, wearing this beautiful vintage mourning gown! The pigs came, but I'd already OD'd on Tuinals and can't remember if they shut it down or not.

Before I passed out Tony Alva would skate by me all the time and I had blue hair, so he'd scream, "Punk rock sucks, Nugent rules!" So we got into this big thing, and I was always telling him, "Alva sucks! You're a piece of shit, you're a fucking hippie…" He loved that. Later I saw Alva at a party and decided I was gonna fuck him. So I get in his car and we drive to Malibu under the pretense of interviewing him for *Flipside*. Yeah, right. So I fucked him senseless, and afterwards I chopped his hair off, and Krazy Kolored it. When he regained consciousness he took off surfing and left his kid brother there unsupervised and home alone … and he got the same treatment! Tony was fucking Kira for a while too—back then it was all of the really fine punk rock chicks, and he wanted some of that! I started going with Alva to skate competitions, and then I met Olson, who I went out with off and on for years. Now I had this entourage of cute skaters all around me … it was that party that changed the whole skate thing, because from that point on, all these guys started skating to punk rock in the competitions! Duane Peters did it first, and I love him for it! I thought he was the shit, because he was like taking Tuinals, all these pills… and skating to the Germs.

STEVE OLSON Gerber is tripping on her ego if she says that her wedding party— this bogus wedding to Henley at the Marina Skate Park—was where suburban teen punkers and skateboarders first hooked up. The mutual awareness thing was going on down in Long Beach as well. No one knew Gerber back then. I thought a fucking big thing, the big milestone in the skate/punk merger was at the Skateboarder Awards in '79. Tony got second and he had some funky glasses and some weird-assed clothes and he still had his long Nugent hair and he threw his trophy in

Gerber's "wedding" to Henley (back to camera). Photo courtesy Gerber.

the trash like "Fuck you, I should have won." And I got first and they were like, "Speech," and I was like "Fuck you, this is a bunch of bullshit. This is jive." And I just spit at the cameras and picked my nose and flicked boogers at them and the kids were just freaking. We were saying, "Fuck you, and your bullshit," and the skateboard industry was like, "Oh my God, these are our top dudes in the reader polls and now this is what they're saying back to us?" They were against us, we were outlaws; all of a sudden they didn't like that we were representing their wholesome little sport any more, and the next thing you know, the popularity of punk and skating was just growing huge. Maybe it all started to blow up from there, but there was a lot of punk shit going on long before Gerb's big day out at the Marina...

With Duane Peters it was all of a sudden, "Here he is now with hair that is no longer there!" He got into punk rock 100 percent ... he was a really good skateboarder ... he was the first cat to do the loop ... he still is a great skateboarder. Back when it started he had this long blond hair, he was a surfer kid, but soon he was into cutting guys' hair off in the bathroom and continuing on the movement.

GERBER You know that trick where they go around the edge of the pool? Duane would do face plants from the edge of the pool—BAM! Straight to the bottom! He would be just so fucked up—his nose was bleeding, his whole face was trashed, and he would just get back up and skate to the Germs some more! He was truly sick! He was a maniac!

This really sick freak lived close to Marina Skate Park. Robbie would skate there, and so this big perv would take pictures of all the young dudes skating the pools. And then R.A. got wind of this, and then all those sick fuck chickenhawks suddenly wanted these skater boys.

Cruising soundtrack lp, featuring the Germs song, "Lion's Share."

Still from *Cruising*. Courtesy: Lorimar Pictures.

CRUISING

O

BOB BIGGS The Germs were invited by Jack Nitzsche to record some tracks for the soundtrack of the William Friedkin film, *Cruising*.

DON BOLLES It was an ultra-noir murder mystery set in the gay hardcore S&M underground.

NICOLE PANTER I thought the *Cruising* soundtrack would be a good thing because Jack Nitzsche was producing it. Before our very first meeting with Jack even began he looked around the room and asked: "Anyone got any Percodan?" Darby said he knew then that it would be okay because this guy was a *real* drug addict. I told Darby that this guy would take him to a whole different place than where everyone else was.

DON BOLLES Jack Nitzsche was an idiot, and Darby and Pat thought he was a bit of an oaf also. He didn't understand shit about what we were doing. He didn't live in the same world that we did. Nicole told us that he was this big time producer-arranger guy who was going to take us to the next level after *G.I.*, but it was nothing. I should have known it was going to be wrong the minute he started saying the songs were too short.

NICOLE PANTER I sat Darby down and told him that this guy isn't just some hippie shithead—this guy is really down for it and he knows his shit! And he handled it all really well; [Darby] wasn't a smart-ass to Nitzsche—he treated him with respect.

DON BOLLES We were in the studio for a couple of days with him, and it sucked. It was an appalling experience. We rehearsed without Darby so he could be alone to crank some new lyrics, but Jack wanted the songs to be twice as long, so we'd do an instrumental break and then play the song again. One day we were in the control room with the great man. He was running a cassette of what was supposed to be a rough mix. The playback sounded horrible, the levels were all screwy. The faders on all channels were in a horizontal line. When I tried to talk to Mr. Nitzsche about it he was busy snorting up a monstrous line, and he just looked up at me from the mirror with this moronic expression, white powder hanging from his nose hairs, and proclaimed, "Hey, man, it's punk ... it doesn't matter, right?"

> RODNEY You're doing a movie soundtrack? Darby, you wanna tell us about that?
> DARBY (sort of off-mic) Sure, we're doing a soundtrack for this homo film, it's all about fistfucking ... where's my whistle? Hold on one minute. We're doing this homo film, and it's all about fist (whistle) ing and Crisco....
> RODNEY Is there any K-Y being used, or what?

DARBY   Just lots of Crisco. And Al Pacino. Seems that Al Pacino likes it up the (whistle)! (laughing)

RODNEY   So what's the name of the film?

DARBY   *Cruising.*

RODNEY   Cruisin' for abusin', it sounds like ...

DARBY   Oh God ...

RODNEY   So how many songs will the Germs be doing in the film?

PAT   Six. But they're not going to use them all ...

DARBY   Did you see the latest thing Jack Nitzsche did in the headlines?

RODNEY   Yeah, I read about that ...

DARBY   He put a gun up her (whistle) and threatened to blow her (whistle) out!

DON   But it's since been reduced to "aggravated assault."

RODNEY   Oh ...

DON   'Cause he didn't actually blow her (whistle) out ...

RODNEY   Phil Spector is sending out pictures of Jack, saying, "He used to work for me!" He was the original arranger for all those records, "Be My Baby" and "Da Doo Ron Ron," in fact, that Christmas album ... (From "Rodney on the ROQ," December, '79.)

BOB BIGGS   The *Cruising* soundtrack sessions were a difficult thing. I spoke with Jack Nitzsche a couple of times, and he told me that he wanted to produce these guys. Now Jack's got a different kind of production thing; he's not a "producer" producer, and I thought it would be interesting to see what he could do with the Germs. They agreed, so they went in with Nitzsche and recorded "Lion's Share," and I think four or five other songs; I don't know how they felt about it, but I felt it was generally a good thing for the maturation of the band, for the experience, if nothing else. I knew they didn't have any more material, and that Jack's demand for new material was going to stress Darby out in some ways, but I thought that that was a good thing; Darby had to go somewhere—he couldn't rest on *G.I.* forever.

PAT SMEAR   They set us up at S.I.R. where we wrote all the songs, learned them and rehearsed 'em, and then we sent Jack a tape. He sent back word that our songs were too short—they had to be twice as long! So we said, "All right," and played them all through twice instead. We'd play the whole song, then there's an instrumental break, then we played the whole song again! So he made us do that, which was dumb, and which we wouldn't have normally done—then he didn't even use any of them, except for ten seconds of one! It's always been a bit annoying to me that they all go twice—they should have been minute and a half long songs!

DON BOLLES   Darby was off somewhere coming up with lyrics for six new songs. The other ones took him how many years?

PAT SMEAR   The *Cruising* sessions were strange ... Jack Nitzsche was the first "real" producer we ever worked with; he showed up for drum sounds, then left and never came back again until it was time for vocals. It was the strangest thing. It was exciting that someone was paying for us to record. I always thought it was really dumb, though—they put us in a really expensive, fancy studio with a hot producer in order to make us sound like we were in a garage. I thought it would be all hot and good sounding, but it just wasn't.

DON BOLLES   The studio was really huge—we set up in one tiny corner of a room the size of an airplane hangar, and from where we were, the curvature of the earth made it tough to see the control room.

NICOLE PANTER   The sessions took a few days, and those tapes were so good! Gold Star was this amazing studio, there were movie people coming in and out—William Friedkin came in when we were recording, and sort of bounced around; he was really funny. Darby was under a lot of stress then—I was terrified that he was going to get so fucked up he wouldn't be able to sing. But Darby handled it gracefully, even though at the point of the *Cruising* sessions I think he was already on that path of getting deeper and deeper into drugs. He took anything that anybody handed him.

DONNIE ROSE   During the *Cruising* recording sessions, Darby was constantly trying to get loaded, but he was having problems, although the singing was better because he wasn't that fucked up. My theory is that the stress involved in having to come up with the lyrics to five new songs on the spot sent him over the edge … that was the beginning of the end of his final spiral…

JACK NITZSCHE   [To a friend after the first session with the Germs] I have never in my life met people like these.

TONY MONTESION   Darby told me that William Friedkin, the director of *Cruising*, offered to set him up with a penthouse in New York City, pay for everything … so he wouldn't have to worry about anything, just write; but Darby didn't go for it. Friedkin saw that this boy could write a lyric, could write poetry.

REGI MENTLE   *Cruising* was the feel-good movie of the year. Darby took me and Donnie to see it on Hollywood Boulevard. It was Fag City protest out front. We walked up to a guy with a picket sign and Darby asked him what was going on. He said, "We're protesting because this movie promotes violence against gays!" We all started laughing and Darby goes, "Well, can we go in and see it 'cause we're, like, on the soundtrack?" and the guy said, "Well, okay, but once you've seen it, you have to tell everyone else not to," and he gave Darby a badge that said, "*Cruising*: Don't See It" and he pinned it to his coat.

GERBER   Darby got pissed off 'cause they only used one ["Lion's Share"] of the five tracks that were supposed to be in the film, but not the one he most wanted.

Jenny Lens: A couple months before Darby killed himself, Malissa said to me, "here, have a look," and she pulled open the bandage on Darby's throat. I was told it was an accident, but come on, how can that be? I don't believe it for a second." Photo: Jenny Lens.

BIRTH OF THE SLAM PIT

O

BLACK RANDY There were all sorts of weird episodes going on around town with off-duty Marines, meth-crazed jocks, and other extremely weird and sick people showing up at punk concerts...

EXENE CERVENKA A lot of kids believed the media accounts of spitting and fighting and that punk was really mean and they kind of got the wrong message. For me the punk ideal was about creating a new art and culture; replacing something shitty with something great, and having a community, which none of us had had because nearly everybody was from bad families. The local punk community was like the first family that some people had ever had, but now it was becoming a dumbed-down mob mentality where we couldn't even play a show because the new kids from the beaches wouldn't let us finish because they hated us so much. Those kids ruined the scene, but we were going away anyway.

MIKE PATTON The Huntington Beach scene killed off the original open interpretation of punk concept ... no rules, no dogma, no stereotyping, no stars, anybody just do it. The original DIY ideology, as we saw it, was that punk was this grassroots thing which could be about anything any individual wanted it to be. All of a sudden once "hardcore" kicked in there were very strict ways of dressing and weird codes of social behavior. When the new kids came to our shows to see what was going on ... we projected a loud aggressive image ... but some of these big surfer dorks took it literally and ran with it ... and the original punk rockers couldn't deal with it, 'cause they weren't fight-back guys.

SHAWN STERN The Olympic Auditorium in the early '80s was the pinnacle for slam-dancing but the Fleetwood was definitely where it started during 1980 ... the Starwood was a place where the old and the new were sort of meeting, that and the Masque four-wall shows put on by Brendan, like at Baces Hall, the Stardust Ballroom, the Polish Auditorium, and Myron's Ballroom.

TONY MONTESION We drove Darby and Amber to Germs gigs at the Fleetwood Club in Redondo. Darby didn't really want to hang with the band any more, he wanted to travel by himself. He had grand illusions. Before one of the Fleetwood shows, he started going off on this one picture on the wall. "Gimme that picture!" Finally, I tore it down and handed it to him.

MIKE WATT Darby had nothing against the South Bay or OC [Orange County], the Germs would play the Fleetwood and stuff ... I think Darby was really influential, but they couldn't handle him as an individual. He was too scary, he wasn't *de rigueur* enough ... "you spit like a pussy" and stuff ... in a weird way they did look up to him as a guy who fuckin' dared cause their thing was so safe, you know?

MIKE PATTON   We [Middle Class] played with the Germs at the Fleetwood. I remember several nights with SWAT teams and helicopters … people running … one night these riot cops showed up and we were outside and the punks were on one side of the street, the cops were on the other, and then somebody threw a bottle at the cops and they charged at us head-on.

X8   Punk started turning really creepy at the Fleetwood … sitting upstairs and seeing guys approach each other and slug each other right in the face; it was too far of a drive to see people fight so I just said fuck it.

BRENDAN MULLEN   Kickboy reported in *Slash* about rows of girls sitting in formation on the edge of the stage with their backs to the performers throughout the show and commented on "hostility between sub-groups … with roving packs of aggro-seeking toughies and girls and boys in separate bunches puking on alcohol." He concluded there were "as many differences as similarities" between the Fleetwood punk scene and the "older, now totally diffuse L.A. one."

MIKE ATTA   I remember playing with the Germs at the Fleetwood and the crowd would have their backs to the bands, and as soon as the band started playing, they would start beating the crap out of each other.

JENNY LENS   At the Fleetwood there'd be these redneck surfer punks and I didn't want any part of that. It was a bunch of slobbering idiots. I hated them cause they hated me, they don't like Jews, they don't like women, they don't like smart women, I happen to be on the fat side, and they especially don't like fat, smart, Jewish women … and then the idea of driving somewhere and having to drive back to Hollywood … please!

BRENDAN MULLEN   The famous *L.A. Times* piece by Patrick Goldstein in June 1980, "Violence Sneaks into the Punk Scene," introduces "slamming" and "slamdancing" into punk vernacular, phrases that Goldstein said later that he picked up from kids at the Fleetwood.
      "Punks don't just dance anymore," Goldstein wrote, "They mug each other. It's part of a new 'dance' craze called the Slam, whose popularity, especially with organized gangs of punk youths, has led to numerous incidents of violence at many area clubs. The accounts of senseless violence, vandalism and even mutilation at some area rock clubs read like reports from a war zone."

JACK GRISHAM   Our first gig [as Vicious Circle] was at the Fleetwood with the Germs and Middle Class, that's a fuckin' good first show. Our band was basically all about a bunch of fucked guys fightin' back … there were a lot of punkers hanging around the South Bay, a bunch of 'em hung around the Black Flag guys, but it wasn't as violent. We were the first to say "Yeah, go on, laugh at my hair and I'll fuckin' stab ya." That kind of "bring it on" thing. We basically beat up on hippies. Maybe the longhairs started it, but the guys I hung out with were fucked to begin with anyway. There weren't very many times when I was a victim ... it was more of the opposite way around. If somebody would drive by and yell, "Hey, fuckin' Devo," we'd chase 'em down and nail 'em. Vicious Circle was more like a gang than a band. There was no thought to the name Vicious Circle ... there was no thought to anything we did. We were So Cal droogs who'd go around stealing cars, torturing people, ripping people off.

DONNIE ROSE The Fleetwood was a nightmare—the worst! God, these fucking assholes were abundant—so much violence and attitude. Darby couldn't sing worth shit—he was so fucked up, he couldn't even function! Everybody in the band was pissed off ... it was awful!

JACK GRISHAM This therapist finally said I was fucked, I was a sociopath, and told me, "You don't know right from wrong." Fuck, man, it was true, and—even worse—it wasn't like we had any cool political cause to justify it. It was just bare-assed FSU ... "fuck stuff up." Our motto was "rape, pillage and destroy." We'd drive around at night and shoot the windows out of banks ... stuff like that. We had records for car thievin' ... burglary, robbery. We were fuckholes who were not gonna make it any other way, whether it was gonna be punk rock or heavy metal, or ska or rockabilly, or whatever ... we were fucked in the head anyway, it just happened we found punk first. We'd been getting our asses kicked by parents, by the schools, and by the police, and now it was like, "Fuck you, we're monsters now, and you're gonna pay for it!" I was 18 years old, six foot three, and two hundred pounds, skinheaded and pissed-off.

DON BOLLES Darby did not like where all the violence was going with the hardcore kids at all. We had no idea about where it was all going until we found ourselves playing at the Fleetwood looking at all these football jocks drooling over each other. They were aware that the Germs were thought to be cool, but they didn't know why. It was like being at some Nuremburg Rally. The crowd was like a blender at the Fleetwood when we played. It was stupid chaos, as opposed to the "dementia of a higher order" concept of chaos that Darby envisioned.

JACK GRISHAM When Vicious Circle became TSOL we got loyalty from people because we were loyal to them. The crowds turned into these big masses of people willing to do whatever we said. Cops would show up and we'd just say fuck you. One time they showed up and I got everyone to lay down on the ground. I'd learned shit from my sister and she'd tell me stuff to do ... like, lay down, stand in the center of the crowd and throw bottles. So I get on the mic to, like a thousand kids, and I said, "Just lay down, lay down on the fuckin' floor, there's nothing they can do to us."

So the cops come bustin' in, and here's a thousand punkers sitting on the floor. They were dragging 'em out one by one, so I said, "Fuck you, there's more of us than there is of you." I said, "Let's get 'em," and you had this raging full-on riot with kids attacking cops. I'm not anti-police ... but when they abuse it, they need to be abused back, like a balance in nature.

MIKE WATT   The Fleetwood crowd were young and they had a lot of testo ... I could see how people would have a problem with them, plus they drove all the chicks away ... looking at the OC scene, they did get socialized ... it was more like high school...

BRENDAN MULLEN   Female attendance plummeted.

ELLA BLACK   The HB's were in full force; they would just like pick on people and beat them up. I got beat up once when the Mau Maus and the Satin Tones were playing at the Fleetwood in Redondo, because I supposedly put a cigarette out in this guy's eye. First of all I've never smoked, and if I was the kind of person who would put a cigarette out in somebody's eye, would I choose some jock that's six-foot tall? What really happened is that they were throwing cigarettes at the Satin Tones and probably one hit this guy, and he decided it was me, so I got beaten up. I was so wary every time I went out anywhere after that.

MIKE NESS   As for Orange County being blamed for all the violence, that ain't right at all. You had guys from South Bay, all over the Valley, by the mid '80s, there became cliques, gangs, and that tears down that Orange County myth: the Northside and the Firm and the Lads ... there was maybe one or two whiteboy gangs in Orange County. That shoots that conception out of the sky. The media blew that up and it kind of like stereotyped us so we'd get those kind of people coming to our shows thinking we were about 'just fuck everything and everyone up' and that violence is cool.

REGI MENTLE   Johnny and I rode down to the Fleetwood with Donnie, Pat, and Jena. It was a long ride, so we smoked dope and told stories. Donnie had us busting up with stories of him fucking [one of the Go-Go's] in the ass and having her bark like a dog and pee down her leg. And this Donnie kid's got, like, major 14-inch Nicky Beat meat! He says the first time was in a practice room at the Masque, and she got shit on his dick, so he rubbed it off in her hair. Jena blew beer out her nose and almost threw up all over John, she was laughing so hard. Pat was going, "Bark! Bark! Bark!"

BILL BARTELL   The last club show the Germs played before they broke up was at the largest venue they had ever headlined—the Fleetwood. That night, Ron Reyes from Black Flag got in a fight with the bouncers, and the whole crowd turned against the security; the bouncers took off running, with hundreds of punk rockers chasing them out the doors, and into the streets! Just then a couple of carloads of drunk hesher types were driving by the club—and they started yelling "Punk Rock—Devo" stuff at the kids. The car in front stopped, but these long-haired dipshits were too busy yelling stuff to notice, and they smashed right into it! By this time masses of punks had hit the street, which caused more cars to smash into each other. Punkers surrounded the cars, jumping up and down on them, stage-diving off the roofs, and generally wreaking havoc! And through it all, the Germs kept playing!

Don Bolles. Photo: Tony Montesion.

PAUL ROESSLER   I think the sound of hardcore punk rock, the speed of it, the guitar style, even the riffs that were used—was absolutely from the Germs. You could say the Ramones, but I don't think the Ramones really captured the same thing. With the *G.I.* album the Germs defined the early hardcore style. Don and Pat totally defined a sound that was so copied it became a generic form that they were the absolute progenitors of.

RIK L. RIK   ... that hardcore edge came from Don ...

PAUL ROESSLER   Nobody played that type of beat before the Germs. You can play downstrokes fast, but most guitar players have the "up-and-down" sound. Pat started those downstrokes; and then he and Don would speed it up together. Before the Germs "punk rock" bands like the Sex Pistols and Ramones were slow by comparison. Punk rock wasn't all about that beat and that guitar style— but hardcore was. Where punk rock was all about a serious cultural frame of reference for some, hardcore thrash was just about the drum beat. Unfortunately, it became about violence, too.

JEFF MCDONALD   The Germs were playful, fun, *and* nihilistic—you can't say the music was "hardcore" exactly as it came to be defined later on; but it wasn't like Sonic Youth art-rock, either. The Germs' shtick was crazed half-step rock with, like, poetry, and bizarre glitter overtones, with Bowie and the image-conscious-ness thing. They dared to present themselves as above their audience, which was really cool to do at a time when everybody was being so pretentious about the "no rock stars" thing. Darby's persona was a post-Iggy Pop "Open Up and Bleed" concept—kind of like a rock Sylvia Plath or something.

215

BOLLES GETS BOOTED

O

NICOLE PANTER   Don was pretty much the odd man out in the Germs.

AMBER   Darby never really felt comfortable with Don the way he did with Pat and Lorna.

JENA CARDWELL   He was very image-conscious; that's why the idea of Don prancing around in a dress was more than he could take.

NICOLE PANTER   Don Bolles wore dresses and make-up. And Darby was mortified: He'd get on Don's case, "People are gonna make fun of us if they see you like that." Darby was not an ironist; he was too deep in his own shit to see irony.

PAT SMEAR   The fact that Don wore a dress was like, whatever, that wasn't it, I don't think—it was that he was in this fucking joke band! I mean, you're in the most serious band in town—how can you be in a fucking joke band?

DON BOLLES   I liked having long hair when everyone else had a spiky punk rock do, but Darby ordered me to cut it, insisting it was necessary for the Germs "image" or whatever. I did once, but felt like a dope, and when it grew back, it stayed. Darby stopped really caring about my hair so much after a while, but the new just-cut-their-hair-off-last-week punks from the 'burbs really hated it.

TONY THE HUSTLER   But Don and Darby had a lot of other conflicts...

JENA CARDWELL   Darby was not happy. He thought Don just wasn't really falling in with the troops, nor was he giving off the right image to be in the Germs. Things like showing up like an hour late for a huge show at the Whisky, holding up the whole show, while they're onstage ready to play—that sort of thing really didn't help. But the dress incident was a real turning point...

NICOLE PANTER   I would try to get to the club guy before Don Bolles did because Don would always try to get the money and take it all for himself.

TONY THE HUSTLER   Don used to antagonize Darby with gay leather terms, like hanky color codes. He'd say, "Hey Darby, why aren't you wearing the brown hanky?" and all this kind of crap. Darby being gay was never really openly talked about. Not even the immediate Germs family would talk about it, let alone the groupies and fans outside the Circle One. Don used to kind of poke fun about him and me living together. He'd go, "You two guys are a perfect couple—leather homos," and, "Which one of you wears the brown hanky in the left pocket?" and

---

Don Bolles playing with Vox Pop, dress included. Photo courtesy of Don Bolles.

all this crap. I thought it was funny, but it kind of got to Darby a little bit. It just drove him nuts.

AMBER When the Germs were on the "Rodney On the ROQ" show, Don was very cocky and egotistical about the band; he spoke out of line in terms of things that were not gelled or ready for announcing. Don was always sarcastic— and he was bold.

> RODNEY So Don, you've been in a lot of groups before joining the Germs, right? You were in the Yvonnes and ...
> DON Funny you would ask me that, Rodney ...
> RODNEY Weren't you in a group with one of the Human Hands at one point, too?
> DON No!
> RODNEY I thought you were one of the Human Hands?
> DARBY He's been with both of them!
> DON I was in the Yvonnes with Rob from the Bags ...
> RODNEY And did you do anything with Nervous Gender?
> DON Lots of things...
> RODNEY And what about Vox Pop?
> DON That's the present erstwhile project...
> RODNEY Who's all working on that now?
> DON It's just me and Michael from Nervous Gender, and Paul Cutler who is the ex-guitarist of the Consumers...
> DARBY (pulls chair out from under Don) I just wanted another chair—
> (From "Rodney on the ROQ," December, '79.)

DON BOLLES Darby said he felt betrayed by me being in a joke band—Vox Pop— when he was so serious about what he was doing. We weren't enemies but sometimes he'd say, "I hate that guy," but it seemed like he at least respected me unless he was with his lair of sycophants. So me getting bounced from the band came as a complete shock.

JEFF MCDONALD I thought Vox Pop was fantastic! They weren't a "joke" to me— at the time, they were one of the only decent bands in town. I saw some incredible Vox Pop shows—twice when I saw them, Paul Cutler was nude. It was total rock and roll!

DON BOLLES It wasn't over the music or my playing, it was about power. It was like because I didn't go through some of the same experiences that he had, how dare I think I was a part of anything? I was always the new guy, I was still an outsider two years later.

Rob Henley, the would-be Germs drummer. Photo: Rooh Steif.

TONY THE HUSTLER   I said to Darby, "You can't replace Don with Rob Henley. He doesn't even know how to play the fucking drums."

PAT SMEAR   Don Bolles was the perfect drummer for us. With everyone else, even Nicky, who was a great drummer, it felt weird, because of the songs, but with Don it felt normal, right, because—well, because it was Don.

DON BOLLES   Darby had Bill Bartell tell me I was out because he couldn't bring himself to tell me himself.

BILL BARTELL   Don went to Darby's house and wrote, "Fuck you Asshole," or something equally intelligent on the door.

FIRST OF THE MOHICANS

O

AMBER   Sometime during May-June, 1980, Darby and I went to London, and the Germs broke up.

NICOLE PANTER   Darby went to London after he announced, "Rob's in, Don's out."

PAT SMEAR   Darby was adamant he wanted Robbie in the band, and when he went to England, he called me up and said "Don's out, Rob Henley's in." It wasn't really Don, or anything he did; it was Robbie. Darby thought, "Well, I can't get rid of Pat, or Lorna ... so Robbie's gonna play drums!" Rob said he could play, and Amber had bought him a full kit. He set up in my garage; but me and Lorna just weren't into it, didn't want to do it, but ... Darby has said the word. So we go there, we play with him—and he can't play at all—at all, at all, at all! Which was a slight problem after Don.

BOB BIGGS   It seemed to me that there was some tension within the band, particularly from Lorna, whether she wanted to continue, or if she had the ability to continue on to the next thing.

NICOLE PANTER   Lorna quit shortly after I did. She was so fed up.

PAT SMEAR   We were just not into teaching someone how to play—that was how the band started, everyone teaching each other how to play, but our attitude was, we're way beyond this, after all this time, we're not getting some guy who doesn't know how to play! I don't remember what the argument Darby and I had was—it was probably, "He can't play!" "Yes he can!" But Lorna quit anyway, and so the band was over.

> RODNEY BINGENHEIMER   So why did you dismantle the Germs?
> DARBY   Because Lorna wanted to travel.
> RODNEY   You couldn't travel with the orig... the regular Germs?
> DARBY   The Germs couldn't travel anywhere, no! (girl's laughter in background) Lorna wanted to travel, so she's in Long Island now.
> RODNEY   So you just, like, split the band up?
> DARBY   No, we didn't, Lorna did—not really, it just fell apart.
> (From "Rodney on the ROQ," December, '80.)

AMBER   We went halfway across the world to get to London, and when we get there it turned out the bands playing were all from L.A.! X, the Go-Go's, Joan Jett—we would go out every night to see our friends play, and get fucked up. We stayed with my friend Jordan, who lived in a little shithole town called Seaford, way outside of London.

"It's not a Mohawk, it's a Mohican!" Photo: Robert Hill.

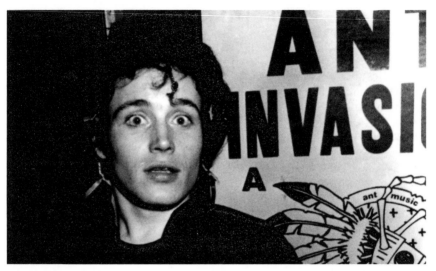

Adam Ant in L.A. a few months after Darby's death. Photo: Gary Leonard.

GERBER Jordan [AKA Pamela Rooke] was some fuckin' stylist-designer chick who worked for Malcolm McLaren and Vivienne Westwood.

BRENDAN MULLEN Jordan remains largely uncredited as one of the major people in the Britpunk fashion look … especially the militaristic dress and the extreme artificial make-up and messed-up hair … McLaren and Westwood fed off her charisma and following, and began to mass-produce her fashion ideas and flogged them out of the SEX boutique where she worked as a shop assistant … the same place where the Pistols got half of their name from … the over-bally-hooed Richard Hell contribution was a safety pin and a torn shirt, but there was so much more to this look than that…

AMBER We had fun, even though Darby didn't like anything in England. He didn't seem depressed, but he was so used to walking into a record store here, and everyone going "OOOOH, Darby Crash, Darby Crash." But nobody in England knew who he was; even worse, nobody cared. I knew people, but for him it was like, "Oh, you're Amber's little punk friend from L.A."

JOAN JETT I was in London with my new band, the Blackhearts, opening for Motorhead. Darby scaled this huge fence, and got up on the 12-foot-high stage; he used to get kind of crazy a lot, and I guess he just wanted to, you know, jump around on the stage or something. Well, the security guys and some of the guys from Motorhead grabbed him, and were going to beat the shit out of him; I had to stop and tell them, "No, you can't do that, that's my friend!" They just wanted to pummel this guy, 'cause they thought he was harassing me.

RODNEY BINGENHEIMER   Darby?

DARBY   Hi!

RODNEY   Can you hear me?

DARBY   Yeah, I can hear you fine.

RODNEY   Hey, can you talk up a little louder?

DARBY   Yeah…

RODNEY   What are you doing over there?

DARBY   Well, it's like six o'clock in the morning right now…

RODNEY   Wow… Have you seen any shows?

DARBY   Yeah, I saw the Go-Go's the other night, I seen the Blackhearts, I went and saw the Bodysnatchers, and um … I think I'm goin' somewhere tonight…

RODNEY   Mmm hmm well … how's the scene? Is it true what everyone says, that punk has died, or what?

DARBY   No way! There's no mods, and there's more punks here than there ever were!

RODNEY   Really? What punk bands are happening? Like UK Subs, Angelic Upstarts, or what?

DARBY   Yeah—UK Subs, and mostly it's Adam and the Ants—everybody's into the Ants!

RODNEY: Really?

DARBY   Yeah.

RODNEY   We'll have to play some…

DARBY   Yeah … like, um, he's staying where I'm staying too, and he'll be here in a little while—and then, um, we're having dinner and stuff. He's on tour right now. I'm seeing him on the 8th.

RODNEY   Hmm—you know X are coming to London next week, next couple of weeks; how do you think they'll do over there?

DARBY   They'll probably do pretty good; they've heard 'em over here. Their album's already over here, I think.

RODNEY   How's your record? Is your record out over there?

DARBY   Yeah. People don't like it, they say it's too fast. It's real weird over here, though—L.A.'s a lot better.

RODNEY   Yeah, everything's real expensive and backwards over there, right?

DARBY   Oh, yeah—like I'm broke!

RODNEY   (giggling) Oh no! They don't have panhandling in London yet, do they?

DARBY   Aww, a little bit, not much; just the old people.

RODNEY   Oh no! Are you guys playing, or what?

DARBY   No, I'm just over here screwing around.

RODNEY   Well you should maybe do a jam or something; get on stage, and…

DARBY   I went onstage with Joan, and her manager got really, really pissed, and they threw me off and stuff, and they didn't understand it at all, and the band tried to explain, "Well, people do this all the time in L.A." But, no, they freaked; they didn't know what was happening.

RODNEY   Really? Who was her manager? She has a new manager?

DARBY   It's just her road manager—some American guy that works with Ted Nugent and stuff like that.

RODNEY   Oh no—that's bizarre! So when are you coming back to L.A.?

DARBY   Um, probably next week—it depends on how long I can last with the money I've got.

RODNEY   Mm hmm, hmmm—so—where are you staying?

DARBY   At Jordan's house.

RODNEY   Mmm ... aaaah ... so, um ... do you want to give out your phone number or address? Maybe people can send money...

DARBY   Anybody that wants to get in touch with me can get in touch with me like through Michelle Baer. Like if Rob needs to get in touch with me, or Iguana, or Bobby, if he could get in touch with me before he goes to jail...

RODNEY   What—Bobby's gonna go to jail?

DARBY   That's what I heard.

RODNEY   For what?

DARBY   Uhh I don't know. He's in some kind of trouble.

RODNEY   Oh no—so if they see these people, maybe they can give them some money and they can send it over to you.

DARBY   Yeah; it'd be great. Hi to Malissa, Pat and everybody.

RODNEY   Yeah! So the Go-Go's are doing really big over there, right?

DARBY   Um, not really—I was at the show the other night when they were opening for the Bodysnatchers, and there weren't that many people.

RODNEY   Mm hmm.

DARBY   The only people that go see them are skinheads, and the skinheads over here are really stupid.

RODNEY   Yeah? What do they do?

DARBY   Nothing!

RODNEY   Oh no! (laughs) Well ... it sounds like fun over there!

DARBY   It's all right, but it's like this punk is dead, and there aren't mods anywhere—you've gotta look all day to find one mod.

RODNEY   Mm hmm. Well everyone's been telling me, like, it's out, and Ska and Mod and everything...

DARBY   No. Not true!

RODNEY   Hmmm. Okay—anything else you wanna say to everybody out here in L.A.?

DARBY   No—just hello!

RODNEY   All right...

DARBY   All right. I'll get going. I'll see you when I get home, or something...

RODNEY   Okay. We're gonna go into "Circle One."

DARBY   Okay.

RODNEY   Okay—take care!

DARBY   All right. Bye.

RODNEY   Bye.

(From "Rodney on the ROQ," June, '80.)

AMBER Darby wasn't used to hanging out and being just another person. He would actually carry Germs albums under his arm! He went to Boy and gave them one, 'cause he liked the clothes—they were punk clothes, but the tailoring was exquisite! We went to some Sham 69 recording, and then we went on to see Adam Ant play. We'd sit and listen to Lou Reed's *Berlin* album and *Stranded* by Roxy Music. We'd listen to these sad, depressing albums. Darby asked Jordan for the Mohawk, and Jordan gave it to him. But, contrary to popular belief, there was no big makeover.

CLAUDE BESSY He was cool when he went to England, but when he came back he looked like a fucking idiot—he had a fucking Mohawk. I said, "Darby! You look like an asshole, man! Just because they are doing it in England, it doesn't mean it suits you. I mean, here you are, you just look like an asshole."

DON GARSTANG Adam and the Ants made a big impression on him. And you had to be very careful not to call Darby's hairstyle a "Mohawk"—it was a "Mohican." Darby was really particular about that—he gave me shit about it more than once.

SHAWN STERN With a Mohawk, Darby was now Mr. Adam and the Ants. He was telling everyone, "They're gonna be the next big thing." The record hadn't come out over here. We didn't know who Adam Ant was. Darby put the record on and it was kind of catchy but when we saw the whole get up it was kinda like, "Fuck, man ... this is pretty lame." But Darby was real into it.

DAVID BROWN One day Darby walked into the rehearsal studio on Selma where the Metro Squad was practicing, wearing the Mohawk and sort of a Clash-y looking outfit, with a big iron cross around his neck and these things dangling from his waist—really gay things. He'd just come back from London. We stopped playing and gave him a big, loud ovation, because we thought his new look was just so dazzling! It was a high, high, hairdo—a combination of a Mohawk and a brightly-colored pony-mane.

RODNEY BINGENHEIMER So how long were you in England for?
DARBY CRASH I went for ten days, I was there about five weeks ... or a couple of months or something.
RODNEY What's the scene like over there now?
DARBY It's great! They say punk rock's dead, but it's bigger than ever. The only band I saw that was really good was the Ants.
RODNEY Remember you said it was like people with Mohawks...
DARBY Mohicans! Not Mohawks.
RODNEY Mohicans? Did you start that? You were the first to have it here in L.A., right? You gonna be wearing that this week, or something different?
DARBY Yeah—I'll probably do that for a while.
(From "Rodney on the ROQ," June, '80.)

Darby and Amber. Photo: Ave Pildas, courtesy of Amber's collection.

"I COULD FEEL IT THROUGH HIS JEANS"

O

PENELOPE SPHEERIS   The trend of the movement was extremely anti-homosexual, so how could a guy like him cop to being gay? That may be one of the prime reasons he killed himself—but not on a conscious level.

AMBER   Darby was very confused about his identity. We used to shop at this shoe store and there was the nicest guy who worked there—he had pictures of his kids and stuff. Darby confessed to me one day that he envied this shoe salesman because of the simplicity of his life. He knew where he was going every day, and at the end of the day he could go home, eat dinner, and play with his kids. Darby's dreams of normalcy were like me wanting to be a mermaid! They just weren't gonna happen. I mean, we talked about having a baby—some of it was joking, but some of it was serious. I don't think Darby had ever been loved unconditionally, and I did love him unconditionally, and still do. I didn't judge him, I didn't tell him what I thought was wrong and right. I loved him when he fell on the ground and I loved him when he stood up straight. I didn't care if he was fucking frogs or whatever.

GERBER   As far as Amber's claim that Darby fucked her, he may have, for the amount of money she was kicking him for dope. For Godsakes, I would've—you would've, we all would've. If I'm sick and she's buying, I would've given her head, given her husband head, I would've given the dog head, for that matter. She bought Robbie those drums that got stolen out of my garage. I had to hear him trying to play drums, in my garage—it was a nightmare! I was always yelling at him to stop it.

AMBER   We started kissing. He got erect, I could feel it through his jeans—he had a full erection and he was getting real passionate—and then, again, he pulled away! I said, "If you go wash your hands and face, you're never going to kiss me again; we're going to be friends." He looked at me, and I said, "What is wrong? I don't know what you want, I don't understand. Your body's telling me one thing and your actions tell me another—I'm totally confused. We've always been honest, so just be blunt with me, you know, if you're not attracted to me, or..." It had never occurred to me that he was a virgin to women. I thought he had been with Hellin! He liked Hellin, he talked nicely about her, except he said she snored. I asked him, "Do you want to stay that way?" and he said, "No." I said, "So?" He looked at me, and said, "You understand," and I told him yes, I understood. He said okay, took my hand, and led me into the bedroom. I had never been so frightened in my whole fucking life. I was shaking, I was so scared. I was terrified! You don't understand, I'm used to guys you kiss, you get a hard-on, you make love! We had different types of sex, and on two occasions we had full intercourse with penile-vaginal penetration and ejaculation. I didn't have an orgasm, but he was functioning just fine. But it scared him. We used to wrestle and make out and stuff.

But when he'd get like an erection he'd freak out—he'd go wash his hands and face! I'm not used to guys who get an erection and then go wash their hands and face. I finally asked him, "Do you not like me, or what's going on?" He said, "It's not you. It's not about you. I don't want to talk about it, I don't want to talk about it."

HELLIN KILLER   Amber claimed, "Yeah, we have sex all the time." And I'd look at her and go, "whatever." It was very degrading and he was so fucked up at that point, like he didn't care and he was desperately trying to grasp onto some of the people that he'd been close to before.

DAVID BROWN   Little punk trashettes were always talking about Darby's dick. To them Darby walking all over them in his boots in their living room was probably "having sex" with him. And I remember hearing it from guys, too. He was available. That's always good, if you're planning on doing a James Dean thing.

The Starwood displays its respect for the Darby Crash Band on its marquee. Photo: Tony Montesion.

THE DARBY CRASH BAND

O

BRUCE KALBERG There was this place called "Flippers Roller Boogie Palace" and one night Prince was playing there. He hadn't quite broken into the big time yet. I think this was probably his first show in L.A. When I arrived I remember seeing these two huge bouncers roughing up Darby and Pat on the street. Two of 'em had Darby up against this telephone pole and they were punching him in the face over and over. As I went stumbling by, Darby kept saying, "Fuck you, man! You can't hurt me. Fuck you, assholes."

DON BOLLES I went to Flippers Roller Boogie Palace where the Germs were supposed to make their debut [May 11, 1980] with Robbie drumming to see what, if anything, was going to occur. Whatever bad feelings I had about being terminated had given way to an intense, morbid curiosity—what the hell were they going to do? Whatever happened, it was going to be pretty weird, and, of course, there was a good chance I would get a bonus gloat or two in the bargain. Predictably, they never even showed up, and I just ended up hanging out in this huge line outside, fielding questions about my ouster as best as I could. Malissa was passing out buttons emblazoned with "Don Forever—Henley Never." To disagree with Darby about anything but the most peripheral trivia was not something normally included in the agenda of Circle One.

DON GARSTANG I saw Lorna at the Starwood after the Rob Henley debacle and I gave her my number and said, "Hey, I'm interested in playing drums with the Germs—if there's a possibility, let me know." I saw her several times after that, and every time she would see me and smile, and before I could even say anything she'd say, "Be patient, hang in there; it'll all work out—they'll call you."

BRENDAN MULLEN Darby returned to L.A. after hanging out in London, and was immediately pressured into forming the Darby Crash Band. After auditioning umpteen potential guitarists Darby panicked and called Pat in at the last minute to bail him out until he could find somebody permanent.

HELLIN KILLER The Darby Crash Band was just kind of sad.

DON GARSTANG When eventually Darby or Amber did call it wasn't to play in the Germs, it was the Darby Crash Band, but we had a hard time putting it together—it was a mess. They had me and Chris Trent on bass. We went through a number of guitarists, but nobody was working out. One guitarist said, "Well, we could just jam, if you don't wanna play the songs," and Darby said, "Don't ever use that word in my presence!" That was it for him. Then the guy from Kommunity FK, Patrick Mata, came, and they decided that he was going to be the guitar player. That was the line-up, and we rehearsed a long time, but it just didn't sound right enough, so they were just going to start over and look for someone else so I suggested, "Hey, why don't you get Pat?" It just seemed so obvious! With Pat it sounded "right" right away. I was real excited, 'cause I thought that was going to be the perfect line-up. But then a week after we got Pat they told me, "The good news is Pat's gonna do it—but Chris is out of the band; we got Bosco on bass." Bosco was good, but Chris and I had already bonded, and were looking forward to it. They wanted it to be something different than the Germs, something which would distinguish Darby as the leader, a solo thing. Amber had this idea that everybody in the band would dress all in black to spotlight Darby with his feathers and the "Mohican," as the undisputed centerpiece. They seemed pretty concerned with having everybody in the background.

BOB BIGGS When Darby started the Darby Crash Band, I knew that the Germs were over—the sanctity of the band had been broken.

PAT SMEAR Then he started the Darby Crash Band, but just never could get his shit together, because he was really too into heroin at that point.

AMBER When the Darby Crash Band got started nobody would touch him, not the Starwood, not the Whisky, not anybody, and I couldn't put on gigs myself. Besides working part-time in a law firm, I was a nanny, and so Darby and I would wheel this baby all over Hollywood. One day I said to David Forrest, who booked the Starwood, "I just need an hour of your time." He said fine, so I put Darby in jeans and a T-shirt and Darby, the baby and I went to David's office. I told Darby, "If he asks if you want something to drink you can have iced tea or Coca-Cola; just smile and fit in with the woodwork—and hang onto that baby." I asked David point-blank why he wouldn't have Darby in his club, and he gave this litany of how he just does horrible things, and bad things just seem to happen when he's around. I asked him if he knew what Darby looked like, and he replied that he wore a leather jacket. I said, "Why don't you just meet with Darby, to see what kind of person he is?" He replied, "You want me to be in the same room?" as if I wanted to put him in a room with a lion, and I said, "Well, you've been sitting in this room with him for the last hour!" He was incredulous! I had introduced Darby as Paul, so he said, "That's Darby Crash? Holding the baby?!" Darby was still on the floor playing with the baby, and I replied, "Yes, that's Darby Crash, that's the man I live with, that's the man I take to my parents' house…"

BRENDAN MULLEN The reception for the Darby Crash Band was not so hot. Worse than flat-out bombing, the audience was indifferent. They wanted the Germs and to see onstage self-mutilation. They were also alienated and confused by the new image, the new get-up. Even worse: one of the opening bands did a song putting him down as a has-been. He was now 21 years old.

Pat and Darb. Backstage at the Starwood before the debut of the short-lived D. C. Band.
Photo: Edward Colver.

SKINHEAD MANOR

O

MARK STERN We had this big house in Hollywood, nicknamed Skinhead Manor, and that became the focal point for meeting people. We moved in during the fall of '79 … we were just sort of hanging out listening to music, and we had a rehearsal studio, a Coke machine filled with beer, we were gonna do a lot of things. We were gonna have a pirate radio station and a recording studio. By 1980, kids would drive in from Oxnard—from Ventura, San Diego, Orange, Riverside counties—for the Tuesday punk night at the Starwood and they'd hang out with us before the gig…

SHAWN STERN For us to get involved in the Hollywood scene was weird. My brother Mark and I went to high school in Beverly Hills where we were the big drug dealers; that's how we got started in business. We would sell drugs and kids would want to hang out with us. We sold everything except heroin … we never sold smack. My brother Mark and I were teens among guys like Gorilla Rose and all the Screamers people and the people at *Slash* who were already in their late 20s and early 30s.

ELLA BLACK Skinhead Manor was weird. My roommates changed every month, and there was a pattern; every other month it was great, and then it was hellish for a month. There were always parties going on. I found out later that Shawn Stern was in a court case with the landlord; he hadn't paid rent in ages, and he was collecting rents from everybody. I came home once and he tells us, "Everyone has to move out by tomorrow." It was really weird timing because about an hour later the phone rang and it was Casey saying she'd found this brilliant house and she needed some people to live in it. Elliot had lived at Skinhead Manor, too, but he'd already moved out.

SHAWN STERN Darby hung out there not too long before he died … he was rehearsing there with the Darby Crash Band just after he got back from England. Other bands that practiced at Skinhead Manor were the Circle Jerks, Youth Brigade, No Crisis … and Eugene had some project. Darby would come over and party and get fucked up, he was hanging out with this little gay kid Elliot Katz. I don't remember who was in his band … Bosco, and I don't remember who else … he wanted to start a new thing, but he was just getting fucked up all the time … he was partying a lot … and there were people shooting speed at the Manor all the time … it was horrible.

TONY MONTESION Darby had a crush on Bosco for a long time before he was in the Darby Crash Band—that didn't last too long.

DON GARSTANG   I don't know how many people knew that Darby and Bosco were, like, going out.

PAT SMEAR   Two weeks before the first gig with the Darby Crash Band, Darby called and said, "We have a show at the Starwood, and we don't have any new songs and we don't have a guitar player; will you just play this one show with me?" It was supposed to be a one-shot deal, but then I ended up doing all of them—but he never got his shit together! I think he even had some other guitarists, at some point, and he said, "They all play just like you!" So we went out and we did mainly Germs songs, except slower and not as good, 'cause it was the wrong drummer and bass player! It was like the Germs, except worse players, and us in black T-shirts, and this total freak in bondage clothes and a Mohawk singing. It was such a horrible experience I don't even like to think about it; it was so weird and pathetic.

DON GARSTANG   We were doing two new songs that the Germs never recorded. Darby was writing new songs, and we were talking about going to New York to record an album. Darby didn't seem sad at all—it seems like if he was thinking bad thoughts, he wouldn't have been planning on going to New York to record an album, or writing new songs or whatever. This was towards the end of August, and during September. He was really friendly; a real nice guy. We hung out sometimes over at Amber's house, where he was staying, and he'd say, "Do you want another beer? Of course you do!" Rob Henley was hanging out with us the whole time—him and Drew Blood. We talked about our favorite bands, what kind of music we liked. I was telling him I liked the Fall and Joy Division. He'd say, "Oh, cool," but I could tell that wasn't what he really liked.

> **DARBY CRASH**   We got a movie coming out ... maybe in October? I think it's called *The Decline of Western Civilization*. It's X, Black Flag, Fear, Circle Jerks—whatever. There's gonna be an album, a soundtrack, we've got one song on it called "Manimal."
> **RODNEY BINGENHEIMER**   Great! That's been on two albums already, right?
> **DARBY**   Whaddaya mean, great? Have you heard it?
> **RODNEY**   No, it's been on other albums...
> **DARBY**   Yeah—it's great on the other albums, but not in that movie!
> **RODNEY**   We'd like to thank Darby Crash for coming by, and we'll see the Darby Crash Band at the Starwood on Wednesday, with the Chiefs...
> **DARBY**   And I really need my rent money, and be sure to bring your feathers. (From "Rodney on the ROQ," circa '80.)

DON GARSTANG   We rehearsed quite a bit at Program Studios at Selma and Highland for the first Darby Crash Band show at the Starwood. Initially, Darby would come, but not sing. The last couple of weeks, when things started to get a bit more solid, he sang as well. It was pretty cool once it finally started to happen. Darby sang really well at rehearsals; into the mic, on the beat, even hitting notes—not incoherent at all. And he wasn't on heroin all the time—although there were a few times when it was pretty obvious that he was.

Pat would play the start of the Queen song "Another One Bites the Dust" over and over, and it was getting on Darby's nerves. Finally, Darby would yell at him to stop. I was thinking "Oh, he won't do it again..." but he would, and Darby would keep getting angrier; it kept going back and forth, until Darby just went off, screaming at the top of his lungs, "PAT! Don't do that again!" And I thought, "Oh, man, he won't dare do it again ..." and, of course ... it was too funny to watch! He'd do it way beyond the point where Darby could take it anymore!

AMBER   There was the Darby on stage, the legendary Darby Crash, and then there was this wonderful boy. Sometimes the wonderful boy and I would be popping popcorn, making beef jerky in the oven, tasting wines ... and then other times the phone would ring and the voice on the other end would say, "Your boyfriend just set fire to a whole building!" Everything that happened in the whole city was blamed on him, whether he did it or not!

DON GARSTANG   Darby was always telling this joke about a "crippled clicking pussy for." The joke was about this guy who heard this clicking sound following him, and he turned around and it was a crippled clicking pussy for. When he told the joke, the person would inevitably ask, "What's a crippled clicking pussy for?" and Darby would say, "Not for fucking!" He thought that was hilarious, and would tell it every chance he got. He also liked ethnic jokes, because they always upset people.

The first show was at the Starwood, in August [1980]. When we got there in the afternoon, we all had to go up and meet the owner, Eddie Nash—the guy they were trying to hang the murder rap on from that John Holmes thing. He wanted to see the band, and he said, "So there's not going to be any problems, right?" It was Amber's idea, to kind of smooth things over or something. The show went well, I think—I was surprised when I read somewhere that Darby was upset or disappointed with the first show, because from my perspective, that was wrong. I know Pat was happy with it, because we saw each other later that night, and he and Darby both seemed really pleased with the way it went. It looked like it was going to work out.

JEFF MCDONALD   I saw the Darby Crash Band ... that was really bad and really depressing! It was like, "What is this?" All he did was like two new songs and some of the later Germs material from the *Cruising* soundtrack, and in between songs he was making all these cryptic statements that wouldn't make sense until later, after he'd killed himself.

DON GARSTANG   I played the second show up in San Francisco, too. We played with Flipper and a band called the Unwanted, at some theater in North Beach. Before the show we all went out to dinner on Fisherman's Wharf; it was kind of a nice place, and right after we got served a food fight broke out. None of the other people in the restaurant were appreciating it, and we got asked to leave pretty quickly.

The San Francisco show didn't go as well as the first one. Probably in part because we had practiced so much before the first show, and then three or four weeks went by and we didn't do anything. We never rehearsed after the first show.

Maybe it was 'cause they thought the first show went well enough that we did-n't have to worry about it before going up there. It just wasn't as together. We had our set list for the show, but at one point, Darby turned around and said, "Lexi-con Devil!" We had never rehearsed that one; in fact, I had never even thought about playing it until that moment! I looked at Pat, and Pat was smiling, and just started playing it; that song is not easy to play, and I was playing it for the first time—it was very disjointed. Maybe that's why he got mad. Then we played "Richie Dagger's Crime" again—we had opened up with that one, but we played it again as like a second encore. The show after that, I wasn't in the band anymore.

I didn't find out that I was out of the band until the day of the third show. I went to the show thinking I was going to play, only to find out they'd got some-body else. Darby wasn't mean or anything—I guess he thought Amber or someone else was supposed to contact me, or maybe it was just something he didn't want to do; he said he was sorry, but they had made up their minds.

PAT SMEAR   We played with this drummer at all the rehearsals, and at soundcheck Darby kicked him out. He was awful, but to kick him out at soundcheck was crazy. Lucky from the Circle Jerks filled in with no rehearsal at all; he was pretty good, he knew most of the Germs songs sort of okay—it was weird.

HELLIN KILLER   During the show, which wasn't very good, Amber walked down the staircase that led to the stage, and as she came down the stairs they put the spotlight on her. She walked onto the stage, and right up to Darby and said some-thing to him, with the spotlight still on her. It was kind of disgusting. It was just too much to watch. It confirmed a lot of suspicions that she wanted to be a part of the thing, and all of a sudden she's like co-starring, right there in the spotlight with him ... it was really creepy.

AMBER   Soon after the Darby Crash Band sold out the Starwood on a Wednesday night, the phone rang, and it was the guy who booked the Whisky. Darby hadn't been allowed in the Whisky since the Masque Christmas show problem, but the guy said that Stiff Little Fingers was gonna play, and he wanted the Darby Crash Band to open. Darby couldn't believe that the Whisky had actually asked him to play! He was just fucking thrilled! That night we decided to go to the Rainbow. We get off the bus, and right in front of the Whisky there's an upside-down police car, and all these punks going crazy. I looked at Darby and said, "There are going to be no more punk bands at the Whisky." Sure enough, they called us next day and said they were canceling, and there would be no more punk bands; further-more, if any punks came in the door they'd be frisked, and there would be a "no entry" list at the door of people who cause problems. That was depressing.

Darby always had a key to my house, except that now I had this new boyfriend and Darby just couldn't sleep in my bed with me any more.

Classic punk skankster archetype, circa '80. Used as the Circle Jerks logo.
Drawing by Shawn Kerri.

Ready for war, circa summer '80. Photo: Gary Leonard.

DRAGON LADY

O

CASEY COLA I was neither fat nor had money, and I wasn't some desperate hang-er-on, I'd been hanging out on the punk scene for more than two years already when I met Darby. I'd always gone to Germs shows long before we ever got together, so he'd already touched my life before we actually sat down to talk.[17]

MAGGIE EHRIG After Darby got back from London, Amber was removed from the picture. They were gone a month or six weeks, I think. She paid for the whole trip. Then Darby moved in with Casey Cola when nothing happened for the Darby Crash Band.

CASEY COLA Darby and I were reaching for straws when we decided to develop one of our previous plans—building a family community out of all these people who had nothing and nowhere to go. We drove around until we found a house big enough for our needs. That's when we found the Oxford house. The house was in my name, I put down the deposit, and all rents were paid to me. We moved in on November 15, 1980.

HELLIN KILLER Nobody really wanted to be around him that much when he got back from England because he was so completely fucked up on heroin and booze. He was like this weird Mohawk feather guy … it wasn't him any more … he was trying to be somebody else at the same time these surf punk kids were coming in. It all just fell apart … people sort of split up and bands broke up, people grew up.

  It all fell apart at the Oxford House, where he lived with Malissa, and Maggie and Rob Henley and Ella Black; that's where it just started really going down the toilet, you know?

MAGGIE EHRIG I lived in this old Craftsman building with a bunch of people crashing in all these rooms. They called it "The Oxford House." The only people who fixed the place up nice were Casey in her room and Darby in his. Casey did hers all frou-frou … and Darby did his all industrial grey. He had his own little kingdom, his palace cave at the back of the house. He stayed home a lot.

AMBER He went there thinking he was going to have this whole big room, and he took my portable typewriter. But Casey put him on *display*! He'd come home, and there'd be like a million little punks—she didn't charge admission, but it was like, "Come! See! Live!" I'd come home, and he'd be in my bathtub, reading, and I'd ask, "What's going on?" He'd say, "Oh, it's horrible over there—it's horrible!"

Casey in the kitchen. Photo: Jenny Lens.

ELLA BLACK   It was a really big house with a huge living room; it had an L-shape with a dining room, which had no furniture in it. Darby's room was just around the corner and everyone else was upstairs. His room was a proper room, but it probably was meant to be more like a den. That was one thing people said, that he couldn't have been going to kill himself because he built his shelves.

MAGGIE EHRIG   I thought that Casey was just his latest enabler. It just seemed like that's the only reason they were friends. She enabled him, she got cash all the time, I don't know if it was from her mom or whatever, but she was definitely picking up for everything after Amber was ousted. Darby never had any money of his own.

CASEY COLA   Maggie and I were pretty good friends at first, sharing my bed, taking pictures, but that was before Darby. Then she got displaced and she resented me. Many others in Darby's Circle One group were jealous of our relationship, how he fussed over me. Darby and I had the same kind of mood swings. If we were drinking, we'd forget the same things and we'd remember the same things. It was a joke that we both went up and down at the same time, but that was also what hurt us. We'd been kidding around about it … we always talked about how we would kill ourselves and stuff.

MAGGIE EHRIG   Casey had hard cash everywhere in her room … in socks, inside clothes, there was just money everywhere, in drawers, under the bed … everywhere you looked there was cash, and we were always rifling through her shit, ha ha. Me and the rest of the Oxford House folks.

CASEY COLA   I was a lot more than Darby's enabler. I *never* did drugs prior to my relationship with him. I didn't know how or where to get them, had never seen or touched a syringe and I didn't have the money, anyway. I was on welfare.

MAGGIE EHRIG   The cops came to the Oxford house and woke us all up and there was about 15 of us crashing in this one room, but they never went into Darby's room where he would have had needles, he would have had shit, they could have busted him, but they only came upstairs to our room…

CASEY COLA   Maggie stuck around, but she resented her non-status with Darby, as he was always telling her to go in the house and leave us alone.

MAGGIE EHRIG   I could never picture Darby going somewhere alone, no fucking way, he was too scared. He always had to have somebody around him to back him up or co-sign his fucking meanness or something. There was a side to Darby that made me not want to be close to him. He became too judgmental and I didn't want to be around people like that, not that I wasn't myself, but he was so much worse. He had so much fear about who he was … he was real mean to people sometimes, and he wasn't kidding around, ha ha mean-daddy joking like with Geza ... except Geza wasn't really mean, he was a funny goof ... but Darby ... yeah, well ... he could be a nasty little fucker, I mean it.

JEFF MCDONALD   Darby's onstage persona always seemed just like an act; offstage he always seemed to not know where he was, and appeared really disoriented the whole time, which was all an incredible act. He knew exactly what was going on. His genius was that this whole image was premeditated! The irony of it was that in punk rock everyone had this "we're anti-stars" attitude. So the idea that he was creating this very precise superstar persona was very appealing, and very fresh, considering everyone else was pretending to be a "peoples' band," or something.

TONY MONTESION   I knew a whole other side of him. Once Courtney and her twin sister had a near-death road accident. Darby went to the hospital and stayed with Courtney all day long. I think that's the closest he had come to seeing somebody just hanging on by a thread. She could have gone either way, and thank God, she pulled through, but it was very touchy. Darby was there every day, holding her hand, talking to her, telling her to hold on, he kept laying out all this positivity...

MAGGIE EHRIG   Once we got in this heated conversation, like he just got so angry and kept yelling real loud, "You're fuckin' weird ... you're so fuckin' *weird*." I said, "Darby, why the fuck are you saying this to me?" Darby would find your worst fears and try to fuck with you on them, and I didn't like that. He wanted to affect me in a big way, like he wanted to fuck with me ... not cool in my book...

RODNEY BINGENHEIMER   Darby was always really nice. He was a gentleman. He was really sincere. My favorite song I used to always play was "My Tunnel" from the *Cruising* soundtrack. I played it all the time.

TONY THE HUSTLER   He was becoming more popular by the day ... there were so many fans and all these little groupies who wanted to buy him things.

BOB BIGGS   I also thought that Darby was exercising his control over the band a little bit more than he really had to—in very subtle ways that are difficult to talk about, mostly with posturing, making sure people were places and doing things, in the studio, that sort of stuff.

Shawn Kerri was haunted by her drawing for this flyer, which features a death's head with Mohican days before Darby Crash's suicide.

CRYING WOLF

O

JILL ASH Within five minutes of being introduced in early 1977 he told me was going to die young...

PAT SMEAR Darby was very specific about when and how he was going to kill himself. When we were rehearsing for the reunion show, he said "The only reason I'm doing this is to get money to get enough heroin to kill myself with." He'd said that so many times I just said: "Oh, right..." and didn't think about it any more.

TONY MONTESION Underneath the punk front he was very childlike, he was extremely fragile, but then he'd turn around and say "I'm not gonna be here one day soon..." or "You're gonna miss me when I'm gone—and I'll be gone by this time next year!" But he said it so many times nobody believed him, they'd just say, "Yeah, Darby—right!"

DON BOLLES In almost every interview he said that he would never be old, that he was going to kill himself. When he was done, he wanted to die, and he said it so much, people thought he was a crying wolf kind of boy.

PHILOMENA WINSTANLEY Darby would say it regularly, "I'm going to die young."

CLAUDE BESSY He told me once he wanted to die and I said, "You're full of shit Darby, just get on the stage."

SHAWN KERRI [When Darby asked me to design a flyer for the Germs reunion show]. He had no idea what I was going to do. He didn't tell me what he wanted. He just said, "Do a flyer." When I showed him the art, he was strangely excited by it. I wondered later if he liked the death's head motif because he had suicide on his mind.

DON BOLLES He said at the rehearsal before the reunion a few days before he offed himself that he was only doing the show to get the cash to buy enough heroin to kill himself.

PAUL ROESSLER I can't think of him specifically saying it that blatantly, although I can say that when he did it I felt that he had been planning it. I couldn't stand what he was doing to himself, I did not understand it, and I wouldn't accept it; I told him, "I can't watch you kill yourself on heroin, I can't be around it."

DON BOLLES There was never a shortage of "Darby's dead" rumors. We'd get at least one phone call every couple of weeks asking if it was true that he had killed himself or OD'd. Still, the way Darby would talk about suicide and the "five year plan" all the time, it was always a definite possibility, no matter how many false alarms there were.

PAT SMEAR   We had always talked about suicide and doing it at this certain time, this certain time in your life. So it was not a surprise. When his timetable came up, he was, coincidentally, fucked up enough in the head to want to do it anyway. He had a choice. He could either have been happy and said: "What a stupid idea that was" and just gone on with his life, or he could go: "Well, since this is the time I was going to kill myself anyway, and since I'm so unhappy, and my life's so fucked up, I may as well really do it." I don't know. That's sort of my theory.[18]

NICOLE PANTER   Darby came to visit me a month before he killed himself. He said he was going over to this monastery in Claremont—the one where Leonard Cohen was. I didn't ask him why at the time, but you know ... people do spiritual things when they feel a need... I thought it might be a career move, something he was doing to start a buzz about him again because the Darby Crash Band was failing so miserably, and I just assumed he needed to regroup. He asked me if I would be interested in managing his new band and I said no, that I was a housewife at that point and didn't ever want to manage a band again.

HELLIN KILLER   Not long before he killed himself Darby would show up and knock on our door and just hang out late at night watching TV ... for hours ... he'd just sit there ... finally we'd go, "Well we're gonna go to sleep now." and he'd go, "Oh, okay," and leave. We thought, "What's up with Darby?" We didn't get it. Afterwards it was like "if only we knew."

NICOLE PANTER   He said: "I'm going to kill myself before I get old, I'm gonna do it at a time when it takes everybody by surprise and I want a statue erected of me for people to go to." To him this was a form of immortality. Darby didn't know when to stop. If he couldn't stand or couldn't move his jaw of his own volition he would mumble and these girls would fling pills into his mouth.

JOHN POCHNA   [Sometime around early December of 1980] Darby showed up at the Zero and the staff didn't want to let him in because he'd gotten in free like five times without paying the five bucks. Even X and the Blasters and all the other bands were kicking in their five bucks so Carlos Guitarlos from Top Jimmy's band who was the doorman kept thinking that this was just too much. Why was Darby so different from John Doe, Dave Alvin, or any of the others, Carlos was demanding to know ... but I said let him in anyway, so he came in and then he came over to thank me. I thought he was overdoing the thank you's. Sure, I'd just saved him five bucks—big deal—but he was saying, "Oh, thank you, John, thank you ... oh, and you've been such a good friend, and it's been nice knowing you." He was shaking my hand, and I just thought that he was overdoing it. He was walking around and shaking other people's hands, too, he was thanking them for knowing him ... for being his friend. Other times Darby had been just like a typical quiet guy walking around talking to people at a party.

DARBY CRASH   I'm not going to save up for my old age because I'm not going to have an old age.

Nearing the end. The calm before the tempest. Photo: Gary Leonard.

THE REUNION

O

BRENDAN MULLEN   Darby told Donnie Rose the purpose of this show was to demonstrate to the new punks how it was, what it was really all about in the old days. The reunion was an overwhelming success with the opinion shared by band members and audience alike that it was one of the best Germs shows ever. The logical sequence would have been to quit screwing around, finally, and get back to work to write a new album. Deluded by drug-impaired judgment he insisted on going solo. He also apparently decided to go ahead with a plan to kill himself—literally days after this gig.

DON BOLLES   I think it was Pat who called and cautiously asked me if I'd play a Germs' reunion show at the Starwood in December. I was still peeved about the whole Rob Henley thing, but the Germs was a lot more important to me than some stupid grudge, and if our leader had finally come to his senses, I was more than happy to bury the hatchet and get back to work.

PAT SMEAR   We decided to do a final reunion show at the Starwood. I figured that this would be the last time I'd ever play a show in my life, so I thought, "Hmm, I think I'll buy my first guitar." I didn't know anything about guitars. I had no idea of what was good or anything like that; I just wanted the cheapest guitar I could find for the show. You have to realize that after the Rickenbacker I used with the Germs was stolen, it was simply a matter of showing up at soundcheck, and whoever was opening that night, I'd ask to borrow their guitar and amp. Guitar Center advertised a sale where you bought two Super-Distortion DiMarzio pickups and they'd give you a Hondo Les Paul copy for free, so I went in there to get that deal. But then I saw this red Hagstrom. I was like, "Whoa! I WANT this!" They gave me a really good deal on it.[19]

JOHN DOE   When the Germs played the Starwood for the last time there were probably six or seven suburban kids, and we didn't know everybody in the audience personally anymore. The club was filled with those strange characters you'd see in the *Decline*, who weren't in it for art, but because they were these damaged people who felt like this music was speaking to them.

PAT SMEAR   While we were rehearsing for the reunion there was still a distance between Darby and me, and something was definitely different. He was noticeably less standoffish than he had been just before the split, and when he did call me "arty" or "hippie" or whatever, he would do it with a little more good humor again. I assumed that maybe the lukewarm response to his solo efforts had finally led him to the realization that the Germs was a unique and unduplicable entity, somehow far greater than the sum of its parts, no matter what he thought about my personality or aesthetics. For better or worse, I had become an integral element,

---

The last show. The Starwood, December 3, 1980. Photo: Rooh Steif.

so maybe it was better to just agree to disagree and get on with it. Whatever the case, the rehearsals went well; so well, in fact, I found myself thinking that maybe we were going to be a band again, like for real. It made sense—not only were we sounding a million times better than the Darby Crash Band, but better than the Germs had ever sounded before.

DON BOLLES The soundcheck—a rare event for us—went smoothly; everything worked, for some reason, even Pat's distortion unit. And by this time, Pat, Lorna and I could play the intro to "Another One Bites the Dust" almost perfectly, much to Darby's horror. The Starwood was wall-to-wall punk rock types, old school Hollywood punks, and a bunch of young beach baldies, some already sporting Mohawks—er, I mean Mohicans. There were more new people than at any other Germs show.

PAT SMEAR It was scary—we had never played so fast, hard, and tight. It wasn't like "the old days" Darby was going on about—it was far more efficient and intense, focused—a well-oiled chaos delivery machine. And that was at the start of our rehearsals. By the day of the show, nothing could touch us.

DON BOLLES I puked behind my floor tom about two-thirds into the set just from the intense physicality of playing. We did a version of "Public Image," with a Darby twist; he sang "public scrimmage" to the sea of moshing manliness below, and he turned an impromptu "Another One Bites the Dust" into "Another Crowd Bites the Dust"—not all that clever, but better than "Public Scrimmage!"

PAT SMEAR That last show was our best ever. We played the best, and were the most comfortable, the crowd totally loved us, fans lined up all down the street, we sold out. We thought "Wow—maybe we should go back, this is really good." But it was one thing for me or Lorna or Don to go back. None of us had failed, but for him it was, "Oh, I have to go back and do the Germs again, because I failed with my solo band." I don't think I'd have been very happy about it either.

DARBY CRASH I've got money, I've got drugs.

DON BOLLES At one point between songs when Pat was tuning up a bit, a guy with a bunch of blood on his nose jumped up onstage and grabbed the mic, and said, in a tone that was sort of halfway between a whine and a bellow, "... dudes from Huntington Beach thrashed on my node—look ad my node—look ad it! Awright? I didn't do nothin' to their shit—dey fuckin grabbed me like dis and dey go, 'Hippie.'" Then Darby says, "It was an accident." "It wasn't no accident! I'm just sayin'—we know who he is; and when he comes back here, we're gonna get his ass!" Later I found out that our mystery guest was none other than Mike Muir, who later fronted the band Suicidal Tendencies.

During "My Tunnel" Darby's spontaneous lyrical revisionism took a darker, more ominous tone, as he replaced one verse with, "What are you doing in MY tunnel? You paint your faces—you wear my clothes—but you don't know; you don't know..." And boy, was he ever right about that one. As the show ended, he quietly said, "Goodnight, and we'll see you all at Oki Dog!"

GORILLA ROSE At the end of Germs shows he'd go, "Hey, everybody ... we're going to Oki Dog!" and he'd invite a hundred people to this Japanese burger joint in West Hollywood.

CASEY COLA After the Germs played all their people were in the dressing room and they wouldn't let me in. I said, "What are you gonna do, leave me out here standing alone? I really am with Darby." He opened the door real fast and in front of all these people he goes, "Casey, where's Casey?" and I said, "Right here," and he threw his arms around me and kissed me and said, "Don't worry, I've got drugs and don't worry, here's the money ... go divide it" ... he trusted me.

PAT SMEAR It was weird—right after the show he was begging me to come to some party at Oki Dog. He was saying, "Please come to this party; it's really important to me." Afterwards, I thought, "Oh shit! I didn't go to his goodbye party? My God! That was sort of rude!"

DON BOLLES Our reunion was great in every way. Me, Lorna and Pat were so happy. It was like being in love and having the best sex in your life. That night we thought we could actually be a real band ... and so for me, we went out on top. When he died a few days later I wasn't pissed. I didn't talk to him after the show, although we'd been totally civil to each other during the rehearsal, but I remember he tried to get Pat to go to a party.

BRENDAN MULLEN Darby, Lorna, and a few others went to Oki Dog to wait for the arrival of the punk pilgrims, but the throng never made it. It was bucketing it down with rain. Everybody went home. Darby somehow failed to notice the torrents and took the low turnout as a personal affront, a mass scale abandonment; forsaken just before the Last Supper. It was here that an alarmed Lorna decided to call John Doe to ask the X-man to talk to Darby. She was concerned about his depressed state and recurrent suicidal talk and didn't feel there was anybody else that Darby respected enough to talk to about such things.

JUDITH BELL It was a day or so after the big reunion show at the Starwood when Darby told John he wanted to kill himself. John said he'd approached Darby to talk about it after Lorna had called him saying she was extremely concerned about Darby's suicidal state. "Perhaps he'll listen to you ... he looks up to you," Lorna said. Darby had previously told John he was petrified of being outed; he thought the new beach punks might beat him up, and that Claude would throw a fit, or something. We were supposed to convene as a group to discuss a plan of action, to somehow intercept for the sake of Darby's well-being, but Chris and John had day jobs and by the time they could figure anything out, it was too late. Darby was gone...

PAUL ROESSLER   Right before he died he came by and sat and watched TV with us. He said, "Come on, Paul—come outside, let's go do stuff," and I replied, "No, man, it's like four in the morning, I feel like watching TV; just got off tour, I haven't seen my wife in two months..."

TONY THE HUSTLER   Two nights after the reunion gig at the Starwood, I visited him at the Oxford house. His room was way in the back. When I walked into his bedroom, I couldn't believe what I saw. Here's a man who was obsessed with toys and gizmos. His jackets and all of his clothing were covered with buttons and clutter everywhere in his life. Especially when he lived with me. We used to have all these weird toys and bizarre little things laying around everywhere. But there was nothing in this room at all, except a foam rubber mat on the floor. No clothing, not a thing on the walls, not a thing on the floor, except the mat and his stereo system, with a small, little stack of tapes and a small, little stack of records. No pillow, no sheets, no nothing. I said, "This is where you sleep?" He goes, "Yeah." I said, "Are you sure you're okay?" and he goes, "Yeah, I'm okay. I'm going to be fine. Don't worry about me, Tony. Everything's okay." He gave me a little bit of the white heroin that he was doing at the time. He did some and let me do the rest. He said, "It's real strong. You probably won't like it anyway."

HELLIN KILLER   People wanted him bad, and they dragged him down. Amber, Casey—the scum of the earth—they just sucked him in and dragged him down. He lost touch with the people that weren't like that; they didn't wanna be around that element. It was like, "Dude, you're going somewhere we're not gonna go!" Nobody would hang around him when he was with those people. He realized that all the people he'd been really close to that he'd loved and who loved him had kind of written him off and moved on. He'd gone in a different direction too far and too deep into drugs. Nobody could help him.

TONY THE HUSTLER   Darby knew that the China White he got from his Hollywood connection was raw. You cannot shoot raw heroin, I mean, even a small amount will kill you. Right then, I knew it was the last time I was going to see him alive, and that I could not do a thing about it. I didn't cry. I just looked at him, then I grabbed him and hugged him, and kissed him on the side of the head. That was the last time I saw him.

HELLIN KILLER   I've only ever known two other people like Darby, who were that much above everyone around them that they couldn't relate to anyone any more ... it drove them nuts ... they think it's never gonna be what they want it to be, so they go, "fuck it," they kill themselves. "Yeah, I wanna rule the fucking world!" That was what he wanted to do; that was his "plan." But he also had that "five year plan," that "I'm outta here before I'm 25" thing; that was SOOO Bowie! "Five years." That was the thing.

SHUT DOWN

O

GERBER My band Sexsick was playing a show at the Hong Kong that night. I talked to Darby on the phone that day. We were fighting, as usual, about Robbie who was staying with him at Oxford. Darby said, "So, I'm coming tonight." I said, "Well, I know, but don't bring Robbie. If you bring Robbie, we're just gonna get into a fight, and I don't wanna fight, 'cause I have to play a show. Please don't bring him. Can you please just not bring him?"

CASEY COLA We drove Rachel to work at the Hong Kong Café early on the night Sexsick was playing. I think it was me, Elliot, Rob, Darby and Lane who were in the car. Then we went and picked up Rachel and Kurt. We went to the Hong Kong, dropped everybody off, and said we're going to go to this party and that we'd try and make it back in time for the Sexsick show. By now it was just me and Darby in the front, Elliot and Rob in the back. We stopped and got champagne. And then we went to this party at Victoria Sellers' place in Bel-Air—but we couldn't get in. It was so fucked; we just stood at the gates. It was one of those nights where everything goes wrong, you know? On the way back to the Hong Kong we were talking about how easy it would be to die, what we'd have to do, and how much money we had. We got back to the Hong Kong at about 11. Rob went off his own way, and so did Elliot. Rachel let Darby and I in.

GERBER I was drinking Tanqueray and tonics all night and I was just wasted. Halfway through the set Darby and Robbie fucking marched in, right in front of the stage. Darby had his hand and was hauling him along, like a puppy dog. I was pissed. My intention was to throw my drink in Robbie's face—that was truly my intention, but I missed and hit Darby in the face with it, glass and all. There wasn't really anything he could do, except get into a fight with me right there, which he wasn't about to do. So he stormed out, Robbie in tow, and they went to the bar next door. They got even more drunk, and then got in a fight about me, because of this weird triangle problem that Darby and I have with boys.

CASEY COLA When you're trying to put things together and you're really trying, and then things fuck up the way they've been fucking up for the last 10 years, or 15 years, or 22, you know, you just finally lose it; you lose conception of how much better tomorrow might be—that becomes the moment when you want to die.

GERBER We finished the set, and some kid told me, "Darby's waiting for you next door—you better get over there, he's flipping out." So I went, sat down with him and Robbie, and had a couple more drinks. We were all screaming at each other—and it just escalated. Then Darby and I started hitting each other, so we took it outside—we were, like, fistfighting, in this little skinny walkway

that led to the back alley behind the Hong Kong. He was pushing me against the wall, I was punching him and kicking him in the balls while he was smacking me in the face and kissing me. We'd get in scraps like that all the time. A big part of it for him was to piss off these boys; kind of like, "Yeah, we're fighting over you, but I could take her from you like that." Robbie got involved, too, and there was like bottle throwing, and I think I hit him with bottles in the head. It was so balls-out people were staying the fuck away from us. Finally, we were both so tired from beating each other up, and he was crying and we were hugging.

CASEY COLA Darby was saying to Robbie, "Well, are you staying over tonight or not?" and Rob was like, "Just fucking leave me alone, man!" and pushed him up against the fence.

GERBER Then he said this statement that he had told me, almost on a daily basis, since I first met him; "Well, when things get too bad, I'm just gonna kill myself anyway." He said that to me all the fucking time. Even in the early acid trips, he would tell me that he would "check out" by 22. I always felt he was threatening me with it so I just lost it. I screamed out, "I am so fucking sick of hearing you threatening to kill yourself! If you're gonna do it, then why don't you just stop whining and go fucking do it! And stop trying to take other people down with you!" And that was the last thing I said to him. I don't know what happened to Robbie—he just sort of disappeared, but Darby left crying with Casey.

CASEY COLA We stopped at the liquor store on the corner of Fairfax and Sunset, where we bought grapefruit juice and 100 proof vodka. Big mistake. That's what Darby and I used to always drink ... unfortunately, the worst kind of friend you can ever have is somebody who, when you get fucked up together, you're exactly the same. We could dare each other to do anything, you know—anything. We blacked out, we got in fights we didn't remember; we had a habit of irritating everybody around because we were just back and forth, all the time.

For about a month, we had been really trying; trying to make the house a home, trying to put a life together and get things the way they were supposed to be. But you get discouraged really easily because it's not working.

We just turned around and said, "Fuck it, let's do it. Fuck this shit, it's not gonna ever change, it's not gonna get better." We said, "Fuck it—we're going!" Elliot said, "No, no, wait for me," and hopped in the car. On our way back to the house we talked about things, like how we were going to do this, whether we could get enough drugs, how I couldn't hit myself, because I have a manual dexterity problem, and he was real nervous about that because he would have to hit me up, and it would be murder if he did. And Elliot's in the back seat of the car, flipping out, not knowing what to do.

It was a whole string of events; plus our whole life was falling apart. We came up with a plan for this great house and everything was fucking up—it was just really a drag.

He was supposed to be writing, he hadn't done any writing; was supposed to be recording in a month, he hadn't done anything for it. You see, it's so hard to explain people who don't plan and have everything go bad for a long time, and then all of a sudden you really try to make things work, and then it still doesn't work.

Darby and I had been consistently doing drugs all during that time, for like a month and a half. Both of us were like, "Are you sure?" "Are you sure?" "Yes I'm sure. If you're gonna do it…" It was like putting two little kids in a room, and they end up doing something that maybe they wouldn't do alone—it just makes it a little bit easier when there's another person. He didn't coerce me into it, and I didn't talk him into it. We never talked each other into anything. We couldn't, so we didn't bother. It was a really close, really strange relationship, but we had each other, and because we had each other we figured that if we did it, then we'd still be together. It was a very safe feeling for us to do it that way. Yes, we probably would've done it alone, but the logistics of figuring it out and working it out alone would've been more complex somehow—I couldn't have bought the drugs on my own, or hit myself on my own.

It was a trade-off. I held his money, okay, if you want to blame me for that, I kept his money for him, I doled his money out for him. See, the girls he'd always been around mothered him, and that was one of the reasons he liked me—I never mothered him. He babied me, I didn't baby him. Those other girls always stepped in, if he ever got the idea into his head he was going to kill himself, it was, "Oh no, Darby, let's go to the beach." "Oh no, Darby, let's do this."

So then we had to go back to the house. He sent me upstairs to get the money, and made the phone call for the drugs.

ELLIOT KATZ   I was walking around the house going, "I don't know what to do, I don't know what to do." After they left I was going to call the police, but I thought, "Oh no, what if I get them busted and they don't actually do it?"

CASEY COLA   We were set; we weren't changing our minds. We just really needed to talk alone. Elliot came around to the car, and Darby said, "Get the fuck out of here," or something like that, 'cause Elliot was trying to let the air out of the tires. We just wanted to get away!

So we went up to get the drugs. We parked the car and he said, "Do you want to come in?" I had paper and a pencil in the car and said, "No, I'm going to write a note." He said, "Fine," and went up to the house. I started writing—I don't even remember what I wrote. After about three minutes, he came back to the car and said, "I want you to come in with me." His excuse for buying $400 worth of junk was that it was for everybody in the house. So we went inside, said "hi" and everything, and got the drugs. F……. and his China White Phenytol.

ELLA BLACK   Part of the $400 they spent on heroin was my rent money, and Elliot's, too.

CASEY COLA   When we left there I said, "Well, are we going back to the house to do drugs?" and he goes, "No way, they'll bother us there." If we were alone for more than 20 minutes in that house everybody had a pee fit. So he said, "Let's

<table>
<tr><td>

12

</td><td>

AUTOPSY REPORT

I performed an autopsy on the body of   ➡

at _____ the DEPARTMENT OF CORONER

</td><td>

No. 80-15734

BEAHM, JAN PAUL

</td></tr>
</table>

Los Angeles, California on _DECEMBER 8, 1980 @ 1100 HOURS_
                                 (Date)   (Time)

From the anatomic findings and pertinent history I ascribe the death to:

(A)   ACUTE HEROIN-MORPHINE AND ETHANOL INTOXICATION

DUE TO, OR AS A CONSEQUENCE OF

(B)

DUE TO, OR AS A CONSEQUENCE OF

(C)

DUE TO, OR AS A CONSEQUENCE OF

(D)

OTHER CONDITIONS CONTRIBUTING BUT NOT RELATED TO THE IMMEDIATE CAUSE OF DEATH:

Anatomical Summary:

1. Acute passive congestion of visceral organs.

2. Tracks of old and recent needle marks on both antecubital fossae.

go to your mom's house." We went to the little house in back where I used to live [137 N. Fuller Avenue]. I went to the main house and got water and a spoon; he fixed it all and everything.

He wrote a suicide note, which I never saw; he didn't want me to read it, it wasn't for me. It didn't say much, other than "My life my leather my love goes to Bosco." I don't know what I wrote in mine; I've never seen it, although there were Xeroxed copies going around town.

He hit me up first, and he said, "Are you okay?" and I said, "Um ... yeah." I was sitting up, and he put his hand at the small of my back and said, "Just hold it, stay there—just wait for me, okay? Just wait for me." He held me up for a second, then he hit himself up; then he laid himself against the wall and pulled me to him. It was almost like he forgot what we were going to do, and then he realized, and he said, "Wait a minute," then he kissed me and said, "Well—'bye." Like everything was cool, both of us were in agreement, and we were happy with what we were doing.

GERBER   Pat called me. He said, "Are you sitting down?" I said, "No," and he said, "Sit down," then he said, "He's gone." I said, "I don't believe you." He asked me what happened, and I said, "I don't want to talk about it and I don't believe you!" I hung up the phone. I still didn't believe it. Then Kira called me and she said, "No, it's true." Then Pat called me back, and was saying, "You have to go over there with me. You have to go over there with me," meaning Casey's parents' house, and something about identifying the body and his mom and all this stuff. I was hysterical and said, "I can't. I can't do it."

THE LORD is my shepherd; I shall not want. He maketh me to lie down in green pastures; He leadeth me beside the still waters. He restoreth my soul; He leadeth me in the paths of righteousness for His name's sake. Yea, though I walk through the valley of the shadow of death, I will fear no evil; for thou art with me; thy rod and thy staff they comfort me. Thou preparest a table before me in the presence of mine enemies, thou anointest my head with oil; my cup runneth over. Surely goodness and mercy shall follow me all the days of my life; and I will dwell in the house of the Lord for ever.

—Psalm 23

In Loving Memory of

JAN PAUL BEAHM

Born
September 26, 1958   California

Passed Away
December 7, 1980   Los Angeles, California

Service
Friday, December 12, 1980   11:00 A.M.
The Wayside Chapel

Officiating
Reverend N.J. Boer

Interment
Holy Cross Cemetery

Directors
GATES, KINGSLEY & GATES
PRICE DANIEL
West Los Angeles, California

AFTERMATH

O

CASEY COLA I woke up in the arms of a dead man, still wrapped around him. There's another false myth on the Internet that he laid himself out like a cross. Some people still swear that Darby didn't think he was going to die, but I know for sure that he wanted to ... he wrote a suicide note, he knew how much drugs he was doing and he did, too, think he was going to die, and he did also think that I was going to die. It's been said that he withheld a lethal dosage from me on purpose, untrue ... he did mean for me to die, 'cause I was dead for a few minutes. The time came and we did it, and, um, he died ... and I didn't ... I did technically die for about three minutes, two and a half, three minutes, according to the police report.

The argument of "he gave me a lot less," is a really bad argument if you saw the police report. It's a very cruel thing to say, because he didn't mean for me to live; obviously he knew what everybody would do to me. And what was done to me afterward was really horrible; he would not have wanted me to go through that, there's just no way. He didn't use me for an excuse to kill himself, and he also knew damn well that both of us would die on 400 dollars worth of junk, so that's bullshit. A lot of people love to say that he didn't really want to die because he built his shelves the week before, or because of this, or because of that.

Malissa, Maggie, and others from the [Oxford] house had come to find us. They hid the syringes and led me crawling and incoherent to the main house where I was left to die in a back room. I was barely conscious, and someone was screaming and berating me to get in the house. I blacked out. Eventually I did die, but the paramedics got me back...

They didn't really think about what had happened to me, because there was a dead person sitting there. They were hysterical. I just couldn't accept that Darby was dead. My mother didn't know what to do—she figured I was drunk. She finally called the paramedics. All I remember is asking, "Is he really dead?"

I was gone, but in my head I saw a big party, in this same house, or rather outside from the street and sidewalk over the front lawn. I saw everyone I'd ever known, but as I greeted people, each one said, "Darby's looking for you!" I moved through the crowd, hearing the same thing over and over. The garage was open and a bright light was shining, brighter than anything, not of this world and I knew, somehow, that Darby was in there. People were pointing and urging me on, they were pulling my arms and saying, "Darby is looking for you. He needs you. He said to come *now!*" As I moved towards him, as I began to float, I heard harsh voices shouting, "He left you, he left you alone, he left you to die in the gutter without him!" It was the paramedics slapping me to try to get me to fight back ... apparently I was saying, "No, no, I've got to get to Darby, I've got to get to him," and they said, "No way, your friend left you in the gutter, he left you to die in the gutter," and all this stuff. And I was like, "No, I have to, you don't understand I have to get to him, he's right there." And they kept saying he left me in the gutter, because they want you to fight back so that your body starts fighting the drug. For two days I didn't talk, because I kept expecting any minute he was going to come walking into the hospital room and go, "Come on Casey, let's go, let's go right now, this is such a joke, let's go!"

JENA CARDWELL When Pat and I went to the house after he died, Rob Henley was there, wailing and crying and feeling that it was his fault; everybody was thinking, "It was my fault, I could have done something," or, "Fuck you—why did you do that?" There was a lot of anger.

JOHN DOE I remember going to save Rob Henley from jumping off the 9000 building, making some dramatic phone call late at night. I don't remember if this was before or after Darby died … the last I heard of him he was up in Spokane, Washington. I think I met this woman who said that she was married to him and had a kid.

GERBER There was this huge, gigantic clap of thunder all of a sudden, out of nowhere, but it wasn't raining.

PAUL ROESSLER The night he died there was this incredibly loud clap of thunder, it was short but LOUD, the most unbelievable thing; we were, like, "What the fuck?" The next day we found out he was dead, and I just thought, "That was him!" And then a week later, Hellin started acting really weird; it turned out she was pregnant with our first son, Alex. Now, I don't really believe in reincarnation, but Alex's middle name is Jan Paul; we both decided that this child will have a mom and dad and a real family; he's gonna have some of the things that Paul didn't have.

JENA CARDWELL When Darby killed himself, it was the first time I ever saw Pat cry. We were still living with his parents; it was early in the morning, and Lorna called. I knew there was something seriously wrong for Lorna to be calling, because Lorna never called. She told Pat, and he told me. I remember it was a shock, but we weren't completely surprised, because he had been spiraling out of control with drugs and drinking, and just being so fucked up, but we were still devastated.

NICOLE PANTER I tried to off myself twice. One time Darby came to see me in the hospital and said, "Don't ever try to do that again. Do you realize how upset I would be if you died?"

JENA CARDWELL There were abandonment issues, like why did you do that to us, why did you leave us? I remember seeing Darby's sister afterwards, and she was gunning for Amber because she felt that it was Amber's fault—a lot of people did, because she got him into the really hard stuff. I have to say that Darby was pretty much in control of his life; he was not the kind of person that could be easily persuaded by anybody to do anything—but his sister felt that Amber was to blame, at least for giving him access to stuff he might not have otherwise been able to get into. She was angry and out of her mind with grief.

DAVID BROWN   I wonder about this sick desire to make Darby Crash the queen of the prom, or whatever. It misses the whole point of what a great guy he was. I remember him as somebody that was fun to sit up all night and take drugs with; he was actually sort of low-key. I really don't remember this heavy-duty poet, and all the rest of that crap. Obviously Pat was very talented, if a bit out of control, but it's questionable to me what Darby had, or what people thought he had. I just thought he was a regular guy who was sort of Bowie-looking—and smashed most of the time! What kind of legacy can you leave behind if you're smashed all the time? He had an amusing look—part crabby, home-town American boy mixed with rum, sodomy and the lash—that sort of jowly overbite kind of thing ever-so-wasted with drugs.

PENELOPE SPHEERIS   I thought "Oh my God, I just did this movie and I have 5000 posters sitting there at Slash with him laying on the floor looking like he's dead!" I had chosen that particular frame for the movie ads because he looked dead, eyes shut—it was really weird. I had just done this movie that was supposed to be all about having fun, and then the guy that's supposed to be the hero of the whole thing kills himself; it sort of took the fun out of it. All of a sudden, it had a terrible feeling to it, a slap-in-the-face kind of reality, like "Okay, you little bastards, you wanted to play mean and gnarly and bad and be as sick and perverted as you could be—well, how's Death for ya?"

TONY MONTESION   He was frightened that if it became known that he was gay, he would be heckled and ridiculed—and he couldn't take that. I don't think he could live with being a punk rocker and being gay—he was young, and he couldn't suss all that stuff out. He was 22 ... what the hell did he know then, you know?

BOB BIGGS   I didn't care in a thousand years if Darby was gay or not; I don't think anyone else did either. But Darby seemed to think that people cared. I think it was all in his head. I think he went out of his way to conceal his gayness and that's how he painted himself into this corner, in part because he couldn't be real.

JUDITH BELL   After we made a specific point of reassuring him it was okay to be gay, Darby seemed able to relax and be openly affectionate with Rob Henley when he was around me and Chris D. and John Doe and Exene. The four of us used to fuck around socially, like a double couple or something, and Darby would sometimes come over to visit John and Exene. We were older, more experienced people. I clearly remember John saying, "We'll support you ... we'll stand by you if you go public." Darby and Rob were so cute together, they really looked in love.

TOMATA DU PLENTY   It's a real shame that punk rock was so in the closet back then. I heard that Darby was despondent over his sexuality and I regret that I couldn't have helped. Homophobia was rampant in the L.A. punk scene and I blame older queers like myself for our silence, but would he have survived even if he had found himself?

PHRANC   I was always out as a lesbian. I can't remember any other out queers at that time. There were the Screamers but nobody ever really talked or sang about being queer. There was that early Go-Go's song "Johnny, Are You Queer?" but that was about it.

PAT SMEAR   Probably until the last year of his life I never even suspected that Darby was gay.

NICOLE PANTER   I didn't find out until after he died.

JOHN DOE   I'd talked to Darby a couple of times, because he was obviously unhappy, and Lorna had asked me to talk to him to try to keep him from doing this. I remember hanging out at the after-hours club that everybody went to, and I remember Darby saying X didn't like the Germs anymore, that we liked the Blasters better. And I remember telling him that that was so high school. And it just wasn't true … I said I thought he was an amazing person. He just needed to get through it. I tried to encourage him to not be so sad. It obviously didn't work. I remember saying that life was worth it even if it didn't seem like it. I put my arm around him and tried to show him that people really cared for him. He had lost that belief. I was trying to tell him being gay was no big deal, especially in the arts…

EXENE CERVENKA   It was his right … he didn't want to be here … and who does? We were making the best out of it at the time and if that isn't enough I guess you check out. We were all self-medicating but I don't know if we had our dosages correct, but I'd much rather that the Go-Go's were on the cover of *Rolling Stone* than Darby commit suicide.

PENELOPE SPHEERIS   I know that people like to put him on that pedestal because we like gods and we like icons, but I can't have respect for someone who killed himself in that way.

AMBER   My husband Don said, "Amber, Darby's dead," so I called the morgue and asked the guy, "Do you have a Jan Paul …" I didn't even get Beahm out, and he goes, "Yeah, he's here." I was just standing there, and I just couldn't feel anything. It was like all my senses went dead. All of a sudden, this car pulls upside my house, and this girl gets out that I'd never met, and she said, "Are you Amber?" and I said, "Yeah." This girl says, "You're the reason my brother's dead." She said, "I ought to just beat the shit out of you and kill you." I just looked at

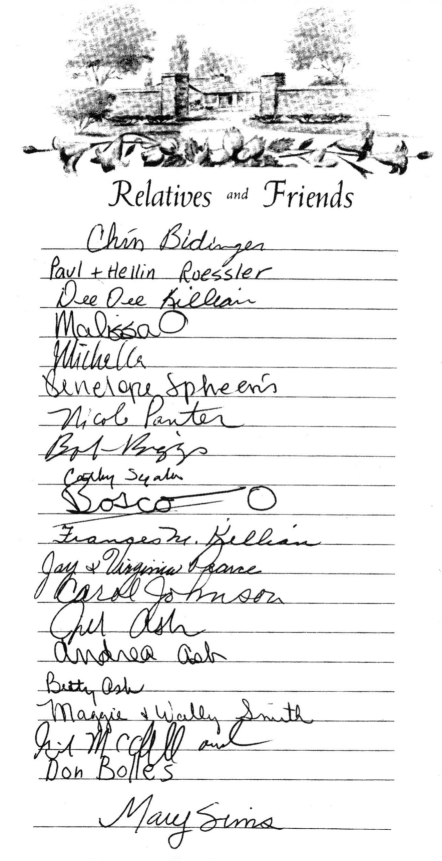

Relatives and Friends

Chin Bidinger

Paul + Hellin Roessler

Dee Dee Killian

Malissa O

Michelle

Penelope Spheeris

Nicole Panter

Bob Briggs

Cathy Scadon

Bosco O

Frances N. Killian

Jay + Virginia Pearce

Carol Johnson

Jill Ash

Andrea Ash

Betty Ash

Maggie + Wally Smith

Gil McGill and

Don Bolles

Mary Sims

her and I said, "You know what? Go ahead." I said, "You can't do anything to me. You can't hurt me. If you shoot me, if you cut me, there's nothing you could do to make me feel any more pain than I'm in right now." She put her fists down, and said, "Will you take a ride with me?"

GERBER   When Casey got out of the mental hospital a lot of people wanted to kill her. I was pretty fucking angry—but I also knew Darby well enough to know that Casey was not responsible for that.

CASEY COLA   I was really messed up after I got back from the mental hospital; not one person cared or wanted to help or protect me. Many spit on me and threw things at me. The general feeling was that I should just go off somewhere and never come back. It was all about Darby. Everybody pointed the finger. It was all my fault. My feelings or well-being after a terrifying near-death experience did-n't count to anyone. While I was locked up in hospital for about a month, they stole and distributed all my things. Not one of them called or tried to visit to see how I was doing ... I didn't count, I wasn't human any more. After Darby died the only thing [Maggie Ehrig] could do was steal from me and kick me when I was down. Maggie admitted that she stole money from me and anything else she want-ed. After Darby died she'd hang out at clubs wearing my boots and clothes and encourage people to boo and hiss and spit and shove me.

AMBER   In the back seat of Faith Jr.'s car is Pat, curled in a ball. His shirt was drenched, and his body looked like someone withdrawing from something. We looked at each other and just wrapped around each other. Faith was driving, and she and her lesbian lover were drinking Jack Daniels. We go down Franklin, get on the Hollywood freeway going the wrong fucking way—up the exit instead of the on-ramp, we're going a hundred fucking miles an hour, and I look up and I see cars coming at us, and I'm thinking, "I'm going to die tonight but I don't care," I was thinking, "I can be with him, great. This is great!"

NICOLE PANTER   If you saw *Suburbia*, you saw the funeral, basically—it was a sad little punk rock funeral. Darby looked like they put green clay on his face, and his hair was dyed black, black, black. I had a lot of compassion for Faith right then; when they were lowering the coffin into the grave she was crying, "Oh, God, please, why not me?"

AMBER   Pat said to me, "I would've done anything. Why didn't he come to me, I would've done anything, I would've died with him, I would've done anything."

GEZA X   About a day after Darby died, Robbie told me he was walking home, and he saw Darby's ghost, leather jacket zipped all the way up past his neck to his chin—typical ghost story kind of vibe—standing kind of like up on a wall in someone's yard. He said that Darby stared at him with this completely ashen ghost face and tried to speak or communicate somehow, but couldn't.

POP REVIEW

BLACK RANDY'S VENOMOUS PATTER

Black Randy is a man of questionable sanity who periodically pops up like a kamikaze to douse us with sleazy, X-rated mayhem. Tuesday night he crash-landed at the Starwood with a typically venomous load of stage patter, an expanded Metro Squad and a new hairdo.

A seminal force behind L.A.'s musical underground born four years ago at the Masque (a short-lived, now legendary punk cabaret), Black Randy is less a musician than a raunchy comedian in the tradition of Redd Foxx. Past victims of his merciless wit have included gays, punks, Rastafarians, Chicanos and L.A.'s favorite local band, X. Tuesday night he made quick work of hippies, John Lennon and recently deceased L.A. performer Darby Crash, whose fans in attendance were less than amused and hurled verbal threats and beer bottles.

Black Randy's humor is staggeringly cruel, his singing voice is barely adequate and he's hardly the rockstar type, resembling as he does a pasty-faced Pugsley Addams grown up into Joe Cocker. What makes Black Randy worth the price of admission is the fact that his observations are more often than not painfully accurate. His backup band, the Metro Squad, is also a show in itself, being one of the few local lineups able to deliver a decent approximation of funk. But then Black Randy's been performing the same set for so long it's no wonder the Metro Squad has it down pat. Mr. Randy needs some new material.

As the name taken by this middle-class white boy suggests, Black Randy's central obsession is the stylish cool of the black word. Bleating out James Brown's "I'm Black I'm Proud" with wild-eyed fervor, he seems to really mean it, but at the same time his sly barbs double back on themselves so neatly that it's difficult to figure exactly whom he's lampooning. Certainly those avant-garde musicians who regard funk with envy and ape it with feeble results are one target. But dressing up like a trashy black pimp for a gloriously ridiculous send-up of "The Theme From Shaft," Black Randy is none too reverent about the black man either.

The climax of Tuesday's show came when a young man wearing a gas mask shaved Black Randy's long hippie locks with electric shears and left him looking as though a rabid weasel had run amok on his skull; obviously, he's not above playing the fool himself. In the wonderful world of Black Randy we're all jerks.

—KRISTINE McKENNA

J. RUBY PRODUCTIONS, INC. LOS ANGELES, CALIF.	DETACH AND RETAIN THIS STATEMENT THE ATTACHED CHECK IS IN PAYMENT OF ITEMS DESCRIBED BELOW. IF NOT CORRECT PLEASE NOTIFY US PROMPTLY. NO RECEIPT DESIRED. DELUXE FORM WVD-2 V-5				

DATE	DESCRIPTION	AMOUNT	DISTRIBUTIONS	
			ACCT. NO.	AMOUNT
12/9/80	funeral expenses for Darby Crash	$1,500.	5070	$1,500.

EMPLOYEE

PERIOD ENDING	TOTAL EARNINGS	SOCIAL SECURITY TAX	WITHHOLDING U. S. INC. TAX	S. D. I.	STATE INCOME TAX				TOTAL DEDUCTIONS	NET PA

Under pressure from Amber and others, Bob Biggs paid for Darby's funeral with funds from a subsidiary corporation.

BRENDAN MULLEN   His half-sister Christine Smith said that after Darby died, there was a visitation; she saw him at the foot of her bed, and he said, "I'm okay, I'm okay."

PAUL ROESSLER   I had dreams where it was like he was sitting next to me. I don't call it a visitation; it's where your memory and your mind takes all the information and assembles it, and gives you—like smells, things you wouldn't even notice you're trying to remember, his essence, his presence. I remember thinking how I fucking knew it was all a joke; that's what a lot of us thought. I looked at him and said, "I knew it was a fucking joke," and he said, "No, Paul—it's not a joke."

DAVID BROWN   Right after Darby died, Black Randy and the Metro Squad did a show at the Starwood. Rudy Ray Moore was on the bill, which was bizarre enough, but Randy had the idea that he should dress up like a cross between Darby Crash and John Lennon. I rented a grand piano. With the stage pretty dark, I played the piano intro to "Imagine," and Randy walked out into the spotlight, with a long hippie hair wig, little round wire-rim glasses, a fringy '60s leather vest, and a Germs armband and he sang, "Imagine there's no Darby…" It was all sort of made up on the spot, and it was great; one of the few things we ever did that actually came off!

BLACK RANDY   Everyone in my band came out in devil suits, and I came out in a blue Mohawk. Everyone just hated it. Somebody like Darby was respected, people looked up to him, little half-baked minds with their blue Mohawks and now they think this is cool somehow … shooting all kinds of speed and shit. When Darby OD'd he helped to destroy the scene, because after the suicide the drug business was certainly out from under the blanket. It was a wonderful negative legend for the authorities and punks in general to think about.

DAVID BROWN   Some irate Darby clone threw a full bottle of Heineken at him which just missed him by an inch—Randy saw it coming and ducked, and it shattered on the wall behind him. We had dared to intimate that Darby was not God, and this kid was pissed off about it, so after the show, Randy invited him up to the dressing room. It was all very jolly backstage. Randy pulled out all these drugs and gave 'em to the kid; "Oh here, have some heroin; have some coke; have some phenytol; have some crank." Now this kid was all wobbling and smiling, and Randy was now his closest friend. Finally, Randy said he'd called him a cab, and he escorted him downstairs. Later, when we were all packed up ready to leave, there was a guy laying there in the alley, making these horrible moaning sounds— a heap of jelly. It was that kid! Randy had paid some Mexicans to beat the shit out of him, after getting him all fucked up! Darby's true fan—it was pathetic! Randy certainly earned some extra points for "Special Cruelty" that night. Like El Duce said, "You don't get a reputation for being an asshole by being a nice guy!"

BLACK RANDY Darby should have had the balls to stick it out. If he couldn't have a band anymore, hell, he could have sold pens, too. There's other things you can do. We were making a statement about his motives for killing himself and we were making a judgment about it. I'm less sure now that I was so righteous and insightful in doing that, but we definitely put the silly-assed Mohawk in the perspective that it belonged.

KIM FOWLEY So Darby died the same day as John Lennon. He died dramatically enough as a martyr but he picked the wrong day to die. That just makes him jackoff fuckboy doesn't it? Now we can all jack off to the futility of his life as the art form.

RODNEY BINGENHEIMER I did a whole show of Beatles and Germs back and forth. One Beatle song and one Germs song as a tribute to Darby and John.

DAVID BROWN It's good that Darby died, or the Germs would have gotten sucked in deeper to that whole Slash Records thing. He would have been lusting after Los Lobos buttocks or something equally distasteful, so it's really kind of cool. Slash had designs on that poor guy; it would have been bad.

PAUL ROESSLER He just loved going through life and screwing up what he could, and he was willing to fucking die for it; impressed the hell out of me, you know? If I was going to pick one martyred fucking saint artist that I know, he'd be the one!

BOB BIGGS Darby was ambitious. Not so ambitious that he didn't kill himself. Darby wanted to be a big rock star like David Bowie but he had such a disdain for the institutions that would enable him to do that that he settled for a cult hero and I think that was enough for him. He didn't want to go through all the machinery and relentless ego maintenance that it takes first to become a rock star and then to stay one.

WILL AMATO I was ranting to Roessler a couple of years ago about how derivative Darby was. For God's sake, he was cutting his chest open and throwing peanut butter into the audience—he took that from Iggy Pop; he took this and that from Bowie, he took this and that from this person, exactly like Bowie did. His lyrics were sometimes really brilliant, and he had all this charisma, but there was something missing. The guy just assembled himself out of other people's shticks! How could he be so blatant in ripping off Iggy, and Bowie, and Adam Ant? Paul listened to all this, and then he reminded me of a startling thing—that Darby was only 22 years old when he killed himself! He was a very young dude! He had barely even started, you know? That put it all in perspective for me.

BOB BIGGS   The "downward spiral" was Darby accepting a role that he had trapped himself in and had started believing in. He created this Darby Crash cult, the Circle One group that gathered around him, and maybe it had begun as a huge joke at everybody's expense among his old high school chums, but now it had all become real, and now how was he going to get out of it? There was just no way out.

HELLIN KILLER   It was some kind of monster, some kind of force. He did a really good job of creating it, but he got sucked into it; he got sucked down... he invoked something he couldn't deal with. It was exactly what he wanted to invoke—he was always trying to pull in all the weird shit … and control people.

GEZA X   Darby was a premeditated would-be apocalyptic cult leader. He chose his doomsday and he did a bang-up job on it, I gotta say. It's lived on as the stuff of mythology. He flat-out said he was gonna do it, and I think he did it exactly when he said he'd do it, according to something he wrote in 1975. He used to say, "I'm gonna kill myself in five years." He'd put some spin on the Bowie song "Five Years." That's how he had all those girls weeping onstage 'cause they knew he was gonna die. He preyed on the female instinct to save things, especially a certain type of female who go for guys who seemed doomed, where the infatuated woman is led into believing she will be the one who saves him from himself, or whatever. Darby was very unhappy and he had it planned out that he was gonna get as far as he could and then off himself.

GENESIS P-ORRIDGE   I knew Darby Crash was doomed the same way I knew Sid Vicious was doomed the first time I met him. I actually shivered. Like Sid, Darby's life became an absolute commitment to recklessness … he had no choice. Some people are like that. They're here for a very specific catalytic reason and their body and soul are here temporarily to perform a function on behalf of the psychic hygiene of the species and then they go. And they should be honored for that. People should be completely non-judgmental of those characters. Some become street people who never get to express their destiny and some are very fortunate and land almost accidentally into a critical position in the popular culture.

BELOVED SON & BROTHER

JAN PAUL BEAHM
DARBY CRASH
1958 ———→ 1980

CAST OF CHARACTERS

O

Will Amato. Artist. Illustrator. Animator. High school friend of Paul Beahm and Georg Ruthenberg who attended IPS with them.

Amber. Patron of Darby Crash. He crashed at her pad and she supported him during 1979, and paid for the trip to London in early 1980 where the two stayed a month or so with legendary Britpunk stylist Jordan (Pamela Rooke). Now a mother and part-time legal secretary.

Jill Ash. High school friend of Paul Beahm.

Chris Ashford. Friend of Paul Beahm and Georg Ruthenberg and founder of What? Records. Drove Georg and Paul to meet Iggy Pop. Put out the "Forming" single in July, 1977, and hooked the Germs up with Brendan Mullen at the Masque. Still a freelance buyer and rare record dealer.

Alice Bag. Lead singer, co-founder of The Bags. Schoolteacher. Occasional member of Cholita. Wife. Mother.

Faith Baker. Darby Crash's mother.

Faith Baker, Jr. Darby Crash's sister.

K.K. Barrett. Former drummer, the Screamers. Art director. Husband to Trudie. Triple progeny family man.

Bill Bartell. (AKA Pat Fear) Founder of White Flag, Gasatanka Records. Producer of Germs tribute album in 1996.

Paul Beahm. Born Jan Paul Beahm. Became Bobby Pyn, and one year later, Darby Crash. Deceased.

Nicky Beat. Former drummer with the Weirdos, and many other bands. Played on the "Lexicon Devil" ep with the Germs. Professional drum tech.

Judith Bell. Co-founder with Chris D. of Upsetter Records. Animation artist.

Iris Berry. Writer. Former member of the Ringling Sisters.

Claude Bessy. Chief reporter for *Slash*. Member of Catholic Discipline. Deceased.

Jello Biafra. Lead singer, Dead Kennedys, the first West Coast punk band to make any impression in the UK. Founder of Alternative Tentacles. Endlessly verbose dialectician. Once ran for mayor of San Francisco. Sliced an artery trying to impress Darby Crash.

Bob Biggs. Former college football star who financed *Slash* magazine and Slash Records. Sold the Slash catalogue to London Records for a reported $14M.

Rodney Bingenheimer. Former owner of Rodney's English Disco, former Mayor of the Glitter Critters Ball. Local Sunday night radio institution since 1976 (KROQ-FM).

Ella Black. Lead singer, Ella and the Blacks. Actress. Currently fluctuating between Manhattan Beach and London where she works for Stephen Berkoff.

Black Randy. (AKA Jon Morris) Auteur, speed freak, coprophile, infantilist, telemarketer; leader of Black Randy & the Metro Squad. Was heavily involved with Pat Garrett and David Brown in the creative side of Dangerhouse Records, financed and owned by Brown. Was responsible for etching his love of the secret male hustler underworld around the early punk scene into L.A. punk lore with the song, "Trouble at the Cup." Died in the mid-'80s of AIDS.

Don Bolles. Former drummer: Germs, 45 Grave, Celebrity Skin. Bootlegger. Rare record dealer. Free music practitioner. Radio DJ. Born Jimmie Giorsetti.

D.J. Bonebrake. Classically-trained percussionist, marimbist, vibraphonist, trap drummer for X and, briefly, for The Germs. Husband, father. Still a regularly employed musician.

Robin Boyarsky. Attended IPS with Paul Beahm and Georg Ruthenberg.

David Brown. Berklee School of Music alum. Keyboardist-arranger for The Screamers and Black Randy's Metro Squad. Financed Dangerhouse Records. High priestess of sadistic L.A. punk vitriol Black Randy style.

Dez Cadena. Former member of Black Flag, DC3, Vida.

Charlotte Caffey. Guitarist-songwriter for the Eyes, the Go-Go's. Mother. Wife of Jeff "Redd Kross" McDonald.

Ginger Canzoneri. Former manager of the Go-Go's. Graphic designer-artist.

Jena Cardwell. Former scenester, longtime girlfriend of Pat Smear.

Belinda Carlisle. Formerly Dottie Danger, initially a drummer of The Germs who never played in even one rehearsal. Became lead singer for the Go-Go's. Former '80s pop star. Made in the shade in the South of France, Belinda enjoys a Lifestyle of the Rich & Famous family life with Morgan Mason and children.

Sean Carrillo. Former scenester from East L.A., co-founder with Bibbe Hansen of Café Troy (the coffee-shop successor to the Brave Dog).

Exene Cervenka. Singer-writer for X. Poet. Mother.

Bob Clark. Artist.

Casey Cola. Former scenester, roommate of Darby. Lived through her heroin overdose and suicide pact with Darby Crash.

Cherie Currie. Former lead singer, the Runaways.

Chris D. Lead singer-writer the Flesheaters, the Divine Horsemen, co-founder of Upsetter Records. Conceptualist of Ruby Records, an imprint of Slash. *Slash* magazine contributor.

John Denney. Lead singer, the Weirdos. Artist.

John Doe. Bassist-singer-songwriter for X. Poet. Actor.

Lorna Doom. Germs bassist. Lives with parents in Thousand Oaks. Born Theresa Ryan.

Tomata du Plenty. Lead singer, the Screamers. Deceased.

Maggie Ehrig. Ex-roommate of Darby Crash. Mother.

Eugene. Former skinhead. Troubled teen in *The Decline of Western Civilization*. Recording artist. World traveling itinerant musician.

Kim Fowley. Former manager-producer, the Runaways. Song publisher, record producer, recording artist.

Don Garstang. Drummer, Darby Crash Band, Ella and the Blacks. Married to Mary Rat from the Plunger Sisters.

Tommy Gear. Former keyboardist-songwriter, the Screamers. Journalist.

Pleasant Gehman. Former 'zine editor, Lobotomy, former member of the Screamin' Sirens and the Ringling Sisters. Author.

Gerber. Queen of L.A. Punk. Born Michelle Bell.

Terry Graham. Former drummer, the Bags, the Gun Club.

Jack Grisham. Lead singer, Vicious Circle, TSOL.

Matt Groening. Illustrator. Creator of *Life In Hell* and *The Simpsons*.

Rob Henley. Surfer boyfriend of Darby Crash who was to replace Don Bolles in the Germs. Last heard of living in Washington state.

Fred Holtby. Co-founder of IPS, the alternative high school program that Paul Beahm and Georg Ruthenberg attended. Still instructing at University High School in 2002.

Gus Hudson. *Flipside* contributing editor. First produced Beck.

Barbara James. Former scenestress and Canterbury resident.

Joan Jett. Member of The Runaways, leader of Joan Jett and the Blackhearts, produced the Germs' *G.I.* lp.

Shawn Kerri. Illustrator. Deceased.

Hellin Killer. High school and early scene friend to Paul Beahm and Georg Ruthenberg. Former member of the Plunger Sisters. Mother of three, wife of Paul Roessler.

Tony Kinman. Former bassist-singer-songwriter, the Dils, Rank & File, Blackbird, Cowboy Nation.

Tito Larriva. Child entertainer from Mexico City. Former leader, the Plugz, the Cruzados. Husband. Father. Record producer. Actor. Currently leads Tito & Tarantula around Europe and Latin America.

Craig Lee. Journalist, former member of the Bags. Deceased.

Jenny Lens. Photographer, Mac artist-teacher.

Robert Lopez. Member of the Zeros. Tours the world as El Vez, the "Mexican Elvis." Author.

Jeff McDonald. Former member of Redd Kross. Husband, father of child with Charlotte Caffey. The couple live as a family in the Hollywood Hills.

Allan MacDonell. (AKA Basho Macko). *Slash* contributor. Former executive editor of *Hustler* magazine.

Toby Mamis. Publicist.

Kristine McKenna. Journalist, author, art historian.

Richard Meltzer. Rock critic/philosopher/journalist who was the bridge between the subjective macho "gonzo" style journalism of Hunter S. Thompson and the subsequent pugilistic rantings of Lester Bangs. Author. Brief boyfriend of Nicole Panter prior to her punk days.

Regi Mentle. Former friend of Darby Crash. Convicted killer.

Tony Montesion. Friend of Amber and Darby Crash. Self-professed fomert hardcore junkie. Photographer.

Keith Morris. Former lead singer of Black Flag, the Circle Jerks, icon of American hardcore.

Mugger. Former Black Flag roadie, SST employee. High school buddy of Rob Henley in Huntington Beach. Helped to create the punk rock stage-diving phenomenom by chasing kids offstage so fast they had to dive back out into the crowd to get away from him.

Hal Negro. Singer for Hal Negro and the Satin Tones. Lawyer. Bird-dogger.

Mike Ness. Leader-songwriter, Social Distortion. Husband, father. Orange County real estate speculator.

Jack Nitzsche. Legendary bad boy arranger-producer who deteriorated so far down on hard drugs and booze he was once arrested while under the psychotic impression he was waging a Travis Bickle-style vigilante war against pimps and prostitution which he thought were ruining Hollywood Boulevard. This was shortly after working wih the Germs for the soundtrack of the movie, *Cruising*. Deceased.

Joe Nolte. Former bandmember of the Last, former resident of the Church.

Margot Olaverra. Founder-conceptualist-bassist for the Go-Go's.

Steve Olson. Skateboard champ. Actor. Journalist.

Genesis P-Orridge. Former member of Throbbing Gristle, Psychic TV, conceptualist of "industrial" art culture.

Gary Panter. Artist-illustrator. Lives in Brooklyn.

Nicole Panter. (AKA Nicole-Elena Olivieri) Former Germs manager. Divorced from artist Gary Panter. Instructor at Cal Arts.

Mike Patton. Former bassist, The Middle Class. Not the Faith No More Mike Patton.

Leonard Phillips. Singer-songwriter, keyboards, the Dickies.

Phranc. "America's Favorite Jewish Lesbian Folksinger." Early punk scenester.

John Pochna. Co-founder of the Zero Zero Club. Gallery owner, art dealer.

Kid Congo Powers. Guitarist. Former member of the Cramps, the Gun Club, the Bad Seeds.

Bobby Pyn. AKA Paul Beahm, Darby Crash.

Rik L. Rik. Lead singer, F-Word. Recorded with Negative Trend from the Bay Area. Deceased.

Paul Roessler. Former keyboardist, the Screamers, Twisted Roots. Husband to Hellin Killer, father.

Donnie Rose. Friend of Darby Crash. Hustler. Deceased.

Gorilla Rose. Close friend of the Screamers.

Georg Ruthenberg. AKA Pat Smear, lead guitarist, the Germs, and later for Nirvana, the Foo Fighters. Producer of Harlow.

Greg Shaw. Founder Bomp magazine and record company. Record producer. Major-league vinyl record archivist including the World's Ultimate Anglophile collection.

Andy Seven. Tenor sax player, Arthur J. and the Gold Cups, Trash Can School. Works for the City of Los Angeles.

Penelope Spheeris. Documentary producer-director of *The Decline of Western Civilization* series. Mother. Real estate mogul.

Seymour Stein. The founder of Sire Records, the label bankrolled by Warner Bros. that was going to make punk rock happen nationally. Sends a circular open letter to the nation's FM programmers denouncing punk and dissociating himself and his bands from "punk." The preferred term, he declared, is "New Wave."

Shawn Stern. Co-founder with brothers, Mark and Adam, of BYO Records and Youth Brigade.

Tony the Hustler. Prostitute friend and roommate of Darby Crash.

Top Jimmy. Lead singer Top Jimmy & the Rhythm Pigs. Chef. Bartender at the Zero Zero Club. Deceased.

Trixie. Former member of the Plunger Sisters. Dealer in antiques and rare collectibles. Lives in New York City.

Trudie. Former member of the Plunger Sisters. Married to K.K. Barrett. Mother.

Gregg Turner. Former fanzine writer, former member of the Angry Samoans. Math professor.

Lee Ving. Leader-songwriter, Fear. Actor. Still tours and records.

Mike Watt. Co-founder with D. Boon and George Hurley of the Minutemen. Tours the world playing with umpteen bands and semi-impromptu ensembles.

Sandy West. Former drummer, the Runaways.

Jane Wiedlin. AKA Jane Drano. Songwriter-guitarist, the Go-Go's.

Caldwell Williams. Former high school teacher at Uni High. Conceptualist, co-founder of IPS.

Jimmy Wilsey. Former bassist, the Avengers, Chris Isaak and Silvertone.

Philomena Winstanley. Former *Slash* staff member. Animation artist. Teacher. Resides in Barcelona.

X-8. Cofounder of *Flipside* fanzine. Works in music clearances at Paramount.

Geza X. Producer, former member of the Deadbeats, Arthur J. & the Gold Cups, the Mommymen. Produced the "Lexicon Devil" ep.

Billy Zoom. Lead guitarist for X. Record producer. Runs his own audio and amp repair shop in the City of Orange; plays guitar in the local Baptist church.

U: DO YOU USE A DICTIONARY WHEN YOU WRITE?
D: Once in a while. There are 26 meanings for the word "the", and I like to know exactly what I mean. I learned this from Scientology.
U: WHAT'S THIS ABOUT SCIENTOLOGY?
D: I took one course. I was going to join staff, then I quit.
U: WOULD SCIENTOLOGY DO SOMETHING FOR ME?
D: Sure, if you've got $10,000 to waste.
U: DOES IT MAKE YOU FEEL DIFFERENT?
D: Sure it does. But so does smoking a joint. So does walking down the street with blue hair.
U: IS "SEXBOY" AN AUTOBIOGRAPHICAL SONG?
D: No, I hate it. That's why we don't do it. It was either the first or second song I wrote. I said, watch, I'll write this "punk" song...It fits the Screamers image better.. it's like a comedy.
U: I LIKE THE PART ABOUT THE KNIFE IN THE CUT...
D: You must be into Freud or something...
U: IT'S JUST A NEW WAY OF SAYING AN OLD THING.
D: That's all everything is.
U: IS IT TRUE YOU HAVE A CLIQUE OF GROUPIES CALLED "CRASH TRASH"?
D: They're not called that...they're not groupies... they're more like followers.
U: WHO IS YOUR FAVORITE WOMAN? D: Katherine Hepburn.

U: ANY POLITICAL BELIEFS?
D: No, just us. We don't believe in politics at all. We're fascists. We don't believe in anything that's existing. Everyone else has tried them, and nothing has ever worked. So either you've got to throw it all away and start with something completely new, or keep on going, playing the game, knowing it's not going to work. We were thinking of being Communists like the Dils, but they aren't Communists anyways. They auditioned a drummer in our garage (not the one they've got now.) This guy wouldn't wear straight leg pants and cut his hair, I'm serious, they told him he had to do that, and stop acting like a college boy. One of them, you know the one that looks like Abe Lincoln? He told me, we're not Communists, that was their manager's idea.

DARBY ⓒRASH

U: DO YOU THINK THE GERMS WILL ACHIEVE MASS ACCEPTANCE?
D: No, Germs is exactly what it means. All it was meant to be was a step to go on to something else.
U: EVER BEEN APPROACHED BY A MAJOR LABEL?
D: Bryan Ferry...but when he met us, he wouldn't talk to us.

U: YOU WERE GOING TO HAVE AN AD IN SLASH SAYING 6 MILLION JEWS CAN'T BE WRONG...

D: Yeah, we still are. The first interview we did with Slash they said, well, what would you like to say to America? I said, everyone kill President Carter, and they didn't print it. They're trying to be like a regular newspaper and edit out the bad things. I don't think they could really get in trouble unless someone shot Carter and they tried to blame it all on us.

Darby Crash interviewed by Chris D. for *Upsetter*, circa '78.

LYRICS OF THE GERMS' RECORDED AND UNRECORDED OUTPUT
BY DARBY CRASH

AMERICAN LEATHER

Looking for a way out
I put my foot out of line
Really like to break-out
I feel so confined

American leather
The poisonous members
Not alone—not together
Their American leather

Saw you on a dark road
Brought myself along
Got a sense of conflict
But I know what's wrong

I know that kinda feeling
So I built my place up high
But you'll never find me kneeling
'Cause I'm too occupied

BEYOND HURT—BEYOND HELP
written in 1980 for the Darby Crash Band

Heart can't feel the wine
Blessed kid's got no time
Feel the water running
Through these veins of mine

I saw the future sinking
When I stepped outside
I saw the highway running
In a long and waiting line

No caring where there's care for
No seeing what I've sought
I'm singing through the ashes
Of the ruins for which I fought

I'm speeding through this tortured land
But all in all I'm fine
I'm reading through the torn pages
Of my L.A. Times

Beyond hurt—beyond help
Beyond here—there's no one else
No one else

CAUGHT IN MY EYE

Through your dark eyes
You can feel my
Every sin
When I walk right
Into a straight line
This world of yours
I got you caught in my eye, again

You're the fall guy
In the corner
Of my gloom
It feels like
Everything I see
Is nothing new
I got you caught in my eye, again

There's a door there
That opens
Without you
And the door lies
With its open keys
To my room
Flames of the torchlight
Fill my thighs
And I crave fulfill
And I consume 'em
But I don't give
Got you caught in my eye, again

CAT'S CLAUSE

Down to the feline den I crawl,
To join the feline force that waits.
I strike a sort of katsy stance
As they look into my cat-like face.

From behind their sable masks
Not a purring sound is heard.
Their luminous eyes catch my every word;
Tonight's the night the tables turn.

You've had your chance and now at last
You've been found guilty by the order of the cat...
You've changed our laws and now because of that—
You're going to live in the claws of a cat.

Talons on and operating
We're sure that you're cooperating.
Straighten up that feline face
And put your footsie pads in place.
Practice up your katsy glance
And imitate my cat-like stance.
Tonight's the night the cats return.
We'll corner them by the alley wall
Bite and scratch them until they fall.
Lap their blood and steal their young.
Finish them off just for fun.

Tonight's the night the cats will run.
Mommy I hear the cat at the door.
I think he's cold will you let him in?
Lay them out and leave our mark.
A cat scratch angle above the heart.
On we'll go to another house
To play the game of cat and mouse...
Why do you plead when we don't care?
We're the cats and we don't scare.
You've had your turn and now it's ours...
We're the cats and we've got claws...

CENTER OF DESTRUCTION
[written 1980 for the Darby Crash band]

No face in the mirror
No blood on my hands

I'm heading for the center of destruction

On my way down
I'm looking around
Can't spot a phase
On my way to this place

I see the light
Is the nightmare rising
Think it's right
To refuse the dying

CIRCLE ONE

I'm Darby Crash
A social blast
Chaotic master
I'm Darby Crash
Your mecca's gash
Prophetic stature

I'm Darby Crash
A one way match
Demonic flasher

Deep, deep, deep, in my eyes
There's a round, round, round,
circle of lives

It's a tame, tame, tame sort of world
Where you're caught, bought,
taught, as it twirls...

I'm Darby Crash
A social blast
Chaotic master

Snap, crackle, pop
Snap, crackle, pop
Snap, crackle, pop—in here

Snap, crackle, pop
Snap, crackle, pop
Snap, crackle, pop—out there

COMMUNIST EYES

I'm looking through Communist eyes
I'm seeing planes in bloodshot skies
I see the flag of a working people
Who conceal the lies in the stars and sickle
It's a double edge

Communist eyes—c'mon inside
I can't ever find the way out
Communist eyes—lost inside
I never get a day out

I'm looking through Communist eyes
All I see is an old man's alibi
There's a world outside but I'm unaware
I open my books but the pages stare
It's a double edge

Communist eyes—all so blind
I can't even play the game now

I'm living through Communist times
I wave my flag and hold my head high
I can feel the glory of my comrades in masses
But I'm waiting for the day when this madness passes
It's a double edge...

DRAGON LADY

You walk to the temple on the boulevard
You know the way in 'cause you're
The son of God

She opens the door with
a sardonic glance
You drop to the floor making your plans

It's a real cool parody
That's my dragon lady
In a low society with no variety

She lives a tongue-in-cheek dream
There's something in her eyes
that nature denied

She's a whirlwind creature of cultural ties
A preacher of schemes and self denial
She talks up a storm with news and belial
To live in Brahmin tragedy
Driven it seems by fantasies
A life like this is sad to see

A smile kept quite in reverie
The clock on the mantle hands stop crossed
The rug on the floors a resting place for the dust
The talk of the town yet she's never been seen
A loving relation with a well-trained machine

FORMING

Rip them down
Hold them up
Tell them that
I'm your gun
Pull my trigger
I'm bigger than—

Mr. Prez in his big white house
Listen he sez we're coming out
Infiltration—we're numbing your minds
Concentration—we've done time

Over there the queen she sez
Let's stamp them out and dry those tears
Saturation—we want it in taxes
Flagellation—we've got gashes

In the cold, the czar's claimin'
Just protectin', rockets aimin'
Alteration—the Earth is changin'
Observation—we want action

I the Emperor proclaim
Us the masters we rule this game
Inclination—somethin' to dream on
Deprivation—we are sons

GET A GRIP

I'm the only thing you need
I'm so real you can feel me bleed
I'm the coat you left behind
I'm the one you'll never find

Get a grip, get a grip on me
On the streets another thing
I'll push your knife and pull the string
Put your thoughts into my mind
I'll show you things of another kind

Get a grip, get a grip on me

GOING DOWN

Sifting through apocalypse
All I want's to catch a glimpse
Just another broken day
My whole world's gone away
I feel the ceilings coming down
I watch the deadmen run around
Trying hard to change the course
'cause they know what's best for us
Your whole world's coming down
Close to the bottom—close to the sound
Your whole world's let me down
Drag me down to the underground
Sifting through apocalypse
Already new it would come to this
Just another game to play
How many ways have I got to play
Hear them running faster now
They wear the hooves of Satan's crowd
You came to visit for just one day
But now that you're here—
You're here to stay

GOLDEN BOYS

Go, go golden boys
You've got your war toys
Your haircuts all the same
And your eyes all blue
And you can march one-two
Into your leader's dreams

Tommy was just sixteen
When the fatherland declared
We've watched the world for oh so long
We're sure we can answer your prayers

Betty had a brother too
Who was called off to war
With a little help from somewhere
He knew he could even the score

Mother Mary had a son
His days were spent having fun
Then Monday he got a letter
You can make your country better

Millions on millions of boys lay dead
While mothers weep with upheld heads

LAND OF TREASON

Land of treason—waste no reason—we are breathing fire
We're packs of dogs—we're enemies of men—we are not desired
Our faces show—we've grown cold—but have not conspired
Old hearts gone—the suture's on—mother nations mired

I like a receptacle for the chosen dead, we find our bodies clawed
And with the scent of death, we find that we are not so very awed
Loyalties burned—the words are blurred—overturn your own
Walk the dogs and watch the doors—have your other stone
Stop the toys that march disordered—calculate the thrones
Feel the pulse descending—decaying hallowed tomes

In the starving sense you worship—the nations of debris
You wear a cost of sewage—that you've never even seen
The time is now—the vicious here—a stolen dinner code
The license of the savage land—that you've always sold
So bite the hand that needs you and bless another coal
The virus never issues—from a cotton so very old

As the lights come down and the guilty blaze; another sort of road
You wash your hands and start to climb the ladder that you stole
Slip the latch—and spin the sword—the money lords are poor
Push the tank—that rolls downhill—their sense of doom absorbed
Still the cat that breaks the night—tie him to the core
Chase the virtue that believes—that what's right is scored
It's a senseless cash in of right for right—what's wrong is never gone
And left is just a bastion for the fools golden dawn

LET'S PRETEND

Out on the streets what ya lookin' for
That thing in your bed's just another whore
That tear in your eye's not a tear at all
For that girl that you touch you could never fall
That stream in your mind it's a tearin' sty

Let's pretend you're vicious
Let's pretend you're cool
Let's pretend suspicious
Let's pretend you're fools

Your leather's tight but you wear it full
'Gether is right but you gotta be cool
You cut your wrists but you don't complain
You change your mind but you still feel the same
To dream ain't your kind just another lie

Sell us a story that we can believe
Spend your dollars on pills for relief
Love is a future that you just can't see
Standing answers to questions are free
Scream in your boredom life's just to die

Dive in problems just like stealin' a fix
Is your life to live or is it for kicks
Kick dirt in the faces of angry dream men
Stand on your chairs and spell don't let me in
Don't stand in the light cuz you know you can't cry

LEXICON DEVIL

I'm a lexicon devil with a battered brain
And I'm lookin' for a future—the world's my aim
So gimme gimme your hands—gimme gimme your minds
Gimme gimme your hands—gimme gimme your minds
Gimme gimme this—gimme gimme tha-a-a-a-t

I want toy tin soldiers that can push and shove
I want gunboy rovers that'll wreck this club
I'll build you up and level your heads
We'll run it my way, cold men and politics dead

I'll give you silver guns to drip old blood
Let's give this established joke a shove
We're gonna wreak havoc on this rancid mill
I'm searchin' for somethin' even if I'm killed

Empty out your pockets—you don't need their change
I'm giving you the power to rearrange
Together we'll run it to the highest prop
Tear it down and let it drop... away...

LION'S SHARE

All he sees are death masked stars
The lion's world is cold and sharp
All he wants is much too far
So he stalks the roads of token cars—
He snarls at winds that mean no harm
And takes the thorns in perfect form
A broken ideal rides inside the torture
Lion's denim hide
I want the lion's share
Gather up the broken chairs
Feed my mind unholy tests
Do me in I need to rest
He sleeps when nothing's in the air
Eats the scraps of some that care
He strains the right to overbear
Secrets hidden in the lair...
Pauses long enough to dream
Nightmares push the glowing scream
His shadowed eyes show the toll
Something only lions know

MANIMAL

I came into this world like a puzzled panther
Wanting to be caged
But something stood in the way
I was never quite tamed

I crossed the paths of right and wrong
And saw them take their toll
I saw armies that marched
And like animals they crawled

Evolution is a process too slow
To save my soul
But I've got this creature on my back
And it just won't let go

If I am only an animal
Then I can do no wrong
But they say something better
So I've gotta hold on

MEDIA BLITZ

I've got television
I've got supervision
No decisions for you
Media blitz—media blitz
Immediate hits—we rule

Don't steal your eyes off the TV screen
Can you realize we're what we've seen
Take an injection from the mad machine

Don't read the papers read between the lines
We're vision rapers and we seed the signs
You'll play your part in the master mind

We feed the science
We deal in riots
We play by ideal time
We're a government fix
All social convicts
Watch the idle rhymes

Bleed your heart out—that's all it's worth
Before you ever start—we planned it first
Forget the truth—accept your curse

NO GOD

I've read every book in the Bible Story
And all it ever brought me was another worry
Don't want God, give me a jury,
See ... there's no God to make up my mind—
No God givin' me time...

I peered in every window where I saw a cross
But I could never see just what they saw
In that piece of plaster on the wall
See... there's no God to fear—
No God to hear your cries...

I'd pray to anything out there
If only I was given some sign to bear
But while I wait I'm gonna live
See... there's no God to watch over me—
No God for human beings...

When I was small I obeyed his every word
Handed down to me by some thoughtful blur
But now I am as big as he
See ... no God bigger than me...
No God frightening me...

In my image I made he him and I gave him life
So he burned me, the creature has risen and I
Think you can see just what it is that's drivin'
Me around round...

We are the church we are good and we've got your
Millions God knows we should
I've read every book in the Bible Story
And all it ever brought me was another worry
Don't want God, give me a jury,
See... there's no God to make up my mind—
No God givin' me time...

NOT ALL RIGHT

Feeling not all right
My time's in a sand-slide
So hard not to unwind
Find some wall to climb—
Capsules cover the signs
My thoughts in a land mine
Some lights burn too bright
My nights hold too tight—
Slowed away outta breath
Won't wait to pass the test
Too late to answer lies
Don't even need to try—
Livin' in a fury
Life's kinda blurry
Dyin' in a hurry
Stories kinda lurid—
No time to worry
Gonna hang the jury
Broke up kinda early
All the bribes are working

Livin' in a fury
Life's kinda blurry
Dyin' in a hurry
Stories kinda lurid—
No time to worry
Gonna hang the jury
Broke up kinda early
All the scribes are working

NOW I HEAR THE LAUGHTER

Walkin' down the long road
Ran into a strange man
Said he thought he'd borrowed
Bought himself a game plan
Shook my head and nodded
That's all I ever plotted
That's all they ever wanted
That's all they ever saw then
Pulled music together
Laughter forever
Now I hear the laughter

THE OTHER NEWEST ONE

I feel your body's close to mine
I hear your breath and mine in time
I know I'm nothing but it's you that I need
I touch your skin and it starts to feed

You're not the first you're not the last
Another day another crash

My eyes meet yours in secret glance
Our bodies look in ancient stance
You whisper something and I
know it's good
You're acting crazy just like I
knew you would

You're not the first you're not the last
Another day another crash

Embracing my life between your thighs
We will perform in the deadly skies
Reducing my mind to endless nights
You send my dreams to their demise

Realized by your last breath
I take your hair into my hands
I pull it tight to fit your demands
feel my body into yours
know it's right cause that's
my soul you stir

You're not the first you're not the last
Another day another crash

RICHIE DAGGER'S CRIME

I'm Richie Dagger
I can stomp and swagger
I can take on all your heroes
I'm Richie Dagger
I'm young and haggard
The boy that nobody owns

He sits in his corner like a child despised
A crazy sort of cast comes over his eyes—
That's Richie Dagger's crime

He's the sort of boy who was never much loved
His idea of fun was society's grudge—
That's Richie Dagger's crime

His life was a mess
And his friends weren't quite the best
But he was satisfied—
That's Richie Dagger's crime
Suck me in and spit me out
Devour me in haste

He could set your mind ablaze
With sparkling eyes and visionary case
He stood like the remnant of an outbreak past
Wore something in his ear and
Boy was he sass--

SEX BOY

I take it anywhere, any time that I can
I'm the fucking son of a superman
I got a weapon that's as deadly as life
It's a well-trained tool of a master guy

Every day it's the same regime
A dozen boys are on my scene
Say sex boy will you come into my hand
They're all on the floor, I better do what I can
Take a number, it's supply and demand
Any time that I can

I put my knife into your gut
You gotta be above when you wanna make love
Say it exactly, sex boy, such a sideshow poster
After such a sweet sweet slut
Any time that I can
I'm the fucking son of a superman
I know what it takes
What in the time I can and can't do
I know what it takes to satisfy you
I know what it takes
That's why your time is due in the house of fortune
I take it out and you know it's gonna come from
behind
Just like you, and you, and you, and you

SHUT DOWN

Let me touch the tips of inculcated desire
And brush the fettered veil away
Shut down in the depths I lay...
If you want nothin' then I've got nothin'
I'm your annihilation man
Lemme get control I've got your minds
Now I want
Your souls, lemme get control
I've got your minds
Now I want control, I need control...
If you want somethin' then
I've got somethin'
I'm your annihilation man...

THE SLAVE

It starts in your head
And moves to your hands
Your body starts shakin'
'Cuz you're in demand
You do the slave to the beat
Of the neuro-sutra can can...

You're lashed 'twixt the stars
With your ice and motor cars:
You do the slave to the beat
Of the neuro-sutra can can
Oh yeah! Yeah! Pull out the Zen
I've got a Buddhist principle in my hand
Your life seems wasted your bodies laced in
Don't stop now you've got to trace it...

You put your hands together
Writhe in the shackle
You twist your body round
Till it starts to crackle:
You do the slave to the beat
Of the neuro-sutra can can...

Right here right now shake it in and out some
Lights on off now make it spin and fight now

STRANGE NOTES

Billy Druid's face is marble
He keeps every thought in its place
He lets the days turn tomorrow
Someone's always walking on his grave

He wears the linens just like Garbo
And talks at a saturnine pace
Listening to the strange notes marvel
Only giving what it takes

It's a sad man's world
And for Billy it's sure to crown
Dragging beauty into darkness
Inflicting a pale white frown

And the matter that runs
Through Billy's head
Is too concerned to fail

STREET DREAMS

I won't build my life on your demands 'cause
I get my truths from a tougher test and
I'm pullin' my mind from outta this mess

I've got street dreams—together with plans
I've got street dreams—chaotic new stands
I've got street dreams—ultra magic mess
I've got street dreams—you're gonna detest

I don't like the way the world's progressin'
God's on fire screamin' depressin' yeah
I want a future that's not in the past
I don't want your recycled trash—kill it!

I've got street dreams—together with plans
I've got street dreams—ultra magic mess
I've got street dreams—you're gonna detest

Mr. Bourgeois we're lookin' for you
We want our lives, we ain't got two
We're taking the keys to the locked doors
The future is for us the past is yours
Give us feelings give us more than you've got
Give us everything, everything we want:

Build me a world with nothing restrained
Give me a hand I guess I can't be blamed
If there's a drop to be bled it's for me
Yeah! Everything—everything for free...

SUICIDE MACHINE
(written in 1977)

[******] died yesterday
Put a gun in his mouth and blew his way out
Just a pill and a dream
It's a suicide machine

She danced all night to the storm in her mind
She waits in the gutter, something she'll never find
Just a sill & a scheme
It's a suicide machine

She cried about the world
She slit her throat to fight it
Someone had told her she'd had it
Just a sill & a scheme
It's a suicide machine

Bobby had lost his sacred identity
He saw his masculinity in a glass of Bordeaux
Just watch the show
It's a sparkler to his child eyes
It's a suicide machine

You find his wish
Get yourself some [munitch?]
Click!

It's a suicide machine

THROW IT AWAY

I've been looking, looking so far
You've been this thing, listening so hard
I've been talking, stalking all night
You've been thinking, thinking I'm right—

I've been missing, listing some parts
I've been falling, calling it art
We've been lurking, working for clues
We've been whistling, this thing for you

Trying to make some kinda sense out of it
Throw it away—throw it away
Trying to make some kinda sense out of it
Throw it away—throw it away
Don't know what I really got
Don't know if I even thought

VILE BABIES

I was born wit' a test tube in my mouf'
A rattle that kills—a gov'ment handout
A set life that was waiting for me
My birthplace marked with a simple B:

We're your vial babies
We've got no cravings
No genes for saving
We're the children God gave thee, maybe…

Love was a virgin, mother of decline
Sex was a killer, destroyer of lines
So you took away a natural gift
Thinking you gave the human race a lift:

We're your vial babies
Just your scrapings
We're not depraving
We're the children God gave thee, maybe…

So you got what you wanted, a perfect race
Now you can flaunt your exacto face
And when God frowns down on you
Ask him he'd like one too:

We're your vial babies
No hurt or straining
We're not complaining
We're the children God gave thee, maybe…

WHAT WE DO IS SECRET

Standing in the line we're aberrations
Defects in a defect's mirror
And we've been here all the time real fixations
Hidden deep in the furor—
What we do is secret—secret!

We're influential guys for the D.C.C.
We can lie so perfect
And we've got a party line to every call
It's a very short circuit—
What we do is secret—secret!

Licensed to drill with the torch in our lives
Walking on shallow water
Progressed to the point of no distinction
Dementia of a higher order—
What we do is secret—secret!

WE MUST BLEED

It's Sunday and the streets aren't clear
The traffic's screaming
but we can't hear
The sounds...the metals...
driving us mad...
The sounds...the metals...
driving us mad...
We must bleed, we must bleed,
we must bleed

The crash as the bottle breaks
Flashes its will through my veins
The pain...the colors...
making me sane...
The pain...the colors...
making me sane...
the pain...the colors...
making me sane...
We must bleed, we must bleed,
we must bleed

I'm not one I'm two, I'm not one
I'm two, I'm not one I'm two
I want out now, I want out now
I want out now now now now now
now now now...

GERMS DISCOGRAPHY

LEGAL RELEASES:

Forming/Sex Boy single (WHAT 01. Released 7/77 Through What? Records)
"Forming" (3:03)/"Sex Boy" Live (2:12)
> Note: These songs were recorded in Pat Smear's garage using his parents reel-to-reel. The echo was produced because they had pressed a button they were unaware of. There was one mic for vocals, and one mic for the music.

Lexicon Devil ep (SCAM-01. Released 5/78 Through Slash Records)
"Lexicon Devil" (2:03)/"Circle One" (1:46)/"No God" (1:52)
> Note: These songs were produced by Geza X.

(GI) lp (SR-103. Released 10/79 Through Slash Records)
"What We Do Is Secret" (0:42)/"Communist Eyes" (2:13)/"Land Of Treason" (2:09)/"Richie Dagger's Crime" (1:55)/"Strange Notes" (1:50)/"American Leather" (1:09)/"Lexicon Devil" (1:42)/"Manimal" (2:11)/"Our Way" (1:57)/"We Must Bleed" (3:01)/"Media Blitz" (1:30)/"The Other Newest One" (2:45)/"Let's Pretend" (2:32)/"Dragon Lady" (1:37)/"The Slave" (1:02)/"Shut Down (Annihilation Man)" (9:39)

What We Do Is Secret ep (SREP-108. Released 8/81 Through Slash Records)
"Round And Round" (2:15)/"Lexicon Devil"/"Circle One"/"Caught In My Eye" (3:23)/"No God"/"The Other Newest One"/"My Tunnel"
> Note: "Round and Round" was recorded in 1977 by What Records, produced by Chris Ashford. "Lexicon Devil," "Circle One" and "No God" are from the "Lexicon Devil" ep. "Caught In My Eye" was recorded in 1979 by Slash Records, produced by Joan Jett. "The Other Newest One" and "My Tunnel" was recorded December 3, 1980, live at the Starwood, by Lee Rickmers.

MIA (SR-45239-4. Released Through Slash Records, 1993)
"Forming"/"Sex Boy"/"Lexicon Devil"/"Circle One"/"No God"/"What We Do Is Secret"/"Communist Eyes"/"Land Of Treason"/"Richie Dagger's Crime"/"Strange Notes"/"American Leather"/"Lexicon Devil"/"Manimal"/"Our Way"/"We Must Bleed"/"Media Blitz"/"The Other Newest One"/"Let's Pretend"/"Dragon Lady"/"The Slave"/"Shut Down"/"Caught In My Eye"/"Round And Round"/"My Tunnel"/"Throw It Away"/"Not All Right"/"Now I Hear The Laughter"/"Going Down"/"Lion's Share"/"Forming 2"

Live from the Masque Benefit, 1978. CD only. (Released through House of Punk/Flipside Records, 1994)
"Let's Pretend"/"No God"/ "The Slave"/ "Shutdown"/ "Hang On To Yourself"/ "Forming."

Live from the Masque Benefit, Volume 2. CD Only. Same as House of Punk/Flipside release. Tracking the same, but with different artwork. Re-issued by Year One Records, 1996.

Live from the Masque Compilation. (BA 1170. CD and vinyl. Released through Bacchus Archives/Dionysus Records, 2002). One Germs' song only.
"Let's Pretend"

TRIBUTES AND COVERS

A Small Circle of Friends lp and cd (Crass Records #60150-13038-2. 1996).
NOFX: "Forming."
FREE KITTEN: "Sex Boy." Kim Gordon—v, g, Julie Cafritz—g, Mark Ibold—b, Yoshimi-d.
MELVINS: "Lexicon Devil." King Buzzo—v, g, b, Dale Crover—d.
THE HOLEZ: "Circle One." Courtney Love—v, b, Pat Smear—g, Eric Erlandson—g, Patty Schemel—d.
D GENERATION: "No God." Jessie Malin—v, Howie Pyro—b, Danny Sage—g, Michael Wildwood—d, Richard Bacchus—g.
MIKE WATT & J.: "What We Do Is Secret." Mike Watt—b, v, J. Mascis—g, d,
RUINED EYE: "Land of Treason." Keith Morris—v, Dave Navarro—g, Sean Ysuelt—b, J.—g, Greg Rogers—d.
THE POSIES: "Richie Dagger's Crime." Jon Auer—g, v, Ken Stringfellow—g, v, Dave Fox—b, Mike Musburger—d.
O-MATIC: "Strange Notes." Michelle Bodine—g, v, Rob Tarbell—b, Scott Bodine—g, Will Gale—d.
WHITE FLAG: "Manimal." Pat Fear—g, v, Trace Element—d, Ronnie Barnett—12-string b, Jello B. Afro—g.
THAT DOG: "We Must Bleed." Anna Waronker—v, g, Petra Haden—v, Tony Maxwell—d, Rachel Haden—b, v.
FLEA: "Media Blitz." Flea—b, v, g, d.
SATOR: "The Other Newest One." Chips Kiesbye—v, g, Kent Norberg—v, b, Michael Olsson—d, Hans Gafvert—k, v.
THE WRENS: "Let's Pretend." Kevin Whelan—b, v, Charles Bissell—g, v, Greg Whelan—g, v, Jerry MacDonald—d.
MATTHEW SWEET: "Dragon Lady." All instruments played by Matthew Sweet.
GUMBALL: "Caught In My Eye." Don Fleming—g, Eric Vermillion—b, v, Jay Spiegel—d, Malcolm Riviera—g.
MEAT PUPPETS: "Not All Right." Cris Kirkwood—b, v, Curt Kirkwood—g, v, Derrick Bostrom—d.
PUZZLED PANTHERS: "Now I Hear The Laughter." Mike D.—v, Thurston Moore—g, Kira—b, Dave Markey—d.
L7: "Lion's Share." Suzy Gardner—v, g, Donita Sparks—g, Dee Plakas—d, Jennifer Finch—b.
MONKEYWRENCH: "Shut Down" (cd only) Mark Arm—v, g, Steve Turner—b, Tim Kerr—g, Martin Bland—d, Thom Price—g.
Executive Producer: Bill Bartell

OTHER RELEASES

The Decline Of Western Civilization (The Movie by Penelope Spheeris)
Segments Include: Eugene (Interview)/"Attention..." (Band Intros)/Nausea (X)/"Punk Is ..." (Interview)/White Minority (Black Flag)/Depression (Black Flag)/The Black Flag Interview/Revenge (Black Flag)/The Germs Interview/Manimal (Germs)/The Germs Interview (Part II)/Shut Down (Germs)/Slash Magazine (Interview)/Underground Babylon (Catholic Discipline)/Slash Magazine (Interview Cont.)/Barbie Doll Lust (Catholic Discipline)/Slash Magazine (Interview Cont.)/Unheard Music (X)/The X Interview/Beyond & Back (X)/The X Interview (Part II)/Johny Hit And Run Paulene (X)/We're Desperate (X)/Security Meeting (Interview)/Red Tape (Circle Jerks)/Back Against The Wall (Circle Jerks)/I Just Want Some Skank (Circle Jerks)/Beverly Hills (Circle Jerks)/Wasted (Circle Jerks)/Eugene & Friends (Interview Segments... Includes Pat Smear & Lorna Doom)/Prowlers In The Night (Alice Bag Band)/"Gluttony" (Alice Bag Band)/"The Pogo Dance..." (Interview)/Fear Intro/I Don't Care About You (Fear)/Beef Bologna (Fear)/I Love Livin' In The City (Fear)/Let's Have A War (Fear)

Note: This above sequence is from the order that appeared in the movie, not on the soundtrack.

Cruising movie soundtrack (Lorimar Motion Pictures, released in 1980 through Sony Music Entertainment Inc. JC 36410)
"Lion's Share" (2:29)
> Note: The following songs were also recorded at the same session for this release, and did not appear on the soundtrack, or the released recording, but were included on *MIA* and partially on "What We Do is Secret" (Slash). Session Recordings: "My Tunnel" (2:28)/"Throw It Away" (2:08)/"Not All Right" (3:55)/"Now I Hear The Laughter" (2:46)/"Going Down" (1:49)

What Is It? compilation (W12 2403. Released 9/82 through What? Records)
"Forming 2" (1:37)

Real Punk! The Nasty Years (CLP 9684-2, released 1996 by Cleopatra Records)
"Throw It Away" (rehearsal)

BOOTLEG RELEASES

Germicide—Live At The Whisky (A108: released 1981 by ROIR)
"Forming"/"Sex Boy"/"Victim"/"Street Dreams"/"Let's Pretend"/"Get A Grip"/"Suicide Machine"/"Sugar Sugar"/"Teenage Clone"/"Wild Baby"/"Grand Old Flag"

Rock N' Rule, Live @ the Masque Christmas Party—Whisky A-Go-Go, 12/79 (Released 1986)
"Lion's Share"/"Lets Pretend"/"Richie Dagger's Crime"/"What We Do Is Secret"/"Art"/"Communist Eyes"/"Caught In My Eye"/"Media Blitz"/"Lexicon Devil"/"Manimal"/"Our Way"/"False Start"/"Shut Down"

Cats Clause (released 1993 Munster/Gasatanka)
"Public Image"★/"Lions Share"★/"Strange Notes"★/"Shut Down"★/"Lexicon Devil"★★/"The Other Newest One"★★/"My Tunnel"★★★/"Circle One"%/"Strange Notes"%
> ★ "From the reunion show and Germs riot @ the Great Gatsby"
> ★★ "From the Hong Kong Café."
> ★★★ "From the Fleetwood."
> % "From the Canterbury rehearsal."

Media Blitz (CLEO #37312. Released In 1993 Through Cleopatra Records.)
"Round And Round"★/"Strange Notes"★/"Caught In My Eye"★/"Media Blitz"★/"What We Do Is Secret"★/"Let's Pretend"★★/"Lexicon Devil"★★/"Manimal"★★/"Our Way"★★/"Shut Down"★★/"What We Do Is Secret"★★/"Art"★★/"Communist Eyes"★★/"Lion's Share"★★/"Lion's Share"★★★/"Throw It Away"★★★
> ★ "From the Hong Kong Café."
> ★★ "Live @ The Whisky."
> ★★★ "From a rehearsal."

GERMS' GIG LIST AND KEY EVENTS

O

Assembled by **Brendan Mullen**

1977

April 16, 1977
World debut at the Orpheum, opening for the Weirdos and the Zeros.

Circa May, 1977
The Roxy ... *Up in Smoke* movie shoot.

June 21, 1977
Whisky ... Kim Fowley Presents ... sometimes called the "Sugar, Sugar" gig.

August 5, 1977
Larchmont Hall w/ Screamers, Dils ... Slash benefit.

August, 1977
The Old Firehouse, Venice, with performance art duo the Kipper Kids. While the Kippers perform to a packed room the Germs set up in another. When the Kips finish somebody announces there's a rock band playing in the next room. Most of the art swingers present have never even heard of the Germs. A few who traipse in for a quick look-see on the way out are astonished to see Bobby Pyn wrestled to the ground by two girls who throw beer on him and get in a hair-tugging match. A few audience members get splattered by beer. After about four songs the room empties except for three or four people. Pat yells: "Get out ... you bunch of stuck-up assholes" and launches into "Shut Down" while writhing on the floor. Bobby sits watching utterly bored and disinterested, Cliff Hanger kicks over his drums. Lorna stands there grinning. Bobby finally sticks his head in a sink. The first art performance meets punk event.

September 4, 1977
Labor Day weekend at the Masque.

September 25, 1977
Whisky Sunday matinee show w/ Bags, Weirdos.

October, 1977
Another Whisky Sunday matinee w/ Blondie and Devo.

October 7-8, 1977
Mabuhay Gardens, S.F., w/ Weirdos

November 23, 1977
Masque w/ Skulls, Eyes, Waxx ... Sympathy for the Germs ... benefit to buy equipment.

December 2 & 3, 1977
The Masque w/ Skulls, Controllers and others.

1978

Early January, 1978
The "Local Shit" gossip column in *Slash* reports that the Germs and their entourage were booted from a New Year's Eve party hosted by the Berlin Brats for "setting fires" and "generally acting like animals".

January 19, 20, 21, 1978
Germs attempt to sabotage Greg Shaw's three-night power-pop fest at the Whisky. Pat Smear is booted from the club for allegedly attacking Paul Zone, lead singer of the Fast, and setting fire to his hair. Zone was described in *New York Phonograph* magazine's Who's Who of New York's Class of '76 as "The dandy of the court, a more dedicated follower of super pop fashion would be hard to find. Up until now a seenster, as lead singer for the Fast he's developing into a scenester." Nobody in L.A. is impressed other than Greg Shaw.

February 23, 1978
Masque Benefit at the Park Plaza Hotel w/ 18 other bands over two days. A fight breaks out in the pit during the Germs' set while they're attempting a cover of Bowie's "Hang On To Yourself," the first recorded "punk rock" scrap in L.A. County.

March 10, 1978
Park Plaza Hotel (then the Elks Lodge) w/ Arthur Lee & Love, Needles & Pins. KROQ promotion. A coupling of punk iconography spanning two generations with Lee the king of Sunset Strip '60s hippie-punk and Darby Crash, the king of the new glitter-brat punks. Darby was reportedly terrified of going on because of the majority of longhairs present for Love. True? False? Turnout was actually abysmal.

May, 1978
Slash hawks the Germs' "Lexicon Devil" ep by mail order only, its second release as a label. Biggs now definitely emerging at the helm, slowly edging Samiof out. Bobby Pyn now officially becomes Darby Crash in the self-mythologizing lyrics to Circle One, one of the three songs on this record produced by Geza X.

May 11, 1978
Go-Go's make their world debut at the Masque during a private invitation-only 21st birthday party for Hal Negro. Kickboy trashes the cake and reduces the affair to a slapstick pie fight. The Go-Go's, who are renting a practice room, jump up onstage for an impromptu three numbers. The Weirdos might also have played, as did the Satin Tones. The Germs also jammed on a 20-minute version of "Shut Down"...

May 23, 1978
Whisky ... Lobotomy Night #2 w/ Bags, Stitches.

July 14, 15 1978
Whisky... What God Means to Me. Germs play the Whisky on a bill presented by *Lobotomy* fanzine (Lobotomy Night #3?) with the Red Lights (short-lived band with a pre-Gun Club Jeffrey Lee Pierce on guitar and Anna Statman on bass).

July/August, 1978
X and the Plugz play a private party for Linda "Amber" Hunt at the Masque. She refuses to allow the Germs in.

September, 1978
Some punks, reputedly Germs' disciples instigated by Darby, set fire to the dumpster behind Licorice Pizza, the record store, to protest the Whisky's first of many bannings of punk bands. The culprits pushed the blazing dumpster onto San Vicente, a downward gradient street, whereupon the giant metal box on wheels careened dangerously and spectacularly down the boulevard. Amazingly no one was injured although it did smash into several parked cars.

September 6, 1978

Germs, Simpletones (first gig) and the Brainiacs at the Rock Corporation. Snickers, Rabbit, Jay Lansford, Jerry and some others were the Simpletones from Rosemead, a Posh Boy discovery.

DARBY CRASH   There's no place to play. Like when we played the Rock Corporation a couple of weeks ago. We didn't want to because it's not the kind of people we want to play to. It's all bikers and stuff. And there's murders outside the door. When the Avengers played somebody got murdered right around the corner. Nobody makes any money. It's just ridiculous.

Halloween, 1978

The Youth Party "Holocaust-Ume" Ball at the Roosevelt Hotel with the Go-Go's, the Germs, Mau Mau's and Hal Negro & the Satin Tones. A fun gig turns creepy and ends in violence with cops pulling the plug. Kickboy and Darby egg the crowd on to smash the place up. "Do damage," he said, the same words uttered by Fred D. of Limp Bizkit at Woodstock 99.

1979

January Shows at the Other Masque (Santa Monica and Vine):

January 12

Dead Kennedys, Germs, Rhino 39.

January 13

Dead Kennedys, Germs, Rotters.

January 19, 1979

Germs, the Middle Class, the Standbys play the North Park Lion's Club, 3927 Utah Street, in San Diego.

January, 1979

Yes L.A., the one-sided Dangerhouse release and response to the Brian Eno produced "No New York," features X, Eyes, the Bags, Black Randy, and the Germs' "No God."

February 24, 1979

The last night of the Other Masque w/ Cramps, Dead Boys, Germs, Pure Hell, Wall of Voodoo, Extremes.

March 13, 1979

Germs, X and Rhino 39 scheduled to play the Squeeze in Riverside. Cops bust up the show because of the alleged bad behavior of the Germs contingent. X doesn't get to play at all. Fight ensues with management when X demands to be paid in full anyway since they maintain the cops' interception isn't their fault.

March 31, 1979

Downtown artist Bob Clarke springs $300.00 for a P.A. to set up a party/gig at his 5,000 sq. ft. loft and confirms the Germs, Holly & the Italians, the '80s and Cotton.

Circa May, 1979

Bankrolled by Slash, the Germs sign a recording contract and begin recording the *G.I.* album at Quad Teck, engineered by Pat Burnette and produced by Joan Jett.

July 17, 1979

Germs, Extremes, the Adaptors at the Hong Kong Café. Germs played gratis in restitution for a window which Darby broke on a previous occasion.

DARBY CRASH   Whaddaya wanna hear? Do you know any songs? Pretend you're at a party! Gimme some beer! Everyone onstage!

Circa August, 1979
August issue of *Slash* carries shot of Darby Crash looking like he's having fun on the dance floor with Carla Maddog from the Controllers during an Alleycats gig at Club 88. Same issue also runs a review of the Germs by former high schoolmate Will Amato, who writes that "the spectacle of the Germs is suicide-magnetic ... their white noise version of the black death was ringmastered by DC who barked out incoherent tirades to exort the crowd to frenzy ... his eyes burn in appalling beams and red welts of honor decorate his chest. The crowd kept yelling 'jump.' Crash made his exit half-way through Shutdown and never returned ..."

August 15, 1979
Hong Kong Café w/ B-People and Vs.

Sept 22, 1979
Hong Kong ... w/ Middle Class and Black Flag.

October 31, 1979
Hong Kong w/ Fear, Black Flag, Catholic Discipline, Chinas Comidas.

Circa November, 1979
Deaf Club in San Francisco.

December 14, 1979
Hope Hall (1329 Hope Street, Downtown L.A.) with X and Suburban Lawns.

December, 1979
The Arena (the Veteran's Auditorium in Culver City) is closed to punk following—guess what—a Germs' gig. Punks were reportedly caught having sex in stalls in the ladies' rooms!

December, 1979
Angered gay organizations call for a boycott of William Friedkin's Cruising, a movie that features one song (of five recorded) by the Germs on the Jack Nietzsche-produced sound track. The militants feel the film negatively stereotypes gay male sex culture as nothing more than a bunch of crazed fist-fucking S&M leather freaks performing violent sex in the backrooms of creepy dimly-lit bars across America. Darby goes around telling everybody not to see the movie because it is shit.

December 23, 1979
Whisky ... Masque Xmas Party w/ Arthur J. and the Gold Cups ... as seen in the "Caught in My Eye" video.

December 31, 1979
Germs, Johanna Went, others at the Hong Kong.

1980

January 29, 1980
The Great Gatsby, Redondo Pier w/ Black Flag, Descendents, Eddie & Subtitles.

February 17, 1980
Kings Palace, Hollywood Boulevard. Youth Party Benefit ... Germs announced on a flyer as playing with X, Circle Jerks, Top Jimmy, UXA, Gestapo, Lost Souls, the Men. Wishful thinking on the part of the booker? Or did Germs actually play this one?

March 29, 1980
Circle Jerks and Mau Mau's play the King's Palace on Hollywood Boulevard. Another flyer dated the same has the Jerks playing with Black Flag, the Germs, the Cheifs (sic) and the

Lurchers. Did Germs play this one? Remember Kings Palace was every bit as flakey as the Mau Mau's and the guy booking these shows.

March 13, 1980
Fleetwood w/ Middle Class.

April 26, 1980
Fleetwood w/ Middle Class, Adolescents, der Stab. Germs play their second to last show before disbanding. Four-track tape exists of "My Tunnel" played live probably for the first time. Bedlam. What happened? Group is banned afterwards.

May, 1980
Germs now banned from everywhere, including the Hong Kong and the Fleetwood. To make matters even worse: Darby kicks drummer Don Bolles out to create a place for Rob Henley.

May 11, 1980
Germs scheduled to play at Flippers Roller Disco with the Alley Cats, but Henley wasn't up to it.

June 17, 1980
Germs, Plugz, others at the Fleetwood. It is uncertain if they played this gig at all, and wether Bolles or Henley played drums. No one remembers.

June, 1980
Darby takes off to London w/ Amber who pays for everything.

July, 1980
Lorna and Pat quit while Darby and Amber are in London, thus ending the band. Darby returns to L.A. after hanging out in London with former Sex Pistols designer Jordan plus other people involved with Adam Ant's entourage. He is immediately pressured into forming the Darby Crash Band. There was not nearly enough time. Darby panics and calls Pat at the last minute to bail him out.

August 27, 1980
Darby Crash Band debut at the Starwood.
The reception for the new band is not so hot. Worse than flat-out bombing, the audience is indifferent. The new band has no edge, although they play probably as well as the Germs, but decent musicians playing an okay show wasn't necessarily what made a great show and it wasn't what the crowd wanted either, especially at that moment. The new kids were alienated and confused by the new image, the new feathered, Mohawked Boy of London get-up. To add insult to injury one of the opening bands do a song or make a wise-assed onstage crack putting him down as a has-been.

December 3, 1980
Reunion at the Starwood w/ Middle Class, the Screws. Pat buys his first ever brand new guitar specially for the occasion. The band utterly rocks and some ecstatic spectators say it was one of the best Germs' shows ever.

I'm sure we missed a few gigs. Write and let us know, and we'll get it into the next printing.

ENDNOTES

O

1. Tomata Du Plenty: Excerpted from *The Big Takeover*, courtesy Jack Rabid.

2. Gregg Turner: Excerpted from "Radio Free Hollywood" newsletter, circa June, 1977.

3. Tommy Gear: Excerpted from *Flipside* interview, used by permission.

4. Pat Smear: Excerpted from the academic paper *An Aesthetic Approach to L.A. Punk Music and Style* by Michael Jones and David Jones. Used by permission.

5. Exene Cervenka: Excerpted from *Forming: the Early Days of L.A. Punk*. Courtesy of Smart Art Press.

6. Ibid.

7. Ibid.

8. Jimmy Wilsey: Excerpted from *Punk '77* photobook by James Stark.

9. Darby Crash: Excerpted from *No* magazine. Courtesy of Bruce Kalberg.

10. Pat Smear: Excerpted from *Request* magazine. Used by permission.

11. David Bowie: Excerpted from an interview by Cameron Crowe, *Playboy* magazine, February 1976.

12. Ibid.

13. Craig Lee: Excerpted from *California Hardcore*, Last Gasp, 1983.

14. Seymour Stein: Excerpted from "Radio Free Hollywood" newsletter.

15. Exene Cervenka: Excerpted from the booklet with the X boxed cd set, *Beyond and Back: The X Anthology*, 1997, Elektra Entertainment Group, Warner Communications.

16. The Dogtown Posse: Excerpted from *WET* magazine, circa '79, courtesy of Leonard Koren.

17. Casey Cola: Exerpted from various interviews by Ella Black.

18. Pat Smear: Excerpted from *Request* magazine. Used by permission.

19. Pat Smear: Excerpted from Pat Smear interview by Jennifer Schwartz and Jeff McDonald, *BAM* magazine.

Prisoner of X
20 Years in the Hole at *Hustler* Magazine
Allan MacDonell

Prisoner of X is a savagely funny odyssey through the bizarro world of Larry Flynt's cracker-rich, X-rated empire.

During his tenure in the *Hustler* trenches, punk-rock dropout Allan MacDonell ascends from entry-level comma-catcher to editorial overlord of the unseemly offerings at Larry Flynt Publications. Here's the inside story of running America's most influential porn domain.

Prisoner of X is a wildly entertaining memoir about climbing the bent and fearsome masthead of an infamous magazine, and the bittersweet reward of publicly crossing its hillbilly Caesar. Cover artist Daniel Clowes is the celebrated cartoonist and screenwriter of *Ghost World* and *Art School Confidential*.

5 1/2 x 8 1/4 • 312 pages • 1-932595-13-9 • $16.95

Choosing Death
The Improbable History of Death Metal and Grindcore
Albert Mudrian; Introduction by John Peel

In 1986, it was unimaginable that death metal and grindcore would ever impact popular culture. Yet this shockingly fast and barbaric amalgam of hardcore punk and heavy metal would define the musical threshold of extremity for years to come. Initially circulated through an underground tape-trading network by scraggly, angry young boys, death metal and grindcore spread faster than a plague of undead zombies as bands rose from every corner of the globe. By 1992, the genre's first legitimate label, Earache Records, had sold well over a million death metal and grindcore albums in the United States alone. *Choosing Death*, featuring an introduction by John Peel, conquers the lofty task of telling the two-decade-long history of this underground art form through the eyes and ringing ears of the artists, producers, and label owners—past and present—who propelled the movements.

7 x 10 • 285 pages • illustrated • 1-932595-04-X • $19.95

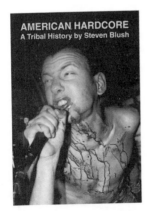

American Hardcore: A Tribal History
Steven Blush

This is the first history of "Hardcore," a genre of music begun as a response by alienated suburbanites to the angst and art of punk and new wave. Angrier, less pretentious and more stripped-down than its artsy, drug-addled predecessor, this harder-faster form of music was not very pretty—an angry and violent outlet to unfocused rage. Containing amazing oral histories interspersed with informed commentary and history, *American Hardcore* explains the gestation, whys and rationales of a scene that began in 1980 and fell apart in 1986. Steven Blush provides a complete national perspective on the genre, explaining all the regional scenes, complete with photos and discographies.

7 x 10 • 333 pages • extensively illustrated • 0-922915-71-7 • $19.95